IMPACT TEACHING

IMPACT TEACHING

Ideas and Strategies for Teachers to Maximize Student Learning

RICHARD HOWELL ALLEN

ALLYN AND BACON

Boston ▪ London ▪ Toronto ▪ Sydney ▪ Tokyo ▪ Singapore

Executive editor and publisher: *Stephen D. Dragin*
Series editorial assistant: *Barbara Strickland*
Manufacturing buyer: *Chris Marson*
Marketing manager: *Kathleen Morgan*
Cover designer: *Jenny Hart*
Production coordinator: *Pat Torelli Publishing Services*
Editorial-production service: *Chestnut Hill Enterprises, Inc.*

Library of Congress Cataloging-in-Publication Data

Allen, Richard Howell
    Impact teaching : ideas and strategies for teachers to maximize student learning / Richard Howell Allen.
       p.   cm.
    Includes bibliographical references and index.
    ISBN 0-205-33414-8
    1. Effective Teaching.   2. Learning, Psychology of.   I. Title.
LB1025.3 .A44   2002
372.64—dc21

                                            2001022141

Printed in the United States of America

10 9 8 7   05

For Tara

Simply the best . . .

CONTENTS

CHAPTER FIVE

The Art of Effective Directions   112

CHAPTER SIX

Language Issues   138

This book is about teaching—the specific techniques, strategies, and practices teachers can use in their efforts to maximize the impact they have on their students. In essence, this book was written specifically for all individuals who are charged with the critical responsibility of expanding the knowledge base and/or skill levels of their students.

The concepts and ideas that will be considered were culled from a variety of different sources. Over the course of my career, I have had a wide range of instructional responsibilities. I have been a high school mathematics and drama teacher, a college instructor at both the graduate and undergraduate levels, a corporate trainer (and trainer of trainers), a lead instructor in an international accelerated learning program for teens, and an outdoor education facilitator. My most recent teaching experiences include roles as an instructor/trainer in schools and businesses in eleven different countries, including England, Sweden, Australia, New Zealand, Malaysia, Indonesia, and Russia. These and other professional experiences have provided a conceptual foundation for this book.

This book also draws on key issues in learning I explored while completing a Ph.D. degree in educational psychology (e.g., recent research findings centering on how the human brain receives, processes, and recalls information). Where possible, I have included academic references so that readers may pursue ideas that interest them in further detail. However, it should be recognized from the outset that much of what is discussed here is based on my own personal "trial and error" experiences. Occasionally I have found that people depend much too heavily on the latest research to raise an idea to the exalted status of fact. You, the reader, are encouraged to consider each idea in its own right and explore ways to make those that seem promising work in a manner that is consistent with your own personality, the students you teach, and any other constraints or freedoms that are unique to your teaching environment.

Simply stated, over the course of my professional career, I have become increasingly convinced that there are consistencies in the language patterns successful teachers tend to adopt, as well as recurring patterns in their styles of instructional delivery. My primary goal in writing this book is to bring to light these language patterns and ways of delivering effective instruction. My expectation is that both novice *and* expert teachers will profit from this analysis. To the extent that this expectation is realized, I anticipate that students will ultimately profit as much from the analyses that follow, or perhaps even more, than the teachers themselves.

I am always intrigued to hear how the techniques may have been successfully implemented. Any suggestions you might have for improving the manner in which these ideas have been presented are also welcome. Please feel free to contact me at my email address and share your impressions concerning the concept of Impact Teaching. Enjoy your voyage of discovery exploring the thoughts, images, stories, metaphors, and examples contained within these pages. Pleasant journeys . . .

—Richard Howell Allen
Lake Tahoe, California
rich@impactlearn.com

ACKNOWLEDGMENTS

Looking back over seventeen years of teaching and training, I can scarcely believe my great fortune at having had the opportunity to work with so many extraordinarily gifted individuals. Each, in his or her own way, has contributed significantly to the development of both my talents and the ideas presented in this book. They are a cast of infinite variety all of whom have given something unique to my understanding of how to conduct successful learning sessions.

Rob Abernathy
Susan Adams
Carole Allen
Tim Andrews
Scott Bornstein
Laura Bowen
Linda Brown
Phil Bryson
Dr. Stephanie Burns
Michael Carr
Peter Coldicott
Bobbi DePorter
David Edwards
Dr. Billie Enz
Dr. Donald J. Freeman
Judy Green
Sean Hall

Allison Helstrup
Jan Hensley
Pete LaGrego
John LeTellier
Dee Lindenberger
Dr. James McCray
Doug McBride
Dr. Cristal McGill
Jim Moore
Kate Neal
Bill Payne
Mark Reardon
Timothy Giles Rickett
Richard Scheaff
Sarah Singer-Nourie
Lance Tomlinson
Larry Wilson

A special "thank you" is due to three people for their help with this book. With their invaluable input, the quality of the final product has been greatly enhanced. Dr. Cristal McGill supplied most of the background research for the references that are woven throughout the text, and has assisted in the overall development of the project from the very beginning. Dr. Donald J. Freeman of Arizona State University offered numerous conceptual suggestions, the value of which cannot be overstated. And Dee Lindenberger voluntarily edited several early versions of the manuscript. The clarity with which the ideas are presented here is due greatly to her suggestions and contributions. All errors are purely my own. In addition, I am grateful for the insightful comments of the reviewers Michael L. Jacobs, University of Northern Colorado, and Courtney W. Moffatt, Edgewood College.

This list is by no means all-inclusive. For those who have contributed to my growth but are not mentioned here, I extend my humblest apologies—and my deep appreciation.

Finally, a warm thanks to my family: Tara Allen; Howell Babbitt and Edwina Wolfrey; Joanne and Axel Neimer; Karen, Lauren, Ben, and Angela McCutcheon; and Barb and David Young.

CHAPTER ONE

WHAT IS "IMPACT TEACHING"?

> This chapter provides an introduction to the underlying philosophy and psychological presuppositions of the information contained in this book. It addresses the key issues of what the concept of Impact Teaching means, where it came from, and how it relates to other information currently available in the field of teacher education.

Impact: (verb) to affect; (noun) the power to
move feelings, influence thinking
—Webster's New World Dictionary

It's always best to start at the beginning. In this case, that means addressing the following question: What is meant by "Impact Teaching"? The idea for the title of this book came from the definition of the word *impact*, as shown above, combined with an understanding of the main objective of classroom teachers. The ultimate goal of these individuals, regardless of subject matter or grade level, is to have a significant *impact* on the students, **an impact that results in a measurable increase in students' knowledge or skills**. As teachers, we want "to affect" them in some meaningful way, to have "the power to move their feelings" and "influence their thinking." If we don't accomplish these things, nothing has really been taught, and consequently nothing has really been learned. If you want to learn how to maximize your impact on your students, and facilitate a depth of learning that moves feelings and influences thinking, the strategies and techniques outlined in this book can help. Consider the following metaphor:

SETTING THE SAILS

Imagine a sailboat cruising across the ocean. The captain of the vessel sees an island off in the distance, and wants to go there. He eagerly sets his course, and the adventure begins. However, the captain has not set the sails correctly, and, despite his initial enthusiasm, the voyage rapidly loses its luster. As the water becomes choppy and rough, the sea turns into a battlefield. The ship is buffeted back and forth, and the captain must call on all his reserves of strength, energy, and determination to maintain control of the vessel and hold his course for the island. Progress is slowly made, but only with a supreme effort. Finally, after a much longer period of time than might have been expected, the ship reaches its destination. The exhausted captain collapses on the island's beach, wondering if it was really worth it after all.

Many teachers will recognize the obvious, albeit distressing, parallel between this episode and their own experiences as educators. They begin a lesson with an objective clearly in mind. Like the captain, they are excited about the adventure in learning that is about to take place. But, all too often, just as with the captain of the sailboat who had to battle the elements to make any significant headway, they too find themselves immersed in a struggle, a test of their willpower, determination, and stamina. When this happens, teachers must exert a tremendous amount of additional time, effort, and energy to achieve the educational standards they set for their students. When this struggle is repeated time and time again, teachers may find themselves questioning whether or not their efforts are worth the physical and emotional price they are paying. Too many caring, committed educators choose to leave their profession of choice as a result of being tired and burnt out.

Whether nurturing young students or guiding teen, and even adult, learners, most teachers want a relaxed, pleasant cruise toward learning objectives. The key for the captain of the sailboat is to know how to properly set the sails of the vessel so the energy of the wind guides the ship easily toward the island. Similarly, the key for the effective teacher is to know how to set the sails of instruction so the natural energy and enthusiasm of the students guides the learning process quickly and efficiently toward the stated objectives. That is the basic goal of this book: to provide educators with information that will help them to determine whether they have correctly set the sails of the classroom experience in order to maximize the impact of the lesson on their students.

The concept of expenditure of energy is a critical issue for most teachers (Larkins, McKinney, Oldham-Buss, 1985). Personally, I've encountered very few who, after teaching all day, are bursting at the seams with energy and exuberance. Not many stand at the door of their classroom, watch their students depart, then race home for a long night of dancing, revelry, and general debauchery! More common is the opposite; they go home exhausted and crawl into bed for a nap before dinner. Therefore, the development of teaching techniques that are impactful while also being energy-efficient is a critical component of long-term instructional success. We need to move away from the teaching style in which the teacher is doing the majority of the work. To move towards this goal, perhaps it is useful to recall the following proverb:

Tell me, I hear.

Show me, I see.

Involve me, I understand.

The wisdom in these words leads to the conclusion that for the most effective learning to occur, teachers must *involve* their students. While the idea is simple to

express in words, and one that many educators would fully endorse, at the same time
it can be challenging to actualize in the classroom (Greenco, Collins, & Resnick 1996).
Creating high levels of student interaction requires that teachers pay careful attention
to a wide range of details. What specific concepts, ideas, and skills does the teacher
need to master to create this result? Which approaches will work best to assure the
highest levels of retention of the information? How should directions be given to efficiently move learners into an activity? What details of language and communication
styles will be most useful in creating a safe, interactive learning environment?

These pages contain a collection of possible answers to these kinds of questions.
The techniques are intended to stimulate the thinking of both new *and* experienced
teachers regarding how to maximize the impact they can have on their students. Naturally, how each teacher chooses to incorporate these ideas into his or her presentational
style depends on the unique combination of his or her personality, students, subject,
and the learning context in which he or she teaches.

The issue of context plays another important role in relation to the information in
this book. The book *Contextualizing Teaching* by Joe Kincheloe, Patrick Slattery, and
Shirley Steinberg (2000) argues that teachers would be wise to focus their instruction
on information that is related to the real world. What strikes me as odd is that this is
such a revolutionary thought that someone would need to write an entire book about it!
Yet the need for such a book is apparent from observing how many teachers have
become trapped in the paradigm of teaching for teaching's sake, without any apparent
connection to society in general, or to what it means to be human. Instead, they become
mired in the day-to-day activities that—while certainly necessary—ultimately distract
them from keeping in mind some of the higher purposes of the educational process.

Making learning meaningful is a critical aspect of the Impact Teaching approach.
Central to most discussions in this book is the issue of how teachers can help learners
see the relevance of their experiences in the classroom to their lives outside of it. It is
not enough merely to identify the importance of this issue; concrete steps must be taken
to bring this reality into the classroom. While this may make immediate sense to many
readers, the question then becomes, "How?" Those who are bringing new teacher candidates into the field must take the next step and highlight specific ways in which
teachers can make this happen in their own classrooms. Practitioners need to know precisely what to say and what to do to create the intended results.

It is certainly not the goal of this book to cover all such strategies. Rather, the
intention here is to isolate and highlight some practical, realistic, down-to-earth ideas
that both novice and experienced teachers may not encounter in other courses, books,
or even over the passage of time in their classroom. The clear-cut strategies outlined
here are based primarily on recent research into how the human brain encodes,
processes, stores, and recalls information. At the very least, we know that for effective
learning to occur students need to be physically and emotionally engaged in the learning process. How teachers can build, maintain, and facilitate this kind of environment
is the focus of this book.

This central issue in Impact Teaching is also consistent with, and supported by,
the theory of creating an enriched environment for learners, as put forward by Marian
Diamond in her book *Enriching Heredity* (1988). Simply stated, she spent years

conducting experiments comparing the developing neurology of the brains of rats in enriched environments (these guys had plenty of things to do) with those raised in more mundane environments (these guys were bored most of the time). The results are clear: the more enriched environment, the better the brain develops. The approach to effective teaching discussed in this book builds on this idea: How can teachers create an energetic, "enriched" environment where learners feel free to be fully engaged in the learning process? This book strives to take the next step and introduce numerous specific strategies teachers can use to make this happen in their own classroom.

As mentioned before, understanding precisely *how* to generate these results is critical, and is the aim of this book. For example, without an awareness concerning many of these techniques discussed here, teachers may accidentally create an environment that contains unacceptably high levels of implied or unspoken threat. Few of us operate our best in these kinds of situations. At the physiological level, computer-enhanced images reveal that in situations involving threat or anxiety, our brains function differently than they do in normal circumstances. Brain activity decreases around the midbrain and neocortex, while it increases in the brain stem and cerebellum. At this level we get behaviors that are instinctive and habitual, and less higher order processing of information occurs (Hart 1983). Simply put, higher order processing is necessary if we hold the expectation that students will make meaningful connections with the material.

For successful teaching, the implications are obvious. Even in a relatively mild threat state, learners will not be performing at their best, nor will they be processing and encoding information at a level that is conducive to long-term retention. It is clear that for effective learning to occur students need to be relaxed, focused, and at ease, generally feeling pretty good about themselves and the learning environment. Many of the strategies covered in this book center around the idea of reducing or removing any trace of threat from the learning situation, so students can engage fully and easily in the activities and discussions that are a part of their classroom experiences.

Here is where the last two decades of rising interest in the constructivist approach to teaching come into play. At the simplest level, constructivists do not believe that knowledge is simply transferred from the mind of the teacher to the mind of the student. Instead, as the teacher speaks, they believe students are processing the information and *constructing* meaning from it based on a wide range of factors. These factors might include, but are certainly not limited to, any previous experiences the students might have had with the topic, such as their emotional state at the time of the lesson, their feelings towards the teacher, and their feelings towards the topic. The discussions in this book are consistent with this philosophical approach to instruction, seeking to explain methods that teachers can utilize in their efforts to design instruction so the meaning students construct most closely matches the intentions and objectives of the teacher.

In 1995, *The Manufactured Crisis* by David Berliner and Bruce Biddle was published. Their primary contention in this work is that the general state of education in the United States is much better than the press tends to lead people to believe. The authors' analysis compares the statistical methodologies used in this country to those used in other countries around the world. In the end, they conclude that the educational system in the United States is at least on a par with, if not better than, most other countries. Basically, we're doing fairly well educating our children. Not that we can't improve our current educational system. There are definitely challenges that need to be faced as we move forward into the next century. Some of them are enormous, while others are fairly simple and straightforward. Generally, things are moving along quite nicely in many schools.

The intention of this book, and in fact the whole concept of Impact Teaching, is to further this idea. In general, not only in the United States but in many places around the world, the educational process is surprisingly successful. It is also responding to the ever-changing needs of a fast-paced, computer-driven society in an admirable manner. Given this, what adjustments can be made to our current approach to education that can help the system keep moving forward and perpetuate the process of continual improvement? What strategies can we teach new teachers that will keep students engaged and responding? Based on the explosion of information in the last three decades about how the brain functions, what specific strategies can teachers apply in their classrooms that will keep teaching and learning exciting? Impact Teaching is one response to these important questions. It is certainly the hope of this author that many more such works will keep entering the education field as we continue to learn more about how the brain functions, and how to create an effective learning experience for students.

Another important question also drives the content of this book. Where do teachers actually learn to do their job? Where do they learn to teach? Ask experienced teachers and they will most likely tell you the obvious answer, "In the classroom, of course!" This statement is a serious downer for those few professors remaining in the ivory towers who still cling firmly to the notion that it is the courses they teach that produce individuals fully ready to survive, and even thrive, in their first year in the classroom. But experience—and research—shows something radically different. In the excitement and chaos of a real classroom, all those ideas teachers gleaned from the numerous Foundations of Education and Educational Psychology classes they were required to take fly immediately and directly out the nearest window, as they come face-to-face with two fundamental questions:

1. "What do I do?" and
2. "What do I say?"

It's not that these classes are in any way invalid; in fact, the information is invaluable, *if it is given to the students in the right way and at the right time.* The challenge is simply a matter of understanding how teachers naturally come to handle those first years in the classroom. While the student-teaching experience of most teacher trainees is designed to meet this need at some level, perhaps there are other things we can do to help prepare them for the awesome task they face when they begin their first full year of teaching.

Imagine, for one wild moment, that there was plenty of money to be spent in the preparation of new teachers. (OK, it's a stretch, but just go with it for a moment here.) In this fantasy world, perhaps teacher trainees would be given an experienced coteacher to work closely with for the first three or four years they are in the profession.

Then, they would be given a one-year paid leave of absence to take a series of university courses. During these courses they would spend most of their time relating what they have learned from their real-life experiences to well-researched educational principles. From the vantage point of personal experience they would more fully understand the various terms and expressions Educational Psychologists and Foundations of Education professors use so frequently. After a year of this intellectual stimulation they would return to their own classrooms, armed with a series of well-understood principles from which to build the most dynamic learning experience possible for their students.

It's clear that I'm having a momentary breakdown by daring to dream of such a thing ever happening! Given the financial constraints currently placed on education institutions and the system in general, such a scenario is unthinkable. However, in its absence, perhaps there are other ways we can best assist new teachers. What they need most at this point are specific strategies and precise language for survival in certain teaching situations. Why not simply give them these tools? They would become the building blocks from which the educational principles can *later* come to make perfect sense.

It's likely that some readers may inadvertently misinterpret what's been said here, and believe I do not fully appreciate many of the time-honored and well-researched educational principles that are taught in these teacher-preparation classes. Nothing could be further from the truth. If this discussion makes any sense, the question is simply one of how teacher candidates will bring these excellent ideas into fruition. There's that word again, *how*. It has been repeated several times in this initial discussion for an important reason: It is the entire basis for this text. The ideas and concepts you'll read about here are very specific, focused directly on how to bring to life all the wonderful theories teacher candidates will learn about in these courses.

From the literature viewpoint, the majority of these teacher education classes will utilize traditional Educational Psychology or Foundations of Education textbooks. I fully endorse many of these texts. Three of my favorites are: Anita Woolfolk's *Educational Psychology* (2000), N. L. Gage and David Berliner's (1998) book by the same name, and Jeanne Ellis Ormond's *Educational Psychology: Developing Learners* (2000). Other classes may use equally effective, yet perhaps more nontraditional texts, such as Eric Jensen's *SuperTeaching* (1988), Bobbi Deporter, Mark Reardon, and Sarah Singer-Noire's *Orchestrating Student Success* (1999), or Louis Schmier's *Random Thoughts: The Humanity of Teaching* (1995). All of these books are excellent resources, and beginning teachers would be helping themselves greatly by reading them at some point before their first year of teaching. The books mentioned here are only a few of the many excellent texts that abound in the field of teacher education. Perhaps, then, it is both fitting and important to conclude this opening chapter with a few remarks concerning how this present book relates to other texts in the field.

Impact Teaching is definitely the second type mentioned above: It is a nontraditional text. To a traditionalist, this book may very well seem an oddity. It does not focus heavily on well-known theories and principles, nor does it frequently quote hallowed names from the field. Also, it certainly makes no pretense of comprehensively reviewing every educational idea, term, and approach that teacher candidates might want to acquaint themselves with before stepping into the classroom. While both theories and researchers are occasionally mentioned, as they should be, they are not the central focus of the book. Instead, *Impact Teaching* attempts to take the solid foundation provided by these books and add to it by supplying a series of specific strategies, techniques, and approaches that may not have been covered previously.

Why are they not covered in these other books? Quite simply, because they are based on a combination of two things: (1) fifteen years of involvement in the growing field of brain research and its applications to the teaching profession, and (2) my own extensive experiences in educational systems throughout the world. This combination has created a surge of ideas, strategies, and specific distinctions that should prove useful to both the experienced as well as the novice teacher. Certainly there will be parallels between this book and certain ideas in other texts, and, where possible, I have pointed these out. Yet I suspect that many, in fact most, of the concepts and strategies may well be unique to most readers.

Given the background that has become the foundation for this information, it is possible to say that this is a very personal book. It does indeed reflect my own beliefs about the nature of effective education. At the same time, the primary reason this book exists at all is that these ideas seem to be so easily generalizable to a wide variety of classroom circumstances. I certainly do not intend to cover every new strategy out there; such a book would be impossible to create, given the ongoing explosion of ideas in the brain-based teaching field. Instead, it is meant more as a handheld library of empirically proven ideas and strategies, where both new and experienced teachers can occasionally drop by and browse, seeking new ideas they might use in their classrooms.

However, while most of this book is indeed focused on specific strategies and techniques, it begins in a different place. It opens with a brief look at some of the precepts and principles underlying the concept of Impact Teaching. Readers may well wonder why I decided to begin a book of specific techniques in this manner. The reason is that both the precepts discussed in Chapter 2 and the educational principles illustrated in Chapter 3 may well be unique as compared to others mentioned in more traditional texts. It feels wise to handle the issue of where we are going on this journey before detailing precisely how we're going to get there.

In addition, the world is rapidly changing. Examples can be found in more traditional educational psychology texts that perpetuate beliefs and principles that may simply not be true today. While it would be silly to ignore what we have learned from the past, at the same time we would be wise to adopt a policy of continually updating our view of what provides a foundation for effective education. Both the precepts as well as the principles discussed in these two chapters are intended to give the reader food for thought. Do you agree or disagree with the ideas presented here? If some of them make sense, how will you actualize them in your classroom?

The basic concept behind *Impact Teaching* is simple: Take what we have learned from the past about how to be an effective teacher, add to it what we are learning about how the human brain functions, and create specific strategies for designing an enriched learning environment that excites the child. That is the focus of this book: identifying and demonstrating ways that teachers can become more effective and efficient in their endeavors to create a positive, dynamic, high-impact learning experience for their students.

CHAPTER TWO

INSTRUCTIONAL PRECEPTS

> This chapter introduces five main precepts for creating an effective approach to instruction. Each one is considered from a variety of angles, while focusing primarily on how to apply it to specific classroom situations.

OVERVIEW

Teachers' abilities to clearly articulate their precepts, thoughts, and opinions about what makes learning happen is an integral part of their effectiveness as educators. These precepts become the vessel within which all future teaching ideas are contained, and the perspective through which new ideas are filtered. They are the criterion on which the success or failure of current instructional strategies is judged, as well as the mental framework from which decisions are made regarding future instructional choices. Perhaps most importantly, teachers' ability to articulate these foundational beliefs can assist them in maintaining a focus on the long-term objectives of a learning situation.

The functional definition of the word *precept* in this situation is *a conviction that certain things are true.* For teachers, this is meant to incorporate all of the various ways they view the nature of instruction. It includes their ideas, feelings, viewpoints, expectations, and conclusions about learning that have been developing since they were first exposed to the educational process.

This chapter contains five of my precepts concerning the nature of effective instruction.

1. Teach People, Not Content
2. Awareness Leads to Choice
3. Learning + Enjoyment = Retention
4. Application Is Everything
5. Stories Are Great

These are just a few of the perspectives that help to form my personal approach to instruction. They are highlighted in this chapter for two primary purposes.

The material in this book is based on these ideas. For example, the second precept focuses on creating greater awareness of choices. A central tenet of this book is that, through exposure to the material contained here, teachers will have an increased awareness of some options they could use in different classroom situations. As another example, the fifth precept assumes the power of stories when used to convey information. The presentation of the material in this book was written with this premise in mind. The vast majority of the content covered here is illustrated through the use of numerous stories, examples, and metaphors. A clear understanding of the precepts that form the philosophical foundation for the material will promote a better understanding of how to apply it in practice.

The identification of these precepts is meant to spur you, the reader, to a consideration of your own ideas regarding effective, impactful instruction. Certainly, all teachers are invited to adopt these five concepts as part of their own teaching pedagogy, their personal teaching style. However, it's important to recognize that each teacher brings to the educational process a different set of developmental factors, including his or her own unique personality, background, and life experiences. Based on these diverse influences, the combination of beliefs that ultimately guides each teacher in his or her approach to teaching is inherently unique. It is a teacher's personal clarity on these issues that facilitates the ability to bring them to life in a learning context.

TEACH PEOPLE, NOT CONTENT

Several years ago, I was teaching a series of one-day in-service programs for public school teachers. Each of these programs had over eighty teachers in attendance. Early in the morning I would ask the group a sequence of questions in an attempt to get an idea of the composition of the audience that day. An interesting pattern began to emerge in response to these inquiries. One question was usually something along the lines of:

"What do you teach?"

Their answers mostly dealt with the content they taught, such as math, history, literature, or music. The use of the word *what* in the question had prompted a focus on the content. At this point I changed the question to:

"Let me rephrase what I was asking . . . *who* do you teach?"

Answers to this new question consistently dealt with the *grade level* they currently taught, such as the second, sixth, or tenth. From one point of view, they were quite correct in their responses. However, I was searching for a particular answer that would prompt the first major discussion of the day. So I paraphrased once again:

"No, really, who do you teach?"

This time the question was greeted with puzzled looks, as if I was a bit dense, and they were starting to worry about what they had gotten themselves into by choosing to attend the program. It was only with repeated prompting that the much sought-after answer finally emerged. Eventually someone in the group would, as if stumbling on a revolutionary idea, say:

"Oh . . . wait a minute . . . we teach *people!*"

The struggle to get to this answer illuminated a trend, which, once highlighted, began to emerge as a consistent theme throughout other in-service seminars. Teachers, like all people, are quick to create categories within their environment. It's a natural human process all of us use to help make sense of our world. However, in a learning environment, categorizing students may place a severe limitation on a teacher's ability to generate effective learning. Whether teachers view their students as *students learning geography* or *ninth graders*, both classifications may prohibit them from understanding the needs of each of their students as precious and special individuals.

Learners are first and foremost *people*, and each person is unique (Tomlinson & Kalbgleisch 1998). Most teachers are quick to acknowledge that, yes, students are people. (Those having a very tough day, of course, might be the only ones to hesitate in agreeing with this statement; some students can seem closer to monster than human on those days.) However, the evidence gathered from the questions asked above leads to the important conclusion that *this wasn't the first thought on the minds of these teachers!* The title of this chapter places this awareness at the forefront of a teacher's thoughts at all times: Teach People, Not Content. Undeniably, content is important. After all, in most cases it *is* what the students are there to learn. However, the primary filter should be one of *people first.* Here are two more personal examples to bring this idea into clearer focus.

First Example

I had been hired to teach a two-week course to eighteen teacher candidates. These students were participating in a special teacher development program, requiring them to spend eight hours a day at a local elementary school. In the morning they practiced their skills with young students, and in the afternoon they participated in classes that would eventually culminate in their teacher certification. This particular course had been allotted a total of thirty hours of instruction. A tremendous amount of content needed to be covered in that time frame, and the lesson plan for each day was packed full of issues needing to be addressed. Time was precious, and everyone was feeling the effect of the pressure.

It was early in the second week. Class had been under way for only a few minutes when an alarm bell rang and everyone had to troop outside for a fire drill. My students had been somewhat quiet so far that day, and I was mulling over how to step up their willingness to involve themselves. As we waited on the grass, I overheard several discussions having to do with an issue that was important to their year-long program, although unrelated to the topic of the current class. As we waited for the bell to ring, indicating it was safe to return, the intensity of the discussions grew rapidly. Although they attempted to keep it to themselves, it was apparent by their body language and the tone of their voices that this issue was weighting heavily on them. The bell finally rang, and everyone headed back into the room.

I needed to make an important decision at the point. The course I was teaching had some clearly stated objectives that needed to be covered by the end of the week, and little time remained. Was it more important to keep the students moving forward with the course content, or would the time be better spent sidetracking for a few moments into that seemingly unrelated issue? Hindsight is always 20/20, but at the time it was a difficult decision to make, given the sense of pressure under which everyone was operating. The guidelines for making this decision ultimately came from the theme of the current section: Teach People, Not Content.

They settled down for the next section by forming their chairs into a circle. I surprised them at that point by mentioning the conversations that had been going on outside, and asked if anyone had any further comments to make about this issue. At first there was silence. Then one student spoke up, then another, and suddenly it was as if a dam had burst, and the room was flooded with heated argument. Everyone in the class became involved as the debate raged on. The remaining two and a half hours of class time were spent on this topic. My role had shifted from teacher to facilitator. As I observed their interaction, I couldn't help but feel the urge to return their focus to the material. However, it was readily apparent that they needed to be spending their time doing *exactly* what they were at that moment. Finally, at the end of the session, that particular issue had been brought to resolution, and several action steps had been formulated.

Question: Had we just wasted a class session? The answer depends on each teacher's outlook on learning. For me, in this particular case, it was a resoundingly clear, emphatic "No! That was time well spent." From a content point of view, certainly nothing had been gained by the time spent on the discussion. However the higher priority was one of *people first.* In this particular case, had we not taken the time to address the topic that was emotionally critical to them, there was a strong chance that little of the information presented that day would have registered with them because their thoughts were focused elsewhere. For my part, why waste my energy trying to teach when no one will be able to remember what was said? Placing content as the top priority in this case would have created a losing situation for everyone. Instead, by responding to the needs of the human beings in the room, a win had been generated for that session. Another win appeared the next day, when the course returned to the content. This time, their focus was much better, and they were able to listen, participate, and engage themselves at a high level of involvement now that the issue had been resolved. Far more material was covered, and at a deeper level, than would have been possible without the previous day's interaction.

It's important to conclude this example with a distinction. Most experienced teachers have countless strategies for keeping learners focused on the necessary content. In this situation, had one of these strategies appeared likely to be successful, it would have been utilized immediately. However, the students' level of agitation during the outdoor discussions made it apparent that the issue needed to be addressed. It was the extreme nature of the level of their distraction that justified the course being temporarily diverted from its focus on the intended content.

Second Example

The setting was an intensive, ten-day accelerated learning program for teens, in which I was leading a class on speed-reading. One male student was restless, appeared disinterested, and wouldn't focus on the material. As the morning continued his behavior grew progressively more disruptive to the other students. I found myself rapidly becoming irritated with him. At the next break I pulled him aside to find out why he was behaving this way. He hung his head, staring at his shoes, and was generally uncommunicative. After much prodding, however, the truth came out.

He was a long-distance runner on the team at his high school. The program he was currently attending required the students to stay within the bounds of the campus during the entire ten-day period. Now, on the seventh day, the lack of exercise had finally gotten to him, and he was going crazy to the extent that he was acting out his frustration within the classroom. As with the previous example, I was caught in a difficult decision. The speed-reading course was critical to each student's overall success in the program, even though it was only one day in length. If students were to miss even a small link in the chain of learning for this content, it might significantly affect their results at the end of the day. How could I honor his need for exercise while still providing him with the necessary information?

Teach People, Not Content. In this situation, it would not have benefited him, me, nor the other students for him to have stayed in the class any longer. I gave him special permission to leave the campus with one of our staff and go for a ten-mile run, as long as he left immediately. His eyes grew wide with excitement at the thought, then he dashed for his running clothes and took off. (On a side note, the staff member who had to accompany him was not quite as enthusiastic when he found out what he needed to do, but he did survive.) To keep that student current with the material, I had to meet with him over lunch and review what the rest of the class had been working on while he was out, which took away some of my personal time. However, the result was worth it. He was successful with the speed-reading component of the program, and, for those last three days, he was focused, attentive, and a star student.

People First

The two examples shown here were developed in depth to demonstrate the concept of putting the needs of the people above the needs of the content. However, this idea comes into play in a much wider variety of situations than I have illustrated so far, and may occasionally challenge some of the basic beliefs a teacher may hold regarding instruction. For example, in the middle of a lesson it may become apparent that the group needs to take a break. If no instructional strategy can be found to keep the presentation useful to the students at that point, then it is best to honor reality and simply take a break right at that moment. Over the last ten years it has become apparent to me that breaks are most useful if they are taken *when they are needed,* not necessarily as scheduled when the original lesson plan was designed. Sometimes they will work quite nicely at those preplanned points, and other times they won't. Respond to the needs of the group and the situation. Teach People, Not Content.

For the teacher to maintain a focus on *people first* requires a basic shift in thinking. Another way to state the same idea is to use these words: Don't teach *to* people, teach *with* them. Teaching *to* a group assumes that instruction happens only in one direction, from the teacher to the student. Teaching *with* the group acknowledges that effective learning is at least bidirectional between the teacher and students, if not multidirectional among everyone! Working within this framework acknowledges that the teacher's point of view is not always the most important one, and should not always determine the direction and focus of the learning session.

Finally, it is important to emphasize that the primary focus of this belief is the effective delivery of content. Curriculum is always important. The critical issue is that, if the needs of the people in the group are interfering with learning the content at a particular time, then the quality of subsequent instruction is greatly reduced. Responding immediately to the requirements of a group, or an individual, will allow for enhanced concentration on the material at a later point. All learners are people first, and adapting to meet their needs respects them as unique individuals.

AWARENESS LEADS TO CHOICE

The profession of teaching is fraught with potential illusions. These educational myths are tricky because they may be true in the majority of situations, while they may be false in other, perhaps less obvious, cases. For example, as discussed in the previous section, some teachers may believe that a focus on content is always the most important consideration. Other teachers may hope that the push for grades will motivate students to achieve higher levels of success, another generalization that can lead to trouble in some circumstances. What of the belief that a final exam is an accurate reflection of a student's understanding of the material? True or false? How about the belief that a college education will lead to a higher paying job? (Come on, be honest, you heard that one somewhere too, didn't you? Think about it: Is it necessarily true?) But of all these "illusions," perhaps none is so powerful as the belief that teachers can control the behaviors of their students.

Imagine the following three hypothetical situations: (1) a boss informs an employee that he or she will be fired if a report isn't completed by 5:00 P.M.; (2) a teacher tells a student that to receive a high grade in his course it will be necessary to pass the final exam with a perfect score; (3) a mentor teacher tells her training teacher candidate to follow a certain instructional methodology or find another mentor from when to learn. In all three cases, is one person necessarily controlling the behaviors of another person? The answer is no. While each situation has some clearly delineated consequences for choosing certain actions, in the end, the individual is responsible for his or her behavior.

Control and Influence

A key distinction lies in the difference between *control* and *influence*. The intention of the implied consequences given by the boss, the teacher, and the mentor teacher is simply to influence the other person's behavior. The concept of influence is itself a broad topic (Cialdini 1984). For the purposes of this discussion, however, it is enough to note that, in the end, the employee, the student, and the teacher candidate all have complete freedom in their choice of behaviors. Influence is possible—control is not. Nowhere is this more evident than in family relationships. Parents learn rapidly that it is impossible to completely control their child's behaviors, although it may be possible to influence him or her. This astonishing discovery is frequently made by parents while raising their first child, much to their chagrin!

Applying this knowledge to a learning situation leads to an important theme in education. *Teachers cannot control what students learn.* As much as they may wish to, they cannot know for certain how learners are interpreting the information they are hearing. They cannot know how learners intend to apply the information. They cannot reach inside the learners' heads and simply plant the information in the appropriate part of their brains, much as they may occasionally wish to use this more direct approach. In reality, all they can do is influence each learner's process in the acquisition of knowledge.

Certainly the extent of this influence can be far-reaching, and will apply to a variety of factors. For instance, teachers can have a powerful effect on how information is perceived by learners simply through their tone of voice, their words, and their use of gestures. The decision to use visual aids to supplement instruction may influence certain learners to conceptualize the information in a particular manner. Teachers can clarify for learners how they might choose to apply their understanding of the information through the use of examples. The length of time teachers choose to devote to a particular topic will demonstrate how important they feel it is, which may bias a learner's perception of the content. These are but a very few of the numerous ways in which teachers *influence* a learner's perception of new information.

Teachers are constantly making choices that affect how learners encode, process, and relate to information. In fact, one way in which teachers judge their effectiveness is through their ability to transfer the information they know to another human being. While this is certainly one valid parameter for evaluating a teacher's competence, the ability of the learner to make choices should not be ignored as an important factor in the knowledge transfer equation. In the end, it will always come down to what each learner chooses to do with the information that has been presented.

All about Choice

This distinction leads to a critical conclusion concerning learning. As frightening as this may seem to some of us, effective instruction boils down to the simple concept of influencing the choices learners make. The weight of this influence can affect choices made both in the present and in the future, and it has a logical connection with the behaviors people choose to engage in:

"Given all they know, people *always* make the best choice available to them."

At first glance, this statement may seem to go against common sense. Consider, however, students who gets labeled as the "class clown." The disruptive behaviors exhibited by such students may appear to be negative choices, because they may constantly be finding themselves in trouble with their teachers. On closer examination, however, it might become apparent that their need for attention clearly outweighs their desire to learn. From their perspective, the best choice of behavior is to make off-the-wall comments and play around during class. This way, their primary need is being served.

It is not the intention of this book to delve into a psychological discussion nor open a conversation on attribution theory or Maslow's hierarchy of needs. Suffice it to say that even the most aberrant behavior can usually be quickly traced back to a choice that someone feels is the best one available at that time. People always choose the behavior they perceive to be the best in any given situation.

If it can be accepted that, on a general level, people make the best choice available to them, then the first part of the previous statement must also be considered: "*Given all they know . . .*" Now the goal of the teacher becomes clear. If he or she wants learners to make effective, powerful choices, students must be aware of the choices they have available to them. This can be summarized as:

"Awareness Leads to Choice."

Perhaps the metaphor of a buffet will serve best to illustrate this point. Suppose a chef desires that diners choose certain dishes. He will then make every possible effort to create a beautiful presentation of these dishes. Still, the diners will always have free choice as to what they put on their plates, and how much they place in their mouths. The only moment the chef can exert influence is when the food is offered to them. The goal of the teacher is to offer not only palatable information, but to make it attractive enough that learners will come to view it as a *viable choice* among those available to them.

A Different Slant on Choice

Choice plays another important role in learning contexts. Too often, learners feel they are being told what to do. This can eventually generate an undercurrent of resentment. This can be true with primary school students all the way through adult learners. Providing people with choice may open doors that release this energy so they can focus on the information. Choice moves learners toward feelings of ownership and responsibility. For example, when working with teenagers, I have often told them to locate themselves anywhere in the room where they are comfortable, as long as they can focus on the information from that position. At the start, they usually need some encouragement to move, given that they have spent most of their class time sitting in a chair in the usual way. Soon, however, they are scattered throughout the room, some lying down, others sitting cross-legged on the floor, and still others perched on tables at the back of the room. This may create an *appearance* of chaos for those more traditionally trained teachers. However, the sense of freedom mixed with responsibility frequently creates a much more focused learning environment.

In programs that I teach, I give choice about taking notes. This is true whether I am teaching young learners or adults. More traditional teachers may require that every student take copious notes during the lecture. However, with experience, I've found that learning styles and preferences vary greatly even within a small group. While some students may in fact do better if they take notes while the teacher is speaking, other students flourish if they are given the opportunity to simply listen and interact during the presentation. Later, these students can either take notes from the chalkboard or white board, from visuals posted on the wall, or from other students' notebooks. As long as they are aware that they are responsible for the material, students given permission to do it their own way are frequently more involved than they might have been otherwise.

Another aspect of choice that applies to teens, in particular, concerns my experience with teaching in special longer learning sessions, such as an all-day Saturday program. As an individual with experience in a traditional learning context, I was operating under the misconception that the students would all return to the classroom after a break—on time. How deeply misguided *we* are sometimes. It quickly became apparent during these programs that some of these teens had to take care of other issues during the break, which occasionally did not allow them to return on time. Often they felt guilty entering the room after the next session had begun, so they chose not to return at all! In response to this, several years ago I began to make the following announcement at the start of the first break for each of these classes:

> I understand that all of you are adults. You may have some things that you need to take care of during this break. Please know that the next session will start on time. However, if you are still busy, please come back as soon as you can.

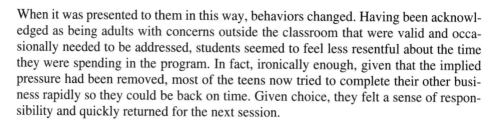

When it was presented to them in this way, behaviors changed. Having been acknowledged as being adults with concerns outside the classroom that were valid and occasionally needed to be addressed, students seemed to feel less resentful about the time they were spending in the program. In fact, ironically enough, given that the implied pressure had been removed, most of the teens now tried to complete their other business rapidly so they could be back on time. Given choice, they felt a sense of responsibility and quickly returned for the next session.

A Final Example

Awareness Leads to Choice is a dominant concept throughout all my training programs. In my seminars for teachers, this idea is presented at the very start of the program. It is held out as one of the foundational beliefs on which the information is based. It is acknowledged that all teachers are unique in the juxtaposition of their personalities, their content, and their teaching environment. It is clarified that the information is always meant to be heard by them with the proverbial "grain of salt." Each person is encouraged to decide which ideas are useful, and which might not apply. Hopefully, you, the reader of this book, will by now have noticed that I've mentioned this quite a few times.

In the classroom, this approach frequently confounds students at first. They are expecting to enter the class and be told "the way" to teach. Yet, from my perspective, there is no single best "way" for instruction to be delivered. The purpose of these seminars is quite simply to allow individuals to become aware of more choices that are available to them. From this "toolbox" they can pick and choose which specific topics will be useful for them, given their situation. Even after it is clearly stated at the onset, this idea is repeatedly brought back to their attention and reinforced throughout the program. This way, they may be freer to assess for themselves the quality of the information.

In Summary

Given this framework, the function of all educators is quite simple. They are present in the instructional environment for the sole purpose of increasing the number of options learners have in their choice bank. A greater awareness of available alternatives can enable learners to make an appropriate choice, whether it is how to solve a math problem, compose an English paper, solve a word problem, or repair a television set. Learners always make their own choices, both in the classroom, as well as in life. An awareness of the full breadth of options available to them in each circumstance will allow them to make a selection that will benefit them the most, and give them the best chance for success in life.

LEARNING + ENJOYMENT = RETENTION

Think back to some early childhood memories. What kind of events are you able to recall now, many years later? If you're like most people, these memories tend to fall into two distinct categories. On one hand are those times when we experienced pleasurable emotions, such as joy, excitement, and anticipation. On the other hand are occasions when we experienced difficult emotions, such as anger, fear, or hurt. The impact created by these types of memories can lead teachers to a useful observation concerning the delivery of content that is readily memorable to students.

These two highly generalized categories—positive and negative emotions—are not meant to provide an in-depth look into our current understanding of how memories work within the human mind. Indeed, understanding how the brain receives, processes, stores, and recalls information is currently one of the most active areas of study in the academic community. For example, some brain researchers debate such fine distinctions as the differences between episodic and semantic, procedural and declarative, or verbal and nonverbal memories. Others are studying the physiology of the human brain, attempting to uncover the secrets behind where and how information is stored. However, a basic understanding of the link between powerful emotions and their effect on recall is sufficient for the purposes of this book.

At some level most teachers agree that emotions can have a significant effect on our ability to remember information. This awareness can have interesting ramifications concerning learning and instruction. If teachers want to use emotions to assist learners in recalling a lesson long after it has been completed, they can follow one of two highly distinct paths. They can either find ways to create a positive, pleasurable, exciting experience for their students, or they can choose to terrorize them!

The idea of deliberately using fear in a learning environment is not so far-fetched as some might think. For example, consider the military boot camp model. This is not meant as an indictment of the military, but it is common knowledge that at times the instructors in these environments choose fear and intimidation as one avenue of creating a motivational learning environment. In this unique case, perhaps this is an appropriate choice, in light of the life-or-death consequences that may directly eventuate from the effectiveness of their training, and the extraordinarily high stress conditions under which their learners must function as they face situations containing high levels of threat to their survival. The instructional style is congruent with the operational state of the learners. In most situations, however, teachers should choose a different approach for making their lessons memorable to learners.

Unfortunately, the military model has been applied to quite a few school settings as well. Strict, stern, domineering teachers who subtly (and occasionally overtly!) terrorize students often feel they are doing it for the students' own benefit. After all, "It's a tough world out there!" is the commonly heard phrase. However, if strong mental associations are created between content and *negative* emotions, how willing are learners going to be to access the knowledge they acquired under these circumstances? If worry, suspicion, doubt, agitation, dread, and anxiety are all wrapped around the information, what are the chances they will want to recall those ideas? In most cases, the answer is not a positive one. In fact, learners may even actively seek to *forget* the material, so they can avoid having the linked emotions brought back into their consciousness.

Fortunately, especially over the last few decades, this approach to teaching seems to be the exception rather than the rule. Consider an imaginary continuum with fear at one end and joy at the other. On the average, where might the emotional feeling level of classrooms fall? In many situations it is located squarely in the middle of this continuum, even though retention occurs best at either end. Learning environments lack danger, yet they also lack any sense of excitement, adventure, stimulation, and exhilaration. The vast majority of classrooms are simply perceived as boring to the learners. And who would knowingly spend time in such an environment? Certainly not me. How about you?

Why No Fun?

It may seem intuitive to some readers that connecting positive emotions with new information should produce longer retention levels. Why, then, aren't more teachers using this approach, adding energy and magic to their teaching? Answers to this question may come from a complex array of factors. Perhaps they have never experienced a successful model of fun occurring while learning is happening. Perhaps they have never been trained in how to make this happen. Perhaps they believe that adults should never be asked to "play." Or, maybe teachers have a need to look "professional," and fear that smiling, laughing, and high levels of audience interaction will negatively affect their credibility in the classroom. Yet, on closer inspection, all of these justifications are open to challenge. For example, if teachers are concerned about their abilities in this arena, books such as this one are tools that can be used by them to develop their skills in creating this kind of environment.

At the heart of this issue lies a fundamentally flawed perception. It is the belief that *learning is hard.* To think that learning could be easy would buck tradition, and slogans reflecting this belief have entered the academic world:

"No pain, no gain!"

While such an axiom may be true in certain situations (for example, when working out in the gym to develop stronger muscles), does it necessarily apply to learning contexts? Or, perhaps more to the point, does it necessarily *always* apply to learning contexts? Must learning always be a painful, distressing experience? Could the learning context have a primary focus on making the acquisition of knowledge enjoyable, yet be interlaced with some serious moments of learner challenge? What would be the effect of such an approach on long-term retention?

Think for a moment about how students go about the process of studying. For years it was a commonly held belief that silence was mandatory for full concentration. Recently, however, with certain learning styles and certain types of material, it has become apparent that some students remember better if music is a component of their studying environment. Other students battle the teacher's or their parents' belief that they must sit still to learn. Yet, for these students, movement and involvement may greatly increase their ability to remember as they encode the information into what is called "muscle memory." Many adults also fit quite well into both of these categories. Some will relax, learn better, and be more willing to involve themselves if there is music in the environment. Others may require high levels of movement to stay fully attentive to the information.

For teachers to create a dynamic environment filled with positive emotions, they must first be willing to challenge this basic assumption about the process of learning. They must decide if they believe that if people have a pleasant experience, they will want to recall those memories and review them. Learners may then spend time anticipating subsequent class sessions, wondering what innovative activities they will experience. And they will go through a natural process of review as they discuss their experiences later with other people in their lives. These potential benefits should overpower any objections the teacher may have about the role of emotions in teaching.

In Summary

There are many ways to bring positive feelings into a learning context. Music, play, laughter, and personal interaction are just a few of the keys that can unlock this potential in learners. One of the highest goals of most instruction is to create a shift in the perspectives of the student. Humor is exactly that—a shift in perspective. Using humor, as often as possible, can unconsciously reinforce this message. Telling stories (discussed in more depth in a subsequent portion of this chapter) allows learners to understand new points of view, and helps them to grasp the advantages gained by learning this material. Giving learners the opportunity to interact frequently with others provides an opportunity for personal expression and human connection, which leads to a higher level of emotional safety. This, in turn, can increase the group's ability to focus on new material. These are but a few of the many ways a teacher can promote positive feelings.

A universal truth about learning is that it is a life-long process. Learners will be ahead of the game the sooner they understand that growth, change, and the development of new outlooks are always going to be a part of their life, most likely forever! There has been a dramatic change in the way people view their professional lives: It is estimated that people entering the work force in the year 2000 will average three to five separate *careers* before they retire. This means a high level of change. Teachers can add greatly to a learner's desire to grow and change by making the learning environment enjoyable.

As a teacher for several different university courses for teacher candidates for the past few years, I have begun to believe that this objective may be the single most important purpose of education—to have the students walk away from a class with an emotionally positive, rewarding experience, while simultaneously learning the necessary content (Sviniki 1990). If learners develop within themselves a healthy outlook regarding the learning process, they will be better prepared to deal with the realities of today's world. Every teacher has an opportunity to add to the development of this outlook by providing an experience within the classroom that is positive and rewarding. Adding positive emotions to the process will also significantly increase the chances for high levels of memory. Long-term retention of the information is what makes instruction effective. After all, if people can't remember it, then they never learned it!

APPLICATION IS EVERYTHING

Why do people bother to learn new information? What's the point of knowing who runs the government, how to solve a quadratic equation, what colors comprise the light spectrum, or when to watch the midnight sky for a meteor shower? Or, as many younger learners frequently express it, who cares? Adult learners frequently, although not always, focus on acquiring information that will be of benefit to them in their professional occupations. Yet, even here they may find themselves circling back to the original question: What's the purpose behind the learning? Why am I spending valuable time focusing on this topic?

At the most fundamental level, the answer is simple. People learn so they can improve their lives. This increased quality of living can occur on either a professional or a personal level. Yet the only way this works is if the new information can be put to use in some practical manner. Understanding basic math helps people keep score in games, tell time, or balance their checkbook. Developing a particular technical expertise may get someone a new job, or even a raise in pay. Insights into different personality styles may help an individual find a compatible life partner. Other benefits of learning may at first be less apparent. Improving internal motivation, gaining respect for other cultures, or clarifying one's personal values are equally important, although perhaps less obvious, outcomes.

Whatever the benefit, *learners must be able to see it for themselves.* The manner in which they can utilize these new thoughts, ideas, and insights should be made clear to them at all times. A parallel can be drawn to the movie *The Karate Kid*. When the student visits a karate teacher for the first time, he is asked to perform a number of seemingly menial tasks, such as waxing a car. Although puzzled, he complies with this unusual request. Eventually he becomes frustrated, because these tasks have no apparent relationship to his personal goal. In anger he approaches the teacher and asks why he has been doing these various jobs. In a dramatic cinematic sequence, the teacher shows him that the motion used to wax the car is identical to the motion used to defend himself from certain forms of attack. Once the connection is made, the student becomes much easier to teach. While it may not always be practical to keep students aware of the applicability of the material, as much as possible they should be kept aware of its usefulness to them.

Keeping a careful eye on the learner's understanding of the value of the material should be a critical part of every teacher's agenda. Consider the following axiom:

> Nothing is taught, if nothing is learned.
> Nothing is learned, if nothing is applied.

By way of contrast, a salesman would never believe that he has *sold* something, until someone has *bought* it. Yet teachers may make the mistake of believing they have *taught* something simply because they have engaged in the act of instruction. Until it can be shown that students can apply the information, then perhaps they never learned it. And if they never learned it, then it was never taught. This may be a challenging stance for some teachers to take, because many times they want to put the majority of the responsibility for learning on the shoulders of the student. While it is certainly valid to point out that learners have some level of accountability in the learning process, teachers also play an important part, and one aspect of their role should be to make the applicability of the material readily apparent to the learners. In a nutshell, *application is everything*.

Applying This Idea

Some content areas may lend themselves more readily to connections with real-world applications than others. For example, teachers of science, geography, or computer courses may find it easy to generate examples. The concept, however, applies across all areas of instruction. Demonstrating the validity of the material through association with concrete illustrations assists learners both in remembering and understanding how to apply the information. Here are a variety of ways in which material can be taught so that applications are readily grasped to the learners.

Example #1:   Teaching higher levels of math can be a challenge. One reason is its inherently conceptual nature. Students may become confused as to where exponents, polynomials, sines and cosines, and other alien-looking symbols and formulas fit into the bigger scheme of life. For clarity, as a secondary school teacher, I taught these concepts only as they could be shown to be useful in the world. Polynomials were used to show how a restaurant owner calculates the markup required for a particular sandwich. Students then ran a small lunch deli on campus for a week to test out their ideas. Banking formulas were generated to show how exponents worked to create interest income, and students visited at least one local bank to find out the formulas they used for various types of accounts. Sines and cosines were used to calculate the height of local buildings, and the distance between various points on a map.

Example #2:   In working with high school students during accelerated learning programs, one of the pieces I was responsible for was teaching a memory system. At first, a "peg system" was taught to them, and they were told to use it in their classes, with few examples having been provided. Over time, I received more and more feedback showing that, although students enjoyed the idea and had fun learning it, few actually used it in school settings. Given this feedback, I redesigned the format of these presentations to include numerous examples and applications in a variety of settings.

The final portion of each session now comprised three new pieces. First, I shared at least five examples of how I had used the peg system in a variety of settings and circumstances. Second, students talked with a partner and generated at least two places they thought they might be able to use it. Finally, a large group discussion was held during which people shared the ideas they had generated with their partner, the purpose being to give everyone even more ways to apply it. Given this new ending sequence to the memory session, subsequent feedback showed that a significantly higher percentage of students were able to use the material in their classes. They needed to understand, very specifically, how and where to use this approach for memorizing information before the concept was of any practical value to them.

Example #3:   I teach numerous programs for teachers on the ideas and techniques explained in this book. For many years one of my guiding thoughts was that the more information that could be crammed into the available time, the better. However, this led to a torrent of material being presented, with a low level of long-term recall. Application was rarely discussed in depth, other than through one or two quick examples. Yet if they couldn't apply it, then it was never taught, so some changes were made in the approach.

Currently, after presenting two or three points, I have teachers get into groups and discuss how they might answer the question,

"How might you be able to use this information?"

At least once every hour they have this amount of discussion time. Sometimes this will happen as frequently as every ten to fifteen minutes, depending on the density of the material. The question is simply whether they can use the information, and, if so, then in what way? Similar to the previous example, after they have talked in these smaller groups, a large group sharing of ideas often follows, so that the key links generated in the small groups can be shared with the other people in the room. This further expands their options on how to apply the material. What is critical in this scenario, as well as in the previous example, is that the *learners are the ones generating the applications.* If learners are able to come up with their own connections, it contributes greatly to their ability to remember the key ideas.

Example #4: In the previous examples, clarity concerning applicability was provided after the information was presented. For another approach, consider giving an example at the *beginning* of a session. For instance, when teaching some of the practices discussed in this book, I frequently open with a problem. The first line might be:

"What's wrong with the following situation?"

Then the situation in question is presented. When the underlying problem is clear to everyone, the instruction proceeds to demonstrate ways to overcome it. In these cases, application becomes the starting point of the presentation. Subsequently, during the remaining class time, variations on this particular type of problem, and ways to address it, are presented.

In Essence

Certainly, there are many other means of bringing applicability into the learning environment. These are merely a few variations on this vital theme. Readers of this book will find my commitment to this idea demonstrated through the use of numerous examples that comprise a major component of each section. The bottom line is that application is everything. Without it, nothing else matters. If the learners cannot find a way to rapidly integrate the knowledge into something they know and are familiar with, the information may quickly fade from their memory. As the old expression goes, "Use it or lose it." In the case of learning, it's far better to use it.

STORIES ARE GREAT

Overview

Long before there were computers, before there were movies, and even before the invention of books, there were stories. The collected wisdom of a group of people could be found in their stories. These metaphorical tales of heroism and courage, of love and renewal, of hope and charity, were the primary means these people had of passing on the accumulated knowledge of the elders to the younger members of the group. It was through stories that young children first learned the essential skills of survival, from hunting techniques to which plants were safe to eat. It was also a way of maintaining the group's unique rituals and traditions. The storyteller in a tribe was looked on as one of its most revered and venerated members (Campell 1983). Even the Bible relies heavily on the use of parables to communicate its message.

Today, stories still serve much the same function and hold the same fascination for audiences of all generations. This phenomenon can be witnessed in the effect of popular movies that have the power to create significant cultural change. The best movies are those with high entertainment value wrapped around the solid core of an important social message. The power of a great story can also be seen in the popularity of the

"Chicken Soup for the Soul" series of short stories, edited by Jack Canfield (1993). Stories, myths, fables, tales, and legends are still very much a part of today's culture.

In teaching, however, the use of stories and metaphors are frequently overlooked as a means of communicating basic concepts and ideas (Sfard, 1998). Yet people learn by example, and stories provide these comparisons for them, developing relationships they can understand. A good story creates a lasting impact and assists the learner in remembering the information. Stories and metaphors should be woven throughout the very fabric of every presentation, from the opening thoughts to the concluding images (McConnell 1978).

A First Example

It was a session on communication skills. The material had focused primarily on how much even a single misunderstood word could affect the outcome of an interaction. At the conclusion of class, the teacher told the students the following story:

> "A man was driving on a winding mountain road. As he approached a sharp turn, a car came around it swerving wildly. It narrowly missed sideswiping his car. As it raced past him, a woman leaned out and yelled at him 'HOG!'
>
> The man was completely startled. He thought to himself: 'Wait a minute, I'm not the road hog here, she is! She's the one swerving all over the place!' With that he leaned out of his car and shouted back at her 'SOW!'
>
> He grinned in satisfaction to himself, rounded the corner, and ran promptly into a hog standing in the middle of the road."

Why did the teacher tell this story at the conclusion of the class? For the simple reason that it provides a humorous shift in perspective on the use of the word *hog*. This further illustrates the central concept the teacher was trying to teach to the students. In this case, the story that was used was a joke. While jokes entertain the learners, they also serve another purpose directly related to learning and long-term retention of information. If the learners enjoy them, there's an excellent chance that they will retell it at a later time to their friends. When retelling it, they are *unconsciously reviewing at least one idea from the material*. Using jokes, anecdotes, and humorous stories is effective in learning situations on a variety of levels. As mentioned previously, humor is essentially a matter of a perspective shift, which is exactly what the teacher is trying to create. Effective use of humor reinforces this fundamental notion for learners.

A Second Example

The teacher in the previous situation told that particular story at the conclusion of the class. This is a wise timing choice, especially if a story or metaphor can be found that sums up the essential point of the lesson. Because it is the last thing the group will hear, it is often the image they will most remember when they walk away. It is also a good idea to *open* a session with a story if one can be found that sets the stage for the content that is to follow.

I have frequently used the following true story to begin some of my programs on teaching and training:

> "I was teaching in New Zealand. A young man attended the three-day course and was an active, involved student. However, at the conclusion of the course he went home thinking to himself: 'This is Rich's style, not mine. I don't think I could create such an effective interactive learning environment.'
>
> The next day he woke up with a different thought: 'How do I know this isn't my style? Just because I've never taught this way doesn't mean I couldn't!' So he called three local schools and offered them each a free one-hour seminar. He figured that, because it was free, he could try some different teaching methods.
>
> At the first school he was only twenty minutes into the seminar when he realized that the students were enjoying themselves more than they ever had before in his courses; they were more actively involved, they were moving faster through the material, and even appeared to be understanding it at a deeper level. At the other two schools the students also reacted in this manner."

I use this story to create a positive mental framework for the information the students are about to receive. Hopefully, they will remember this success story as they proceed through the program. Then, if for some reason they can't immediately see the applicability of the content, they will understand that it might very possibly become much clearer to them when they try it for themselves, just as it happened to the person in the story.

Both the beginning and the ending of many learning sessions should contain at least one story. Of course, between these two points, even more stories should be used to illustrate, highlight, exemplify, and clarify the material. The basic idea of this chapter is quite simple. Remember to start with a story, end with a story, and in-between tell even *more* stories!

More Thoughts on Stories

Stories can be anything. As shown above, they could be simple jokes. They could also be real life examples, situations you have personally experienced. Or perhaps they are events that have happened to someone familiar to you or someone on television. They can also be metaphors, such as some of the stories included in Appendix F. Each of these gives the learners a different slant on the material. In fact, there are stories, metaphors, and examples throughout this book, and they are included precisely to show how a particular idea might play out in real life. Or, stories can come from popular myths, fairy tales, or fables. Basically, they can come from anywhere.

Stories also assist learners in encoding the information for later recall. Much has been written about the benefit of having prior knowledge when attempting to learn new material. If the teacher can relate the current content to something the learners are already familiar with, the effort needed to recall the material later is greatly reduced.

Certain areas of instruction may lend themselves more readily to the inclusion of stories and metaphors, such as creative writing or history. However, storytelling should never be limited to these areas. Instead, they should be present in every context, from stereo repair to philosophy. As a high school mathematics teacher, I told stories about gambling techniques in Las Vegas to help convey the concept of probability and to show that it isn't just something created to annoy math students. At other times I used stories about being an actor off-Broadway to illustrate certain points in my drama classes. Every arena of instruction offers opportunities for the recounting of stories unique to that topic. Teachers should take advantage of these moments and find ones relevant to their material.

Where do teachers find good stories? The truth is that they are everywhere around us. They are happening to each of us every day. You can start developing this talent for yourself by simply beginning to take note of events as they occur around you. People often say, "But nothing interesting ever happens to me!" The truth is that many interesting things are always happening around us. The question is whether we are willing to look at them from the perspective of a storyteller. What message is contained in the moment? What could be learned? What is this situation similar to? Addressing these questions will begin to open your eyes to the endless possibilities that are present in each and every day. Additionally, collections of jokes and stories abound, including the Canfield series mentioned earlier. Another excellent source is the children's section of the library, where countless books have very short stories that can be utilized to emphasize a particular point of instruction. Original stories always add a unique, personalized twist to each teachers presentation. Finally, there are several unique stories included in Appendix F. They are meant specifically for you to use as a starting point in your development as a storyteller in the classroom.

In Summary

Our lives are full of stories. Some of them are positive, some are negative, and all of them can teach us something about the world in which we live. The greater purpose of most learning environments is to increase the quality of the lives of the learners. Stories help students gain insight into how to apply the knowledge and make connections for themselves. Bringing storytelling into the classroom is not only an effective way to teach, it is common sense.

INSTRUCTIONAL PRECEPTS: A SUMMARY

The consideration of a teacher's precepts about effective learning is a process, not a product. It is insufficient to clarify these ideas once and assume they will remain the same over the course of your entire teaching career, or even over the next few years. A switch to different content may promote a change in your approach. Exposure to new strategies may alter your perceptions. Over time your teaching style will naturally mature and grow. This process may require you to reexamine the foundation on which you have built your current model of learning and instruction. These chances to reset the basic tenets of your approach to teaching should be viewed as opportunities to further enhance the excellence of your teaching or training skills.

The five ideas discussed in this section are an integral part of my instructional mind-set when approaching the creation of a dynamic learning session. Now it is up to you to consider for yourself what you believe to be true in this regard. What are the central beliefs that guide the development of your lesson plans? What are the key assumptions that influence the design of an instructional activity or creation of a course? What are the criteria you use to judge the level of success of a particular class? Your personal clarity on these issues will go a long way toward determining the quality of the students' experience and the impact of the instruction.

CHAPTER THREE

PRINCIPLES OF EFFECTIVE INSTRUCTION

> This chapter covers three principles for maximizing a teacher's impact on student learning. While there are certainly hundreds of principles, these three deserve close attention by all teachers. Several examples of each are provided to highlight how it functions in practice.

CREST OF THE WAVE

If you're not riding the crest of the wave, you'll find yourself beneath it.

The ocean is relatively calm. In the distance, a swell begins to build. It is slow and steady at first. Gradually, as it approaches the shore, it gains height and momentum. It arches up out of the water, growing ever higher. Soon, critical mass is reached and, at the very top, white foam begins to form. Slowly the wave curls in on itself, crashes thunderously forward, then begins to dissipate. The wave gently washes up on the beach, and all is calm again.

This simple scene from nature demonstrates a critical lesson in creating and maintaining an effective learning environment. Teachers who are sensitive to this fluctuating dynamic can provide a powerful, integrated learning experience for their students. If a teacher's timing is off, and she attempts to continue with the same format after the wave has crashed, the feeling is similar to trying to surf after the wave has crashed down on itself. Most teachers have experienced exactly this phenomenon, and it's not one to create pleasant memories. Most teachers who leave the profession do so because of physical and mental burnout, which is often the by-product of trying to work against the natural flow of the group. How can teachers learn to read the flow of the group, then guide it to their own advantages?

Simply put, much like waves building, peaking, then crashing down, there are swells, crests, and tumbles in learning environments. When students' ability to draw useful learning from a given mode of interaction has been maximized, the crest of the wave has been reached. At this point it is in the best interests of both the teacher and the students to shift to some alternate manner of instruction, to engage in some distinct change of pace that will recapture their focus and interest. The following are two examples that may be useful in clarifying this concept.

Situation #1: It is early in the year. The teacher's objective for this sequence is to allow students to meet others in the room on a one-to-one basis. The students form into dyads. They choose who will go first and who will go second. The teacher provides a question to be addressed, and informs them that each person will have two minutes to answer the question. The teacher will tell them when it is time to switch to the second person. The first person begins.

Here is the critical question: Does the teacher always give the first person the full two minutes? The answer depends on understanding the "Crest of the Wave" principle. First, it is necessary for the teacher to observe and listen to what is happening in the room once the conversation between students begins. Initially, the sound level in the room will build. However, as some students run out of things to say, they will stop speaking, and the overall sound level will decrease. At this point, the "crest of the wave" has been reached.

The crest of the wave can also be identified visually. As the first person runs out of things to say, she may begin to feel uncomfortable and look away from her partner's eyes. Or, she may begin to shift, fidget, or twist and turn to see what else is happening in the room. These are visual cues indicating that some of the dyads have reached the crest.

Consider what happens if *nothing* is changed at this moment. As time continues, students will feel increasingly uncomfortable. When the next activity is introduced, they may be hesitant to engage in it, because they have now had a mildly unpleasant experience in this class. While it may be subconscious at first, with repeated experiences teachers may suddenly find they have a "difficult" group on their hands, unaware that a simple matter of timing has created this particular group dynamic.

Once the crest of the wave has been identified, how could the teacher respond? In this case, perhaps the teacher might say, "Please take ten seconds for the first person to complete." With this statement, those who are already finished will be relieved that the discussion is almost ready to switch, knowing they can survive for ten more seconds, while those pairs that are still talking know that it is now time to complete their conversation. The most important point is that the teacher *must react* in some manner to the fact that the majority of the people in the room are ready to move forward.

Situation #2: A lecture has been given, and the teacher has opened the floor for student comments. Several questions have already been answered. As another one is asked, the teacher is aware of several people shifting slightly in their seats and looking around the room. This movement informs the teacher that the questions have shifted from those that were of concern to the large group to those that are of concern only to one or two students.

The crest of the wave for this session has just been reached. The teacher responds to the present question, perhaps adding, "This will be the final question for now. We'll be ending class a bit early today so that those of you with further questions may speak with me individually at that time."

These two examples demonstrate the beginning of how the Crest-of-the-Wave principle can be understood in instructional situations. The most effective teachers are those who are responsive to these waves of interest and attention within the environment and make appropriate responses and adjustments.

On closer inspection it is easy to see that there are multiple "waves" happening simultaneously within most learning environments. There are small ones, such as how many seconds of silence to allow students to observe a newly introduced visual, how much time to give a group to read a particular passage in a book, or when to use directed questions instead of a general question technique. Larger ones may consist of how long to give lectures, how much time to allow for discussion in a small group, or how much time to devote to a particular lecture. It is the careful management of, and response to, these various situations that creates an atmosphere that has the highest level of impact on the students.

A key point of consideration is that, when teachers prepare for a class, they are essentially operating out of pure fantasy. (You knew this, didn't you? And now, someone has finally come out and actually admitted it!) Of necessity, they are simply imagining what will happen when the students actually arrive, the class begins, and the teacher utters those first words. Yet teaching is a *living* art. Its effectiveness is primarily dependent on the ability of the teacher to stay present in the moment and respond to the reactions of the group. Certainly, with sufficient experience, one hopes to be better able to imagine what will happen. At the same time, even the most widely experienced teacher will gain greatly from paying particular attention to what is occurring in his or her instructional room each moment of the day.

Perhaps the most important situation where application of this principle is mandated occurs when information is being delivered through lecture format or direct instruction. Before this discussion continues, however, consider this question:

"How long can you *pay attention* when someone is presenting?"

Paying attention, in this case, is defined as being able to recall and use the information at a later date. Of course, our ability to focus and give our full attention to a presenter depends on a variety of factors. What are some of these influences?

- Environmental Factors: room temperature, comfort of the seat
- Teacher's Presentational Skills: vocal changes, facial expressions, hand movements, use of humor
- Learners' Physiology: Did they get enough sleep last night? Did they eat the proper foods?
- Learners' Internal Motivation: How motivated are they to learn this subject?

There are many more; however, suppose for a moment that each of the factors listed above were *perfect*. The room temperature is just cool enough, the chairs are sufficiently comfortable, the teacher's delivery is both humorous and poignant, each learner has personally chosen to be present at this class and desires to learn more, and so on. (Now this is every teacher's true fantasy!) If everything were perfect, once again ask yourself the initial question:

"How long can you *pay attention* when someone is presenting?"

While answers will always vary from person to person, and from situation to situation, academic studies have established some general figures. Given the previous definition of *paying attention*, on the average, adults can focus up to a maximum of fifteen minutes. Yes, that figure is correct. Fifteen minutes, at most. And the younger the audience is, the shorter that figure becomes, naturally! For teens the figure is eight to ten minutes of direct instruction, and for students twelve years and under the figures are drastically lower. (Middle school teachers have occasionally been caught pondering whether it's possible for some students to actually have *negative* attention spans. While scientists may argue that this is theoretically impossible, these teachers may have a very different opinion!)

What does this mean for teachers? Consider, for example, the length of most high school classes. Most will last somewhere between thirty-five minutes and an hour. For the purposes of this example, let's consider a fifty-minute class. What may happen to the learning in the room if this class is taught in a rigid lecture format? The question takes us back to an educational principle that is well over one hundred years old, known today as Ebbinghaus's Curve (Driscoll 1994). In some of the earliest educational experiments, he demonstrated that, when studying long lists of content, students tended to be able to recall the most amount of information from the beginning and the end of the lists. True, there may not be a direct correlation between serial list learning and lecture format. However, the *tendencies* derived from these early studies can certainly be considered in regards to generating effective teaching.

For fifty minutes of classroom instruction, with our limited attention spans, this means that learners will recall material primarily from the start of the class (the first ten to fifteen minutes during which we can actually give it our best attention), very little from the middle, and some points from the last few moments of the class. True, in the academic example discussed here, many teachers currently make some form of adjustment, such as taking a single break in the middle of a long class, but it may not be nearly enough to achieve the result of efficient learning.

It is important to remember that what is under consideration is maximizing a student's ability to pay attention. It is not that learners will get *nothing* from longer sessions. Most important is the fact that, as time continues, learners will have to work harder and harder to stay focused on the information. Eventually a breaking point will crash in on them. Reaching this point is readily apparent on learners' faces as they fall back on that skill all of us learned as teenagers: stare at the teacher, occasionally nod the head to send message of interest while our brain spaces out by thinking about anything but what is being taught at that moment. We've reached the information overload level, and the wave has crashed down. What can be done to avoid this from happening? Consider the following example:

What's frequently the worst time to teach, and the worst time to learn? Most people would agree that it's directly after lunch, when the food's digesting, taking blood away from the brain, making us want to NAP!

Despite basic common sense, a special high school class was to be taught from 1:30 P.M. until 4:30 P.M. each Wednesday. Students were naturally quite concerned, given the timing. However, it was a mandatory class, so at the appointed time on that first day they trudged in and took their places.

The teacher introduced himself, and the class began. The first thing he did was to hold up a small kitchen timer. He asked if the students could all see it. They could. Carefully, in full view of the class, he set the timer to ring in exactly ten minutes. He said nothing further about the clock, but instructed the students to take out a pen and some paper to take notes. He began to lecture. Ten minutes later the timer rang, and the teacher stopped.

At that point he turned on an overhead projector that had a question written on it and asked the students to discuss this question with one or two others near them. After several minutes he asked for them to share their ideas with the large group. When they were finished, he carefully reset the timer and began to speak again.

This time when the timer rang he stopped the lecture, distributed a two-page article related to the subject at hand, and asked the students to read through it. When they had finished reading, they again formed small groups and discussed what they had read. Following this the teacher reset the timer for ten minutes, and the class continued in this manner, with an extended break in the middle, until 4:30 P.M.

What was the effect of the ten-minute timer? Students in the class quickly realized that this teacher would speak for no longer than the timer allowed. This meant that everyone in the room knew how long the lecture would last, and that there actually was an "end in sight." Students were able to avoid the natural tendency to fade out, knowing they could surely stay focused for the small amount of time required. Another way to say this is that, for once, the students had . . . hope!

The class was taught in this style for the entire semester. In the collective experience of the students, interviewed after the class, most agreed that not only had the class time passed rapidly, but that they could recall considerably more information from this class than many, if not all, of the classes they had attended.

The ideas from this example can be applied to many situations. When a maximum of fifteen minutes has been reached, teachers should look for another method of allowing the learners to process the information. Students given options similar to those created above are in fact creating *redundant retrieval routes* to the information. They are strengthening the primary concepts in their minds, and making meaning for themselves. This, in itself, may result in greatly increased levels of retention. This approach is also known as the *pause procedure* (Ruhl, Hughes and Schloss 1987.)

It should be noted that this statistic has been academically validated only for a carefully defined situation, where new content is being presented in lecture format. Even so, it makes sense, doesn't it? Attention spans for other circumstances may vary greatly. For example, most of us can sit through an entire two-hour movie or forty-five minutes of stand-up comedy quite easily. Despite these differences, however, it should be noted that the same idea may still apply: Of the forty-five minutes of comedy, how many jokes can we actually recall when it's over? How many lines from the movie could we recite from memory? In learning environments, attention spans may be quite different in situations where students are discussing ideas in small groups, or creating a team skit, or reviewing material in preparation for an examination. While it is up to the individual teacher to assess the effectiveness of the time given to students for each component of learning, a useful starting point may be to consider much shorter periods of time than has previously been given their students.

Few teachers lament that they have too much time for instruction. Yes, for some reason you won't often hear them say things like, "Gosh, what am I going to do with all this free time?" It just doesn't happen. In fact, it is often quite the opposite, with frustration setting in over not having sufficient time to cover the material in an effective manner. Given this reality, a common response from many teachers to the idea of lecturing for fewer than fifteen minutes before making a change may be one of fear that they are wasting precious classroom time (Gagne and Glaser 1978). In response to this concern, consider the net effect on learning if the teacher continues to speak past the point where it is possible for the learners to effectively take in new information. The learning curve drops drastically, and it will increasingly become a waste of time for both the speaker and the learners to continue. Who needs that?

Instead, if time is taken to allow learners the opportunity to process the information through a different modality (talking, reading, editing their notes in silence for a few moments), it will become a double-win situation (Litecky 1992). On one hand, learners are being given time to reorganize their thoughts, process the material, and thus be better prepared when the next section of lecture is delivered; teachers have the opportunity to assess the students' reactions, breathe for a moment, and reorganize their thinking for the next section. Given a few minutes break, when teachers then begin the next section of lecture students are likely to be more articulate and focused, and, thus, able to communicate the information more clearly and in a shorter period of time.

When a presenter recognizes the crest of the wave is happening, and moves forward to something else, he is changing the "state" of the audience. The word *state* in this situation refers to the audience's physiology, their physical and mental state. An expression commonly used in active learning environments is that the teacher is using a *state change*.

> Definition: A *state change* occurs when an educator changes the method of instruction for the audience from one modality to another modality.

There are countless ways in which state changes can be accomplished. Several have already been mentioned in this section. For example, after a brief lecture, having the audience switch to small-group discussion is a state change. Moving then to a large-group discussion would be another state change. State changes can be very brief or continue for some time. They can be subtle, such as moving from direct instruction mode into telling a story, which would cause a subtle change in how learners listen to and process the verbal information. They can also be quite dramatic, such as moving from indoors to outdoors for the next section of the class. Here is another fairly obvious example of the use of a state change:

> It is early in the year. The teacher has just completed delivery of a short section of content. She asks the students to stand up. Next, she asks them each to sit in a new seat somewhere else in the room, next to people they don't know very well. Finally, the students are invited to introduce themselves to two or three people seated somewhere near them. When this has been done, she asks them to look forward and continues with her next piece of information.

The conscious use of state changes, even quite subtle ones, can have a powerful influence on the audience's ability to stay focused on the material. For example, simply by varying the tone of voice a teacher uses, *vocal inflection*, can add greatly to learners' ability to focus for longer periods of time. Most dynamic teachers change their method of presentation quite frequently, even within a single class session. They will alternate between storytelling, focusing on main points, brief audience involvement, and the use of humor. Teachers using direct instruction techniques that effectively incorporate these ideas may be able to continue well past the fifteen-minute time frame discussed previously.

Teachers of younger audiences may want to consider this same discussion from the opposite perspective. Given that younger students are quite naturally full of adrenaline, motion, and excitement, perhaps instruction should be geared toward activities that *release* that boundless energy. The crest of the wave may then come in the form of those brief, quieter, more focused moments when the primary content is delivered.

When a state changes occurs in a learning environment, it causes the brain to refocus its attention to what is happening (Schacter 1990). For a brief period of time, it will feel like the start of something new. When things are new the brain tends to be in a heightened level of awareness. The use of frequent state changes may allow the audience to maintain a higher level of attention than might otherwise be possible. However, be aware that the use of state changes can be overdone, and it will be up to the discretion of each teacher to determine which kinds of state changes to use and how frequently they can be introduced, given the audience, the content, the time frame, the physical learning environment, and other important factors.

Is it important for the presenter to pay attention to the audience's physical as well as mental state? You might try this right now, wherever you are sitting:

> Slouch down in your chair. Slouch *way* down. Slump your head forward, let your shoulders sag. Now, in this position, feel . . . Happy! Excited! Joyful! See if you can feel those emotions while your body is in that physical posture. Is it slightly difficult to follow both these directions simultaneously?
>
> Now try the opposite: Sit tall in your chair. Head up, eyes up, shoulders back. Take a nice, deep breath. Remain in this position and feel . . .

Sad. Depressed. Wait, keep that head up and keep trying to feel unhappy. Again, it's challenging to sink into negative emotions when seated up upright!

If you had difficulty maintaining the postures while trying to experience those particular feelings, as requested, it's because our brains and bodies are linked in what is known as an "inextricable loop": Each element is always having an effect on the other. It's the same reason top athletic coaches inevitably spend valuable practice time on the mental aspects of the game. For teachers it is often just the opposite: They must remember to address the physical aspects of their "game." They must read the physical and auditory cues from their students and make adjustments when necessary.

This brings the discussion in a full circle back to the idea of reading the crest of the wave. Even when teaching highly technical content, teachers should remember the reality of the physiological link that exists between the human mind and body. There will always be evidence of the crest of the waves for both the physical and mental aspects of learning, and teachers need to respond to these cues as rapidly as possible to maximize the learning effectiveness.

The bottom line is to become aware of, and respond to, the changing needs of the audience. This is not to imply that students have no responsibility. Quite the opposite. If teachers demonstrate a responsiveness to the needs of the students, students often respond to the needs of the teacher and the situation, choosing to become much more actively involved than they might otherwise have been. With continued exposure to this form of instruction, learners frequently demonstrate a greatly increased level of personal responsibility for their education. Isn't that a nice outcome?

Here is a recommendation for those teachers who choose to use this concept on a regular basis in their work. Below is a list of state changes, some already discussed and some additional ones. Consider this as a beginning point. As you discover for yourself which state changes seem to work best for you, create your own personal list. Carry it with you at all times. Build on it whenever you can. Then, when you realize that the crest of the wave has been reached and the learners are ready for a state change, you will have some prepared options to fall back on in case your creative genius is unable to spontaneously generate an idea.

- Find a new place to sit.
- Stand and stretch.
- Tell a story.
- Exchange back rubs.
- Play a thirty-second game.
- Stand and shake hands with several people nearby.
- Have someone stand and read a part of the text.
- Role-play a related scenario.
- Give students two minutes to edit their notes in silence.
- Meet three people wearing the color blue.
- Take a three-minute walk outside, perhaps in pairs or trios.

Here is a further example of how one teacher currently makes creative use of one simple state-change idea:

> The teacher lives in the southeastern United States. He is a calm, soft-spoken individual. In addition to teaching math, each fall he also tours the schools from several states and gives two-hour lectures in an auditorium setting to high school students, usually in groups of over 250 at a time. The topic he covers is, "Getting involved in today's politics." Attendance is frequently mandatory for the students at these assemblies.
>
> As might be expected, the audience is seldom very pleased to be present. However, at the appointed time, he quietly begins his lecture. After about ten minutes, he pauses to ask the audience an innocuous question. He waits until someone responds. When a student finally does answer the question, he turns around in silence, takes something off of the table behind him, and tosses it out while saying thank you.
>
> When this happens, many in the audience sit up and take notice, wondering what just happened. What was thrown out to that person? There is the sound of crinkling paper, and suddenly it becomes clear: It was a piece of candy! With this realization, the game has begun.
>
> Meanwhile, the lecture continues. The teacher has made no reference to what happened. However, another few minutes passes, and the teacher now asks the audience another question. What happens? Many hands are raised. The question is answered and another piece of candy is distributed.
>
> Throwing candy out to audience members is the *only state change* this teacher uses in his entire presentation, and the audiences stay right with him for the entire two hours. It is never done to the point of completely distracting them from the information he is delivering. To keep it lively, he has a number of variations on this theme, such as occasionally announcing that he feels "random" and heaving out huge handfuls of candy. But that simple state change is enough to keep his audience focused, smiling, and paying attention to what is happening in the room. His goal is quite simple: If they pay attention, it will increase their ability to recall the information when the lecture has ended.

Ideally, state changes should occur at the crest of a particular wave. Yet perhaps the most critical moment of awareness for an teacher regarding the audience's state comes at the *beginning* of any learning session. Consider the following idea:

> Suppose a man decides to grow a crop in a new field. What is the first thing he must do? He must till the soil and prepare it for the seeds that are to come. Metaphorically, this image transfers easily into a learning environment. It is necessary to prepare each learner's mind before the seeds of knowledge can be effectively planted and reasonably expected to bear the fruits of higher learning.

Imagine the first moments of the first class of the day. The students walk in, sit down, and begin to organize themselves. Where are their thoughts? While a few may be looking through past notes, perhaps even previewing sections of a text in preparation for the session, experience has shown that these individuals are few and far between. (Some teachers may have never met even one of this rare breed of student!) Most students will have their thoughts focused elsewhere. Some may be thinking about their drive to school or perhaps the bus ride. Others may be remembering a discussion they had with their friends that morning. Still others may be daydreaming about the weekend ahead, looking forward with excitement to their "free time." The social ones in the crowd may be talking with those around them, inquiring about movies they have seen recently, people they've dated, or which restaurants have the best food. What they are *not* thinking about is the material, the content, or the class in general.

The key is to get the audience mentally focused in the room, ready to fully engage themselves with the topic at hand. Failing to do so is akin to the farmer walking out into the unplowed field, throwing out a handful of seeds, screaming "Grow, dang it!" and *hoping* that *something* takes root out there. Does this make agricultural sense to you? If so, please feel free to consider occupations other than producing our nation's food supply. And if not, then why would it make educational sense? Woe to the teacher who causally waltzes in and starts the day by announcing:

"Good Morning. It's 8:00. Let us begin."

The mental field is not yet tilled. The ground is unturned. The likelihood that the seeds of information will bear fruit is greatly reduced. A farmer would be wasting effort in this case, just as a teacher would be who chose to ignore the opportunity to prep the minds of the students. Here is an example, similar to one discussed earlier in this chapter:

> It is the beginning of class. The first thing the teacher asks the students to do is find a partner. When everyone has a partner the teacher gives them thirty seconds to discuss a topic that he provides for them, such as, "What did you do last night?" This is repeated with three to four different partners, each time with a different topic, such as "What's your favorite late night munchie?" or "Where would you like to go on a dream vacation?" In the final pairing, he provides them with a question to discuss that relates to the topic of the day's class. Total time for this opening: three minutes.

As students interacted with each other, they became more mentally present in the room, more aware of their classmates, and more comfortable in the environment. The final question began to focus their attention on the topic, and now, as they seat themselves, they are ready to involve themselves in the issue to be discussed during this class session.

The example provided here has a high level of *social* interaction. There are several reasons to consider opening the class with state changes that involve students interacting with each other. In general, human beings are *social* animals. As such, our social reality can have a powerful influence on our state of mind. If learners are comfortable with those around them, they may be better able to relax and focus on the topic at hand. I strongly recommend that teachers experiment with opening state changes that provide learners with the opportunity to engage in casual conversation with each other. Even those teachers who are not outgoing by nature may wish to explore this concept and gauge the results for themselves. Learning environments with groups of people are, by their very nature, social environments. Allowing this feeling of a positive social dynamic to unleash itself may provide people with the chance to release their inner energy, thereby giving them a better chance to focus on the day's lesson.

Here are some additional examples of options for opening a session. Notice that some are content-related, and others simply serve the function of getting people to become more mentally present and comfortable in the classroom.

- Form groups and have them introduce themselves. Ask them to discuss the key point from the previous class.
- Early in the year, introduce a name memorization game.
- For math classes, write a mathematical puzzler on the chalkboard. Have them work with a partner to solve it.
- Give students two minutes to browse through last session's notes in silence.
- Play an active, fast-moving game, such as tag.

As before, the type of state changes used by a teacher is entirely dependent on individual choice. One teacher recently came up with a creative, novel idea, one that many new teachers could borrow. Because she was a first-year teacher, she did not know many different ways to start her class. She needed to generate some additional options. For the first two classes, she provided the opening exercises. After the second time, she told the students in her class what she was doing, and the purpose it was intended to serve. Then she presented them with a sign-up sheet, and groups of two or three students were to take on the responsibility of creating the opening activity for each class. Some of these activities were successful, and, as you might imagine, some were not quite so successful. When she saw one that worked well, what did she do? She wrote it down and put it into a file to use the following year. After just her first year, she had more ideas than she could possibly use in her class.

The purpose of this book is to provide the reader with insight regarding some of the theoretical issues related to teaching and training, with concrete examples provided for clarity. It is not the purpose of this book to provide an endless list of state changes, openings, and closings, as those have been done quite well by other authors. For further ideas, please refer to the various examples provided throughout this book.

In conclusion, the principle of Crest of the Wave is quite simple. When the possibilities for maximum learning in a given situation have peaked, it is time for the teacher to switch to another learning modality. Use state changes when needed to keep the audience's attention focused where it will be most useful.

OPEN LOOPS —good

Situation #1

The first day of class had arrived. The subject of this class for high school seniors was "The Psychology of Reading." The teacher was fiddling with a TV monitor and an attached CD-ROM. The time came for the class to begin. Instead of introducing himself, or handing out a class syllabus, the teacher simply said:

"Watch this."

The class watched. On the monitor appeared a cartoon character who proposed to introduce the students to the exciting world of reading. Letters began to appear, a lively musical tune was heard, and the character took the class through the first portion of a popular instructional reading program. When ten minutes had passed, the teacher turned off the monitor and turned to the class. He asked:

"So, how effective do you think this reading program really is?"

The students looked at him in silence. After a significant pause, he asked more questions:

"Will children who learn to read from this program be actually learning to read, or will they be simply mimicking what they see? Are the letters on the screen large enough, or too large? Does the color of the background have any impact on the quality of the instruction? What age group is this program designed for?"

No one volunteered to answer any of his questions. Then the teacher made a final statement:

"When you finish this class not only should you be able to answer these questions in considerable detail, but you should be able to back up your answers with articulate, well-thought-out explanations. You should even be able to provide references that support your case."

Situation #2

It was the first morning of a special two-day technical class. Students were learning to repair a new walkie-talkie that was soon going to be sold in local stores. As the session began, the teacher passed out a walkie-talkie to each person. When everyone had received one, she asked them to turn them on. None of the units worked. She then said:

"Each device has some sort of problem with it; I personally saw to that. Now, here's a $20 bill. If you can fix your walkie-talkie—or anyone's around you, for that matter—in the next five minutes, you may have the money. Your five minutes begins now."

The students immediately began taking their walkie-talkies apart, discussing ideas with people near them. At the end of the five minutes, no one had been able to fix their unit. The teacher now said:

"OK, let's learn how to make some money fixing these things."

The Explanation

In both of these classes, the teacher was employing a strategy known as an *open loop*.

"An open loop is any statement, action, visual device, or other event that gives learners foreknowledge of what is coming."

Open loops are used by teachers to set the stage for what is about happen, to incite anticipation in learners. Open loops come in an infinite variety of formats. As indicated in those first examples, they can simply be a statement. Other times they may be visual, such as signs or posters placed around the room, or something written on the chalkboard. A guitar placed in plain view, even though never mentioned, may serve as an open loop if it is used later. Or perhaps a teacher brings a box to the room with various colorful supplies sticking out of the top, in plain view to the learners. All of these events can be viewed as open loops: They serve the purpose of arousing learner curiosity (Berlyne 1965; Keller 1987).

The RAS

To gain a clear perspective on how open loops help learners, it is useful to consider one aspect of how the human brain operates. The intention of this discussion is not to provide a detailed analysis of brain functions from a physiological or neurological perspective, but to bring these concepts into a practical focus for use by teachers. As such, the language and the overall concept are presented in a somewhat simplified manner.

A simple demonstration may show how open loops affect the brain. Try the following experiment for yourself:

"Wherever you are as you read this, follow along with the instructions. First, right now, notice the feeling in the bottom of your feet. How do your toes feel? Next, check out the feelings in your legs. How about your back? Your arms? Your fingers? Your nose? OK, relax!"

Were you able to follow these instructions? Probably everyone could accomplish this task. But what about before you were instructed to follow directions: Was there still feeling in your feet, even though your attention wasn't directly focused on it? Of course there was. It just wasn't important at that moment, as your attention was focused elsewhere. Our five senses (touch, sight, sound, taste, and smell) guide stimuli from the environment into our brains. Once in the brain, the information is processed, either on a conscious or unconscious level. It's important to note that your senses are in *constant operation*, and scientists estimate that a human brain is receiving thousands of different bits of information every second it is awake (LaBerge 1990).

Given all that incoming information, the problem is one of potential overload. How does our brain know what to focus on? In fact, it is only due to an amazing process in the brain that we are able to sort out the chaos of incoming stimuli and locate the key bits of information we are seeking. Scientists call this focusing mechanism of the brain the

"Reticular Activating System"

Because that's a mouthful to say, it is more commonly referred to as the *RAS*. The RAS is the sorting mechanism that makes decisions about which stimuli are important to *consciously* focus on and which can be processed on an *unconscious* level (Driscoll 1994: 262–268). The RAS allows the brain to concentrate on what is most important, while moving the other information to the background. In actual practice, this focusing process, which functions at an electrochemical level, is vastly more complex than I'm describing here, but for our purposes all we need to understand is what happens, not how the mechanism functions.

You've probably experienced this RAS phenomena for yourself. See if you can recall being in one of these situations:

> Have you ever been hungry, and decided to walk to a restaurant three blocks away for lunch? As you are walking along the street what do you notice? Signs about food, pictures of food, restaurant signs advertising food. What do you smell? The sandwich in the hand of a man walking past you. Fresh bread from the bakery. Fresh coffee being brewed in the corner deli! Suddenly, food is everywhere!
>
> What is the worst time to go to the grocery store? When you're hungry, of course! Since you're feeling those tummy pangs, suddenly it seems like buying every item of food in the store is vitally important! So you load up the grocery cart to the overflow point, purchasing enough food to supply a small army. Then you go home and eat one meal. Yet, as soon as you're full, you look around at all the other food in bewilderment, wondering why you ever bought some of those items!
>
> Or, have you ever decided that you were going to buy a new car, and you knew exactly which make, model, and color you wanted? Once you were very clear about what you wanted, what happened? Did you start noticing that exact car everywhere around you, passing you on your way to work, behind you on the freeway, and parked at the grocery store! Suddenly it seems that car is coming at you from every direction . . .

Why do these things happen? The answer is actually quite simple. It's because you "programmed" your RAS to become acutely aware of either the food or the car. Once it became clear to your brain that these were the most important elements in your environment, the RAS focused on finding them and registering them in your conscious mind. By the way, did you happen to become hungry right now while reading the food example? Yep, that's another demonstration that your RAS is functioning quite well.

In the demonstration, when you were asked to focus on different parts of your body, your RAS was directing you to experience certain sensory inputs at that moment, though you had been unconsciously aware of them all along. It was the instructions you were reading that were directing your RAS where to focus your thoughts. This illustrates the key point regarding a teacher's use of the RAS mechanism. *Learners can be directed by outside influence to pay attention to what is most important in the learning environment.* This concept is the crux of understanding the principle of open loops:

> "Teachers should use their knowledge of how this aspect of the brain works to influence learners so they carefully pay attention to the most important aspects of the information."

This means that the teacher can deliberately direct a listener's unconscious attention. Used properly, this can create a powerful effect on learner's long-term retention of the information on which it has been directed to focus.

The RAS in Action in a Learning Environment

The following situation is included in this section because it demonstrates how the RAS operates, in a general way, in a learning situation. Later, additional, more specific examples of the use of open loops will be presented.

> I was attending a class on Accelerated Learning. The objective of the class was to teach us to speed-read, spell, understand vocabulary, and master other related learning topics. The room of eighty students was filled mostly with adults, although a few teens were also in attendance. The class lasted Friday night, all day Saturday, and all day Sunday.
>
> The opening session included a series of five pretests. We were told that we were going to take a similar posttest at the conclusion of the program, so we could measure our progress. When the first four of these pretests had been completed, the teacher asked us to take out a blank sheet of paper. She then said she would ask five questions, to which everyone would write their responses on the paper. The most important thing, which she strongly emphasized, was:
>
> > "If you don't know the correct answer, *make one up*!"
>
> This request, as you can imagine, was somewhat startling. Did we really have permission to simply make up an answer? Seeing our looks, she made the same statement again, verifying the instruction. Once the teacher was certain we were ready to continue, she proceeded by asking the first question:

"What is a sperm whale's favorite food?"

No one appeared to know the answer to this curious, seemingly irrelevant question. However, when she saw the baffled looks on everyone's face, she reminded us that it was fine if we didn't know the answer to the question, but it was important that we as least make something up! So, that's precisely what everyone did. In fact, I clearly remember someone near me, equally confused but willing to follow the directions, having a grin come over his face as he jotted down: "Number One: Sperm whales like to eat . . . peanut butter!"

This was followed by four more questions, all focusing on similarly bizarre, trivial topics. When everyone had finished writing, the teacher asked that those pretests be set aside, assuring us that she would explain later the purpose behind that particular one. Despite being deeply mystified, we did exactly that, and the class proceeded.

Nothing more was said about that test for the rest of the night, and indeed all the next day. Saturday evening, however, the class had reached a point where the speed-reading techniques were being practiced. The idea was to read an assigned article as rapidly as possible, then check for speed and accuracy. The room was dead quiet as people concentrated. Suddenly, someone in the back jumped up from his chair and shouted out:

"Hey everybody, it says here what sperm whales like to eat— plankton!"

The room erupted as other people reached that point in the article and started showing each other this seemingly amazingly important piece of information that they had found!

What had happened? As the teacher explained later, simply by asking that question on the opening night, everyone's brain had been programmed to find out what sperm whales liked to eat, and an open loop had been created. While everything else had continued on a conscious level, some part of the subconscious had continued seeking the answer to this question. When it finally appeared, nearly twenty-four hours later, it registered so strongly that it had caused someone to announce it as if this was earth-shattering, groundbreaking news! The act of making up answers and physically writing them down had further emphasized the importance of finding the correct response to this question, increasing the impact of the reaction as it was found.

This experience illustrates the most important aspect of the use of open loops in classrooms. Had we not been "programmed" to have our RAS subconsciously seeking this information, when we did encounter it we would have simply passed over it and kept moving forward. While it would still have registered on the conscious mind, the use of an open loop *made it stand out as significant*. That information now has an excellent chance of staying in the memory of the learner longer.

As mentioned at the start of the example, I told you about this situation for a very particular purpose. No, what whales like to eat really isn't the issue here! Instead, the key is the impression the information makes on the student if an open loop has been used to precede it. Similarly, learning will be enhanced if a teacher isolates the most critical points in each presentation and uses an open loop to stimulate learner curiosity.

Closing Loops

Open loops create a dynamic that drives students to find a way to "close the loop." Closing loops is important to almost everyone, as it brings a sense of closure to a given situation. For instance:

> Have you ever been in a car, listening to one of your favorite songs? You're enjoying this tune as you cruise on down the road, happily singing along. However, right at the very end of the song, the DJ fades it out. Instead of hearing the final few notes, you experience the highly questionable joy of listening to an advertisement for a toilet cleanser! Feeling cheated and irritated would probably be an appropriate response to this situation. The longer you were listening to this song, the stronger the loop, and the greater the sense of personal dissatisfaction that it had not been allowed to come to completion.

What creates this effect? It's the desire that's within each of us to bring things to completion, although that desire may exist at different levels in different people. There are even unkind labels given to people who like *every last detail* to be brought to completion. For the sake of decency, I will allow your imagination to generate some of these words! Suffice it to say that one of the most common ones is one of those four letter words beginning with the letter "A." Regardless, the key here is that most people require a sense of closure. Another way to consider this phenomenon is to examine this figure:

If you were to glance at it very rapidly, perhaps for as little as fifty milliseconds, you wouldn't register it as a series of stars. Instead, the image that flashes in the mind is that of a circle. This is a demonstration of the mind's desire for closure even in our visual field, a commonly understood phenomenon in psychology.

In the opening examples of this chapter, the teachers were engaging the learners through the use of some seductive open loops. The teacher of the class on reading techniques now has each learner's RAS actively seeking how to confirm whether a computerized reading program is actually achieving its objectives. When these details are discussed and presented in later classes, the students will register the information on a stronger level than if a loop had not been used. Similarly, the teacher with the walkie-talkies now has her audience's full attention, knowing that by developing their skills they are learning how to earn a living.

Examples of Open Loops

Here are eight examples of open loops. Each is followed by a brief explanation showing one situation in which it might be used.

Example #1

"There were three elements we found during this analysis . . ."

A loop consisting of three elements has now been created. To close the loop it will be necessary for the teacher to cover all three elements he has alluded to by his choice of words. What happens if class ends and the teacher had only introduced two elements? There is an open loop still out there, one that he had better be certain to close at the start of the next class if he doesn't want half the class wandering up to him at the next bell asking him to identify the third element. The use of a specified number in an open loop is sometimes referred to as a *framework*. The following statements are further examples of frameworks:

- "There are eight points I'd like to make tonight."
- "There are really only two ways to look at this issue."
- "Four primary factors led to this decision."
- "Five distinct issues led to their downfall."
- "We lead the field because of six things we do well."

In general, if the teacher has a set number of points to make, it assists learners if they know this number in advance. Now they can mentally prepare themselves to receive and organize the appropriate amount of information in their minds. Even within this section, note that the phrase *eight open loops* is a framework used to open this discussion!

Example #2

"In thirty seconds, when I say go . . ."

This phrase, used as a part of a direction-giving sequence, creates a very short open loop that informs learners as to precisely when the specified action is going to occur. This idea was discussed earlier, and in great detail, in the section in this book on giving effective directions. The brief duration of this loop also sparks consideration of a connected detail regarding the use of loops. *Open short loops early in a session and close them fairly quickly.* This builds confidence with learners that all loops will be closed. Now the teacher can create larger and larger loops, and the impact of these loops on learners' attention will be increased. For example, suppose the teacher announces that something will be happening in ten minutes, and it does occur. This builds her credibility. Now when she says that at the end of the week the learners will be able to master this new skill, the students' perception of the validity of her statements will be enhanced.

Example #3

"After the break we'll be taking a look at . . ."

This is a phrase frequently used by teachers across many contexts. It opens a loop by indicating the topic of the presentation that will commence once they return from the break. However, it is included here exactly because it has that familiar ring to it. Familiarity may be useful in some situations. However, if students have heard a particular phrase quite often, they may not pay attention to it, thereby reducing the effect when the loop is closed. Instead, the suggestion here is to be as creative as possible with language to maximize the reaction from the learners. In this situation, the teacher might instead say:

"Let's take a brief break now, so when we return your minds can be focused on the most critical aspect of this entire chapter . . ."

With these slightly different words, the learners may be listening more closely. The more carefully they are paying attention to the loop, the more the RAS will be engaged, and the more powerful the effect will be when the loop is closed.

Example #4

"Here are a few ideas on notetaking, and then we'll take a break."

Suppose this statement were made in a setting where the learners were beginning to get restless. The intention of the statement is to let them know that a break is definitely going to be happening soon. Now they are aware that they only have one more thing left on which to focus. With this clearly in mind, hopefully they will be able to fully engage all their remaining attention and stay with the material being delivered. However, the teacher using this phrase better be sure to get to the predicted break fairly soon. If not, the students may begin to doubt the teacher's integrity, a definite distraction.

Example #5

"This next piece could be the most valuable hour of the entire year for some of you in the room."

With these words, the teacher is focusing the learners' RAS mechanism intently on the value of the next piece of information. Learners will want to pay close attention to the content being delivered, on the chance that *they* are one of the people for whom this would be a useful piece of information! However, it is important to use open loops such as these on an infrequent basis, and *only* when the teacher truly believes it is the single most important piece of information.

Example #6

"You don't have to believe me now, you'll see evidence of this tomorrow."

This statement actually serves a dual purpose. In terms of open loops, students will now be watching carefully for the purported "evidence" in the next day's session. However, it also serves the function of allowing them to pay attention to the information without getting caught up in evaluating whether or not it is true. This mental "editor," as it is sometimes called, can prohibit information from ever being considered if the initial impression of the information is negative. The first half of the statement allows the teacher to at least temporarily filter out some of the possible negative aspects of the learner's internal editor.

Example #7

"Please take about two minutes to walk around the room with your group and discuss the posters on the walls. Which concepts have you already encountered, and which are new to you?"

In this situation, new posters had been placed on the walls of the room that morning before class began. By giving the students two minutes to walk around and review the information, the teacher is creating a huge open loop. Students now understand the general direction of the instruction. They will also be remembering any information they know related to these concepts, which could then be brought into discussions that take place with regard to the material. This validates them as students and acknowledges the work they have done so far in the class.

Example #8

"For you folks on the left side of the room, I'll have a question for you in a few moments. For those of you on the right side, here's your question . . ."

When used correctly, this open loop creates a wonderful effect. The following example came from my observation of a class in Sydney, Australia.

The room was divided into two halves, separated by an aisle down the middle. The class was going to break for lunch soon. The students appeared slightly restless, and the teacher wanted to do something a little extra to keep them paying close attention to the content. She turned and created the open loop exactly as it is stated above.

The right side of the room got a question. However, it was a simple, fairly innocuous question that those students easily answered. When the interaction was complete, the teacher continued teaching. She made no mention of the fact that the students on the left side of the room were still expecting a question. What effect did this have on the audience?

As I watched from my seat at the back of the room, there were two reactions. Both, however, served the same purpose. The students on the left half of the room who had not yet answered a question were closely watching the teacher, anticipating that their question could be coming at any moment. On the right side, students who had already answered a question were also watching the teacher, knowing that she still had to ask a question of the other side of the room. In other words, *both sides were paying careful attention* to the material!

This teacher was excellent at the game of keeping them attentive. Twice during her subsequent instruction she paused, looked at the side of the room that had yet to receive a question, and smiled knowingly before going back to teaching! This both entertained the audience, and kept them tuned in. In fact, she was able to go almost *15 minutes* before turning to the left side of the room and saying:

"Now, I've got a question for you folks . . ."

What was their reaction when she finally said this? As you might guess, there was an audible sigh of relief as they realized it was finally their turn! This occurred even though this second question also added very little to students' understanding of the material! It was not the question itself that mattered, rather it was *how the question was used in the course of the instruction.*

It is important to notice that unless the teacher has a good relationship with the students and is already fairly talented, this situation could potentially cause an unwanted backlash. The audience could easily end up paying close attention to her, but not be listening to the material she was presenting. However, in this case, the teacher was quite gifted, and able to maintain interest during those fifteen minutes through the use of humor, body gestures, vocal changes, and her gift at storytelling. The use of the open loop was simply one more tool in the teacher's tool kit that she used to further the cause of instruction.

Open Loops in the World

The concept of open loops is not limited to teaching environments. They are everywhere around us. Recognizing their universal appeal may help teachers realize the incredible potential of this tool for use in a classroom. For example, open loops play a critical role in marketing and advertising. A well-known jingle can get the consumer thinking about a certain restaurant or food. Colorful, creative advertisements for faraway destinations may create a desire to travel, and the only way to close the loop is to book a vacation. And some ad campaigns focus on making people feel like they are missing something if they don't possess a certain car, a new home, or the latest toy.

Open loops are also an integral element in every book at the top of the *New York Times* best-selling fiction list. Avid mystery readers may remember the books of their youth, featuring Nancy Drew, Tom Swift, or the Hardy Boys. In those classic series, writers frequently ended chapters with the hero or heroine in great peril, prompting the readers to race onto the next chapter. Today's best-selling authors, such as Stephen King, Danielle Steel, Tom Clancy, and Dean R. Koontz, while much more elegant in their delivery, are still utilizing the same concept. One large loop contains the plot of the book, while it subsumes numerous smaller loops that are opened and closed as the story moves forward.

One of the most innovative and effective uses of loops I have personally experienced came during a recent visit to the Arizona State Fair. After an initial entrance fee had been paid, admission to many of the events on the fairgrounds was free, and people tended to wander from show to show quite easily. In one of the larger arenas a hypnotist was plying his trade. The show was fairly standard fare: People were put to sleep, given embedded commands, then awakened and controlled by the presenter.

The hypnotist himself was quite skilled, and the hour-long show kept the 500-person crowd thoroughly entertained. However, it was very hot that day. Although the audience was under a screen, they were still subjected to the desert heat. Sure, it's a dry heat, but it's still hot! As the show started to wind down, and the crowd began to look like it might move on to another event, the hypnotist demonstrated his true genius. He first announced to the people:

"This will be my final act—and, as always, I like to save the best for last!"

This minor loop served the purpose of keeping those who looked like they were about to stand up and leave glued to their seats a bit longer. Then he had three volunteers come to the stage. He put them to sleep and gave each one a hidden command that had to do with a cartoon character. For example, when the hypnotist gave the appropriate command, the first person was going to stand up from his seat and run up and down the central aisle shouting "Beep Beep!" like the Road Runner. The other two volunteers received similar commands. After cautioning the audience not to say anything yet, he woke up all three people and sent them back to their seats among the audience. Then he said:

"Now if you're intrigued by what you've seen today, I wrote a book on hypnotism that I happen to have for sale. If you're interested in purchasing a copy you can see me up here after the show. It talks about . . ."

He proceeded to give the audience a thorough sales pitch about his book. I confess that I am not much into sales pitches; however, when I went to leave, I found I couldn't! Why not? No, I hadn't been hypnotized. I stayed because the hypnotist had created a hilarious open loop with those three volunteers, and I really wanted to see what happened! So I waited through the sales pitch, which lasted approximately ninety seconds. Then the hypnotist gave a command, and the first volunteer raced through the crowd going "Beep Beep!" The audience roared with laughter. When they calmed down, the hypnotist said:

"I also have for sale some cassettes I've made about hypnotism . . ."

With that he launched into a *second* sales pitch! When that was done he gave the second command and the second volunteer did her thing. And, yes, he followed this by a third sale pitch—for videotapes—before giving the final command. This ended his show.

The effect of his use of open loops was obvious. People stayed in their seats, which meant that *everyone had listened to his sales pitches for all his merchandise*. Was it just an accident that many people made their way forward to purchase his products? I suspect not. It was the deliberate use of an established communication tool between a presenter and his audience that enhanced his profits that afternoon.

In Summary

Open Loops come in a variety of forms; however, they all share one common objective: to alert the students to what is coming and its potential value to them. Given this perspective, learners are now more focused on receiving the new information and remembering it. The use of loops can be an effective *component* of a learning strategy, but it is never the entire strategy. Finally, teachers must be certain that all loops they have opened are eventually closed! This provides the sense of closure and completeness that assists learners in locking away the information for later recall.

FRAMES CREATE MEANING

Overview

Painters know it's true. They can spend countless hours carefully crafting a single masterpiece. Every detail may be attended to in excruciating detail: the curve of the lines, the mix of background and foreground, and the subtle blending of hues. All may eventually be just the way the artist first envisioned them. But if the right *frame* is not placed around the final product, it can greatly reduce the picture's overall effect on the viewer. While it will not diminish the picture's effect entirely, it can certainly have a powerful effect on the result. Every picture looks better with the right frame surrounding and enhancing it.

The same phenomenon is true in life as well as in learning. People have certain perspectives, points of view, or *frames*, that exert a powerful influence on their perception of events. For example, imagine a minor car accident in which no one is injured. One driver may view it as a terrible event, because he or she has damaged his or her new car. Another driver may view it as a blessing, because he or she has emerged unscathed from the crumpled metal heap. Both had a similar experience, but their subsequent outlook and attitude are distinctly colored by the frame they choose to wrap around the circumstance.

Translate this idea to the world of teaching. Imagine a setting where there are thirty students in the room. The entire group engages in an activity designed to demonstrate a particular concept. Each learner enters the activity with his or her own mental frame. This frame impacts the learning he or she will extract from the experience. Each student may process the experience along an entirely different line of thinking. To ensure a more common outcome for learners, teachers need to invest time to create a common frame that will help guide students' thinking along the intended lines of instruction (Ready 1978). This section first looks at clarifying the overall concept by examining frames in general, and then moves to a specific exploration of their use in learning situations.

A Broad, Metaphorical Example

Bill is driving home from work one night when a car driven by a drunk driver crosses over the yellow line and hits his car head on. In the resulting collision, Bill is seriously injured. He wakes up in the hospital, only to discover that he has lost a leg in the accident. He is horrified, thinking of how terrible he will now look, and all the things he won't be able to do. This sends him into a severe depression. The doctor tells him he will be able to walk again with the use of a prosthetic device, but he is too depressed to care.

Eventually Bill goes home. He has the opportunity to practice with his new leg. One day he goes outside, and sees a car drive past. He thinks to himself that the driver must be making fun of him, or perhaps worse, pitying him because he walks with a limp. Ashamed, he goes home and refuses to practice anymore. He spends his time watching TV and feeling sorry for himself. That's Bill's way of coping with the experience.

John's story starts out much the same, although it has a different ending. He is driving home from work one night when a car driven by a drunk driver crosses over the yellow line and hits his car head on. In the resulting collision, John is seriously injured. When he wakes up in the hospital, he discovers that he has lost a leg due to the accident. Unlike Bill, however, his initial reaction is one of immense relief that he has survived. The loss of a leg, he realizes, is not as catastrophic as what could have happened. When the doctor tells him that he can one day walk again with the use of a prosthetic leg, he is thrilled. There will always be some things he can't do, he realizes. However, with the use of the prosthetic leg, there will be many more that he can.

Eventually, John goes home. He takes every opportunity to practice walking with his new leg. One day he goes outside. A car drives past. John imagines that the driver sees him, and is amazed at his courage. This inspires John, and he walks further and further each day, proudly showing off his ability to walk. Eventually his walk becomes almost normal, and John is able to return to school and continue with his life.

Two identical stories, but with different results. What creates the difference? It is the perspective, or *frame*, that each individual chooses to place around the experience. Nothing can be done to change what happened, but the future depends greatly on each person's reaction to their circumstance. Their response is intimately influenced by the perspective they have chosen to embrace. Frames are ultimately under the control of each person, so it is best to select a useful one.

A General Perception Example

Many years ago, I was conducting a workshop for teenagers. There were 140 students in attendance. In the course of the weekend workshop, students were shown a movie clip that lasted approximately sixty seconds. It showed a car traveling down a dirt road, and then hitting a barn. While preparing for the workshop, several of the staff become engaged in a conversation regarding how our perceptions influence our realities. Eventually, the discussion narrowed, until someone raised the question as to whether a single word could influence a person's perception of an event.

On a whim, we decided to conduct an informal experiment. Immediately after the film had been shown, the group was given a written list of questions regarding what they had just witnessed. In the normal course of the program, the questionnaire was used to demonstrate how people remember things. However, in addition to the normal questions, this time one more was added. Half of the questionnaires had this particular question phrased one way, while the other half had a single word altered. Half of the students read the following question :

"How fast was the car moving when it *bumped* into the barn?"

The other half of the students had the question that contained the altered word. This time the question read:

"How fast was the car moving when it *smashed* into the barn?"

Would this single word switch create a difference in the students' perception of the event? After everyone had completed their questionnaires, they were turned over to the staff, who totaled up the responses of the two groups. The result was what you have probably already guessed. On the average, the group that responded to the question with the word *bumped* in it estimated that the car was traveling at 32 mph. Conversely, the group that responded to the question with the word *smashed* in it estimated that the car was traveling at 47 mph! It was apparent that the alteration of that single word had produced a significant change in the students' perceptions of the film clip.

Admittedly, this study was not conducted under the rigorous conditions dictated by the standards of experimental psychology. As such, it is not meant to imply a proven psychological construct. Nonetheless, it opened up our eyes. As teachers, we need to consider the awesome potential of the power of framing experiences for learners. If a single word could exert this much influence on their perceptions, what would be the effect of altering whole sentences, or even a string of sentences? The opportunity for positively influencing the perspectives of the learners became readily apparent.

Years later, during my doctoral work, I was deeply immersed in academic research. To my considerable surprise, variations on this concept began to emerge in my readings of the literature on memory (Loftus 1992). What had once been merely an interesting idea was rapidly becoming a proven theory, whose applications ranged from general memory theory development to the very specific task of police assisting individuals in providing accurate eyewitness accounts.

Learning Examples

Understanding the overall concept of framing, as well as the specifics of using it effectively, will enable a teacher to increase the extent and nature of the learning students take from their classroom experiences. The previous two examples were included to clarify the general concept of a frame as a perspective. The remainder of this section focuses on seven specific examples of the use of frames in learning contexts.

Example 1: Use of a Four-Letter Word

Suppose there are two minutes remaining in a test situation. Learners are hunched over their papers, busily working on their math problems. The teacher wants to let them know their time is almost up, so he announces:

"You have just two more minutes!"

In this situation, what effect does the word *just* have on the communication? It can easily be interpreted as putting pressure on the students. The simple use of the word *just* has framed the final two minutes as being stress-filled. But a testing situation is inherently filled with pressure, so teachers should do what they can to avoid unnecessarily increasing this state of anxiety. Most researchers agree that adding significantly more stress only decreases student effectiveness (Covington 1992; Covington & Omelich 1987; Woolfolk 1998). In this case, the four-letter word *just* may unnecessarily produce this unwanted result. Instead, the teacher could simply leave out that one word, and in a calm tone of voice announce:

"You have two more minutes."

Now the communication is more straight-forward, lacking any implied urgency by the teacher. Some teachers may want to take this situation one step further, doing what they can to ease learner stress, and add a few words to the communication, perhaps saying:

"You have plenty of time. Please make sure all your answers are written as clearly as possible during these final two minutes."

Note that the essence of the communication has not changed at any point. In each case learners have been reminded that they have two minutes left. The primary distinction between these frames is the perspective learners may adopt given the words the teacher chooses. In similar situations, teachers might also want to be aware of other words or phrases that might create a similar unwanted reaction, such as *merely* or *only*.

Example 2: A School Summer Class

It was the first day of class. The teacher had given a general overview of how the two-week summer school class would proceed, and what topics would be covered. The next step would involve distributing the reading materials to the students. The teacher turned and picked up a large stack of papers, containing copies of eight articles that all students were required to read. Her hands visibly laden with this frightening collection of reading material, she faced the class again and said:

> "OK, now, I know it's summertime, and reading may be the last thing on your mind. But we have to do this, because it's required by the school that you at least do *some* reading for this class. We'll have to buckle down and do the best we can with it."

Consider the frame the teacher has just created for the students around reading these articles! The first visual image the students have in this moment is a *heavy* stack of papers, definitely not a good start toward making a positive first impression. Next, by *telling* them they shouldn't like reading, because it's summer, an ominous negative image is immediately formed. Then come the words, "But we have to . . ." and "It's a requirement . . ." These phrases build further on the negative base that has already been established. The final blow is delivered as she concludes the frame with a sentence containing the idiom *buckle down* which implies seriously dreary times ahead. Given this frame, even a student with the most positive attitude in that classroom should have contracted at least a mild case of depression!

Before moving on to consider an alternative method for handling this situation, it is useful to note that the words used in this example are not that unusual. Uninformed teachers simply say what's on their minds, and usually *with the best of intentions*! However, because of the negative frame, they have unwittingly communicated a potentially lethal message. It then comes as a complete surprise to them to discover that there is a common reaction among the students concerning the reading material. When the time arrives for them to do their homework, for some reason they find themselves completely uninspired!

Here's a different approach the teacher could have taken with this same situation. She begins by separating the articles into eight *small* piles, a key starting point for visual effect. Now the first impression the students have will be that these are thin articles, and thus quite short. Next she frames the distribution of the articles by saying:

> "I'm not certain if you knew it, but this class was supposed to have a required text. It's this one here, and costs $60 at the bookstore." [She holds up the text, which is quite thick.] "However, in looking through it, I decided that there's no way that we could make use of the majority of the material in it given the time we have available. If each of you were to buy this book it would be a waste of both your time and money."

She sets the text down. This action is no doubt accompanied by a collective sigh of relief from the students. Then she says:

> "Instead, I've spent some time locating a *few* articles that speak directly to the topics we'll be exploring. This way you won't have to spend unnecessary time sorting through a heap of irrelevant material. You should be able to complete the reading quite easily, so you can continue enjoying your summer. Please come forward and take one article from each group."

What a difference a frame makes! The students are now mentally comparing that massive text to the thin stack of articles, and perhaps feeling that they "got off easy." This should begin to put them into a more positive frame of mind concerning the required reading for the class. Additionally, they are pleased to discover they didn't have to spend the $60 on a book which, for the most part, would go unused. Finally, she implied that their reading will go quickly, so they can return to "enjoying their summer," concluding her remarks by foretelling a pleasant future.

Finding the best frame is certainly a key element in any learning situation. Of course, the simple use of this second frame may not turn nonreaders into avid ones. However, it should at least give them a head start toward forming a healthy perspective concerning the articles. This more positive outlook may go a long way in having the students *choose* to do their homework, which in turn may have a significant impact on the results of the class. Yes, there's probably some sort of cause and effect going on here.

Example 3: Framing a Learning Activity

The teacher had decided to illustrate several important concepts relating to her class by involving the students in an experience. The activity she had chosen required the students to solve a maze, a grid of masking tape laid on the floor. As a team, students would need to discover the path of safe steps from one end to the other end of the maze. The exercise was introduced by the teacher saying:

> "Welcome to The Maze! Here's how the game is played . . ."

On closer inspection, it is apparent that this introduction includes no frame at all. Why are they doing this activity? What's the objective? How does it relate to the class they are currently taking, and the topics they are focusing on today? With no frame provided, students are free to think anything they'd like to about the activity. Perhaps they decide that this activity doesn't have anything to do with them, and stop paying attention to the directions. Perhaps they think it's a competition, and lose the point of the entire exercise. Perhaps . . . well, who knows what they'll think?

This teacher later changed her approach to the maze activity. The next time she chose to use it, when she introduced it she said:

> "Welcome to The Maze! The Maze is a puzzle. While solving this puzzle, several issues may emerge that will be useful to our understanding of innovation and creativity. Having experienced them on a firsthand basis will enable us to look closer at how each of us approach these topics."

With this frame, learners become aware that the activity does have a purpose beyond simply killing time. They can be preparing themselves for the discussion to follow by silently observing the interactions of their peers. They now know that in some way this activity will allow them to further their understanding of the concept of innovation. Therefore they have a purpose, a frame, through which to process the experience.

Example 4: Students Teaching Math

While teaching an advanced math class for high school seniors in Hawaii, I made an interesting discovery. The material that this class covered was a partial review for many of the students, so I made them a unique offer. If anyone would like to teach one of the chapters from the book, they wouldn't be required to take the test for that chapter! Of course, they needed to prepare lesson plans, and personally review them with me well in advance of each class. Additionally, they needed to create the final test, plus generate an answer key with the solutions written out completely.

I was concerned because as a teacher I knew the level of work required in preparing to teach a single chapter of math. It far exceeded the work normally required of a learner, whose primary responsibility was simply doing their homework and taking the test. Much to my surprise, students leapt at the opportunity to teach a section of the class. It was only later that I understood what now seems very obvious.

Simply put, the frame of *not having to take a test* was too powerful to resist! I had forgotten that their world was filled with tests, and the chance to avoid one seemed too good to be true, despite the work required. They dove into their respective chapters and produced impressive results. Of course, as a teacher I understood one of the basic concepts of teaching:

"We learn best what we teach to others."

Without becoming consciously aware of it, many students took quantum leaps forward in their overall understanding of math, because they now clearly understood the information from the one chapter they had taught. In most cases they were able to use this solid foundation as a base for understanding material in subsequent chapters. The frame of not having to take one chapter test ultimately produced better results for both the "student teachers" as well as for their peers.

Example 5: Out on the Tennis Courts

The scene was a weekend program for teens focusing on the development of teamwork and self-confidence. The course opened with a three-hour introductory session on Friday night, and was followed by an outdoor adventure experience lasting all of the following day. Some readers may be familiar with the term "ropes courses." They challenge people to "feel the fear and do it anyway." One example was The Pole, where people had to climb a twenty-five-foot telephone pole, clamber onto the top of a small disk located at the top, then jump out toward a trapeze. They were completely secure because they were attached to safety lines the entire time they were off the ground. The experiences students had that day were used as metaphors for the remainder of the class.

One of the primary objectives of the opening session that Friday night was to get the teens comfortable with each other and bonded as a group. Experience had repeatedly shown that this produced much better results the next day. This outcome was achieved through the use of a frame. Early on that first evening the teachers began to develop a very clear frame with the students:

"Listen, everyone. We want you to be 100 percent safe tomorrow. We will certainly do our part to ensure that that happens. You can insure your own safety the following way: Be willing to be completely outgoing, wide awake, and ready to respond to any instructions we give you. This way, if we need to shout out an important last-minute direction while you are very high up on one of the events, you won't be feeling so self-conscious that you'll fail to hear us. Your willingness to look "not so great" and stay present in the experience will help keep you absolutely safe!"

At that point all students were invited to stand and join in a brief activity. The activity was usually one that required them to do something slightly outside their "comfort zone," something slightly beyond what they were previously comfortable with. As the evening went on, approximately every fifteen minutes another activity was done, each moving one step up the gradient of risk-taking. The final activity was usually something so outrageous that three hours earlier they would have never have believed they would have allowed themselves to be seen in public doing it. In one program, the final activity of the evening had everyone out on the tennis court howling at the moon like wolves!

In the end, this approach accomplished dual objectives. The frame was built on a foundation of truth: The more comfortable people feel with each other, the more probable it is that they will experience success, as individuals and as part of a team. While this sequence of activities did accomplish this, on a global level it also brought the group closer together. Later in the program, this meant that they felt emotionally safer with each other, and were able to explore in depth some of the more sensitive issues that they might otherwise not have been willing to approach. The frame of ensuring their physical safety also served to open them up to each other emotionally, creating an atmosphere that virtually guaranteed a high level of success for the entire program.

Example 6: Personal Introductions

In my classes where I help teachers learn about the skills outlined in this book, one component focuses on basic presentation skills. To generate discussion on this topic, these teachers are given an opportunity to take one minute and introduce themselves to the group. The group then gives them feedback about their "performance." When this activity is first mentioned to the large group, their reaction (much like you might have just experienced when you read about it here) is frequently one of intense horror! The only external sign they show, of course, is an uncomfortable shifting in their chairs or a twitching of the eyes as they look for the nearest door through which to escape!

Their reaction is expected. For a variety of reasons, most people don't enjoy diving cold into these kinds of situations, especially with a group of people with whom they are not familiar. As a teacher, it is apparent that, in order to have the activity produce worthwhile results, a frame is needed. In this case a series of points is made that combine to produce a frame that creates the desired effect.

It starts by acknowledging that few people like these situations. Students are asked to raise their hands if they are one of those people who has an intense dislike for situations like this. When most, if not all, raise their hands, general laughter ensues as people realize they are not the only ones. Then the question is raised as to why even do the activity? The answer is that the group's learning can be much more focused if they have just had an experience of the topic currently under consideration. This certainly happens when each person needs to take the stage. Having been prompted in this manner, most people agree that being a part of this activity will generate a more useful conversation and greater learning. With this knowledge, they begin to move closer to a willingness to participate. The frames, however, are not yet done.

The next step is to discuss feedback. This is the part that people tend to dislike the most. What *feedback* means in the context of this class is highlighted at this point. Primarily, it is built around the idea that feedback is just someone else's fantasy! Which, if you think about it, is exactly the case. Feedback is simply someone else's opinion, and we can choose whether or not we believe it provides us with any valid input concerning our presentation style. Just because feedback has been provided does not mean it is the truth, and therefore must be followed. When this perspective is presented to the teachers, people frequently feel a great deal of relief. This sensation is further enhanced when they are informed that, when people give feedback, all the presenter says is:

"Thank you."

They are then invited to *think anything they want to* about that feedback, but do it to themselves. Externally, those two words are the only response necessary. This means, of course, that they will no longer have to explain or defend themselves, and this takes further pressure off the situation.

Finally, these teachers are given several moments to talk with someone next to them and generate ideas on what to say when it is their turn. This piece speaks directly to the idea of doing it while they are unprepared. Given time to organize their thoughts, most people can quickly come up with a few things to say that will fill the required one minute. The frame of time to prepare helps reduce the potential tension even further.

The use of these points within this frame rapidly reduces the teachers' reluctance to involve themselves in the activity. Their internal anxiety will not completely diminish, but that is not the intended outcome. Rather, the goal is to provide them with a perspective that: (1) allows them to see the activity as useful in the context of the class, (2) creates a level of safety in which they feel they can participate, and (3) moves them to a place where they are ready to take action. In practice, the frames mentioned here have done an admirable job in accomplishing this objective. Prior to using these frames the activity was successful only on a limited basis. Since employing this strategy, the end result has been a much more dynamic activity, in which the teachers generally seem to engage themselves with considerable energy and focus. The five to seven minutes required to go through the entire sequence is ultimately time well invested.

Example 7: Metaphors

The metaphor of the jigsaw puzzle provided in Appendix A is an example of a frame that might be useful for you as a reader of this book. Indeed, you are even invited to use that particular frame, or come up with some of your own, perhaps some that are specific ones for the content you are teaching. Especially useful are stories that show how one person has benefited after attending a particular class. If done correctly, these frames can form a useful perspective for the students to consider: If those other people could learn that from this class, what could I learn? In my class I've often told the true story of a woman from Singapore who attended the class and walked away with quite a few ideas he felt would be useful to his development as a presenter. He spent a year offering free classes to others so he could develop his skills, and is now a successful class teacher for both teens and adults.

In Summary

Theoretically, frames fall into one of three categories. They are either useful, harmful, or neutral, although in practice they rarely prove to be completely neutral. People always seem to have at least *some* opinion about *everything*. If left to their own devices, the frames students choose frequently end up being at the very least limiting, and at the worse harmful, to their learning experience. With this in mind, it's important that teachers seek to provide learners with the most useful frame they can create for each activity and section of instruction. With a carefully crafted lens to see through, the experience of the students is maximized.

Frames answer the question, "Why?" When engaging in learning activities, students always want to know what's in it for them. Why should I be doing this? Why is this important to me? Why are we spending all this time on this one issue? A frame provides them with the answers to these questions (Plyshyn 1973).

Perhaps the effect of frames is best summed up by a variation on an old saying, which tells us that *we learn from our experiences*. While this is certainly true, *what* we learn from those moments is dependent on the frame we choose to hold around that experience. In this case, perhaps the following expression would be more useful:

Experience + Frame = Meaning

Without a frame, an experience is just an experience. If teachers intend to focus students' attention on a particular aspect of learning, it is necessary to provide them with an appropriate frame for the experience.

CHAPTER FOUR

CLASSROOM STRATEGIES

Sixteen specific Impact Teaching classroom strategies are covered in this chapter. Each one is explained through the use of examples and illustrations. They are arranged in alphabetical order.

BRIDGES AND ZONES

Meet Jake, an individual who is currently quite upset. Perhaps he is sitting slumped down, holding his head in his hands. George, a concerned friend, sees this and wants to soothe him. He hurries over and offers comfort by gently patting Jake on the shoulder. George then sits down to be with his friend, continuing to maintain the contact between his hand and Jake's shoulder. The next day, Jake is in a much better mood. He and George see each other and get together to chat. In the course of the conversation, George's hand makes contact with Jake's shoulder again, perhaps as he is congratulating him for something he did well. Shortly thereafter, without understanding why, Jake finds his good mood slipping away. In fact, he realizes he is becoming depressed again. Why? What triggered this emotional reaction in Jake?

In the original interaction between the two friends, a powerful connection had been established that linked George's hand touching Jake's shoulder with the emotion that Jake was experiencing at that time. A *bridge* had been built that connected the two together. The next day, when George's hand touches the shoulder again in the same manner, the bridge is rebuilt, and those emotions are rekindled in Jake.

Admittedly, this is a somewhat simplistic example; however, it serves a purpose by illustrating a powerful psychological and physiological concept (Dastoor & Reed 1993). It is the idea that similar stimuli can generate a consistent emotional response in people. This notion can be useful in many facets of life. As one example, psychologists know that it is best to avoid physical contact with a person in the throes of powerful emotions because of the potentially negative side effects that even a well-intentioned person may create. Instead, as a general rule, while it is certainly fine for someone to sit and talk with a person who is upset, it is usually best to allow them to at least begin the process of recovery on their own. The field of Neuro-Linguistic Programming (NLP) also understands and utilizes this idea, although there it is referred to it as "anchoring" (Grinder 1988).

practical?
b ✗

It is also a useful concept for teachers to understand, adapt, and utilize as an educational tool. They should consider building clear bridges between certain physical locations, or *zones*, in the room—and the particular aspect of instruction that takes place when they stand there. These connections can then be used to stimulate the audience's mood, or state. The more clearly these bridges are established and the more consistently they are used, the more effective they can be in guiding the students' internal responses. While this is frequently an unconscious response on the part of a student to a stimulus, it is nonetheless an effective technique for teachers to use.

For example, teachers may want to establish a storytelling location in their rooms. This is the place they choose to stand every time they begin a story. Each time the teacher moves to that location, the students will realize that they are about to hear a story or metaphor. This knowledge should trigger a positive emotional response as they prepare themselves to listen. This establishes a storytelling atmosphere that will ultimately help generate an effective learning environment.

Three Zones

There are three distinct zones of instruction a teacher might want to use to create a specific effect. The first zone is the area nearest the chalkboard or white board, the space furthest from the audience. This is the "instructional lane," where content is delivered. Supporting visuals are usually located in this area. When the teacher moves to stand in this location, students will know that information is about to be presented. In some cases, simply moving to this location may alert them that it's time to take notes, and prompt them to organize their materials for what is coming (Lozanov 1979).

The second zone is the area somewhat closer to the audience. It is used for more casual conversation or interaction with the audience, such as responding to questions. When the teacher shifts into this area, students know immediately that a different level of interaction is expected of them, and they can then adjust their thinking accordingly.

The third zone is for giving directions. This is the area closest to the audience. Proximity adds impact to the strength of directions. When it is time for mobilizing directions to be given, the teacher steps closer to the audience (into the third zone) and delivers the necessary instructions.

The effectiveness of each of these bridges between the location and the expected content can be strengthened if the teacher also changes both his or her tone of voice and gestures when moving between the different zones. In the instructional zone, the voice is evenly modulated for content delivery, with gestures supporting the explanation of the information. In contrast, in the facilitation zone the voice is casual, and the gestures are inviting, and in the directional zone the voice is clear and commanding, with gestures that are large enough to encompass the entire room. When utilized clearly, alternating between these zones (and perhaps between the storytelling spot mentioned earlier) can effectively function as a state change for the students.

A related example shows the power of building a bridge for one area of classroom management. In a typical situation, if students misbehave while the teacher is in the act of teaching, he or she may stop immediately and correct their behavior.

However, handling disciplinary issues this way may unintentionally cause students to build a bridge between being in that location in the room and being disciplined. Because this may be an unpleasant connection, it could negatively impact the students' desire to recall the information. How could discipline in this case be handled differently?

A sixth-grade teacher in California recently related how she deals with this situation. The very first time the students misbehave to the extent that she must talk sternly to them, she says:

> "Let's stop for a moment. Please turn your desks so they face toward the left."

At that point she has all students turn their desks ninety degrees to the left. When everyone has his or her desk turned in the new direction, she walks over to that side of the room and disciplines them as necessary. She takes whatever time is needed to complete this task. Finally, when the situation has been handled, she says:

> "Thank you. Now please turn your chairs back to face the blackboard."

Then she moves back to the front of the room and continues teaching. Using this strategy, she has effectively eliminated the potentially negative connections students might have made between the front of the room and the information had she disciplined them from that location. She has also done something perhaps even more important. As the weeks pass this pattern is repeated. All discipline is delivered after the students have turned their desks in that certain direction. What the students come to realize is that, while facing the blackboard they were *never* disciplined, never made to feel wrong. As a consequence, they felt safe when they are facing that direction, and thus became more involved and interactive when she was presenting material.

COMFORT LEVELS IN PHYSICAL SITUATIONS

The topic of this particular class was teamwork and how individuals can work together to solve problems. The teacher was leading an exercise commonly known as The Human Knot. Clusters of eight students joined hands at random with students on the other side of their group, creating a tangled knot of people. The next step was for them to remain holding hands with each other and begin unwinding this bewildering amalgamation of arms, hands, and bodies. All teams had joined hands and created their human knots. However, before telling them to begin untangling this knot, the teacher said:

> "I bet you're all wondering what you're about to do! Well, actually this activity is something called The Human Knot! That's right, what you are now tangled up in is a complicated knot that you will soon begin to unwind. But I did want to let you know that I'm not the one who first thought up this activity. I learned

it from some other people. They weren't even the ones who made up this idea. As far as I can tell, this game has been around for a long time. Let me tell you some of the history of this human knot activity . . ."

With that, the teacher launched into a three-minute talk about the history of the activity. What's wrong with this situation?

The problem is probably obvious to you, although it certainly wasn't obvious to the teacher at that particular moment. The students had been physically arranged into a human knot. As the teacher spoke, the people were currently standing in various awkward poses, holding sweaty hands with someone they didn't know, and in close contact with other people's bodies! This is an inelegant, ungraceful, potentially embarrassing posture in which to remain for any length of time. In fact, in this case, it wasn't long before the students started releasing each other's hands, and the knots dissolved. Once the teacher had finished his brief historical overview of the activity, the entire exercise had to be started over again from the beginning.

Clarification

In most classrooms, there are occasions when students are asked to physically interact with each other. At those times, teachers should be cognizant of some important interpersonal dynamics that may come into play regarding students' comfort levels in group situations. If not handled appropriately, this sense of physical discomfort can create an unpleasant experience. Sometimes this reaction will be visibly evident, such as students choosing not to participate in a particular learning activity. At other times, students' reactions will be more passive, evident only on a subtle level. While continuing to remain involved, they may mentally remove themselves from the experience. The result in either case is an inhibited and less effective learning experience.

At the very least, this feeling of unease might significantly decrease an individual's willingness to participate in future exercises. If students grow even mildly distrustful of a teacher who has made them feel physically uncomfortable, effective learning can be rapidly squelched. The physical comfort level of students should be one of the top priorities for all teachers, both when designing and when conducting a classroom activity.

Several Potentially Threatening Situations

Following are a few examples of situations in which a teacher might want to exercise caution when approaching the physical aspects of an activity or exercise. While every situation is unique, teachers can use these as general guidelines in considering whether or not their students might feel unduly awkward in certain situations.

- Occasionally, students may be asked to hold hands. For example, this might happen when they are being asked to form a circle. A brief holding of hands occurs in a surprisingly large number of learning settings, even those with teenagers.

However, most people past the age of ten find holding someone else's hand to be somewhat awkward. If a student must hold hands with someone else for any reason, allow them to unclasp their hands as rapidly as possible so they can return to a more comfortable level of physical interaction.

- How long can students stay silent? Whether asked to sit or work in silence, this request can be difficult for many people, and it will become increasingly difficult the longer the silence stretches out. In a group setting, there is a natural inclination to interact with other people. During extended presentations, this is often what accounts for students eventually starting to whisper to each other. Teachers can avoid this disturbance of voices by creating opportunities for conversation as a natural part of their state changes.

- Asking people to close their eyes in a large group setting can be a challenge. Individuals rarely feel safe enough in a group to keep their eyes closed for any length of time. There are two primary means of handling these situations. One way is to keep these moments as brief as possible. Less than ten seconds might be a useful guideline. The other option is to allow students to perform the same function without actually closing their eyes. For example, during visualizations teachers frequently require students to shut their eyes. However, staring at the ceiling or floor often generates exactly the same effect. This way, students are less likely to become distracted by opening their eyes if they begin to feel uncomfortable. Giving them these other options frequently produces the desired result without any unwanted distractions.

- Students may be asked to stand close together in a small group. As with other forms of physical proximity, standing very near other people can be a physically uncomfortable position in which to remain for any length of time. If this is necessary for any part of a learning session, either allow the individuals within the group to spread apart, or get them in motion as soon as possible so they are not consciously thinking about their proximity to other people.

- Sometimes students might be asked to sit in a dyad facing each other. However, if they don't know each other and have nothing to say, this can quickly begin to feel threatening. In these situations, if conversation has ceased, provide students with a reason to turn away from each other, or allow those pairs that are finished to move on to a different task.

In Summary

A critical component for effective learning is insuring that the students have a sense of physical and emotional comfort. Handled incorrectly, these situations can lead rapidly to reduced participation on the part of the students, sometimes to outright rebellion. However, when teachers are able to create a sense of physical relaxation and emotional ease among the students, and handle those potentially threatening situations in a manner that reflects their concern for their comfort, students will quickly develop a bond of trust with that teacher, thus allowing the boundaries of learning to be stretched even further (Maslow 1968, 1970).

COMPLETING ACTIONS

The teacher was out to make a point. At the front of the room a large piece of paper had been taped to the wall, stretching from the floor to the ceiling. Two students were invited to come forward. Each was given a pen. They were told to reach up on the piece of paper and mark the highest point their fingers could touch. When this had been done, the teacher had both people close their eyes and visualize themselves reaching further up the wall. After a minute of imagining this, the two students opened their eyes and tried again. Both were able to reach higher than their first mark. The rest of the group applauded this demonstration. The teacher said:

> "What you just saw did not happen merely by chance. There was a reason they could reach higher the second time. Why? Because they had taken a moment to believe in themselves. When we truly believe we are capable of accomplishing a task, then the chances of us being successful increase immediately."

The teacher continued discussing the power of positive thinking for the next several minutes. He was passionate about his topic, providing examples both current and historical to support his beliefs. However, despite his considerable enthusiasm, as he continued it was clear something was wrong with what was happening in the room. This problem became increasingly distracting to the audience.

What had happened to the two people who had come forward to assist with the demonstration? In this case, nothing! *Both of them were still standing in the front of the room.* Because they had not been invited to return to their chairs, they remained where they were, wondering if they would be needed again. Each was wondering what he or she were supposed to do next. As the teacher continued his presentation, they became fidgety and restless. One eventually sat cross-legged on the floor. The audience became distracted by their behaviors. After a full five minutes had passed, the teacher suddenly realized they were still in the front of the room with him. He paused, had the class give these two students a round of applause, and finally had them return to their seats.

Clarification

In the above situation, the primary action was inviting people to come out of their chairs and assist in a demonstration in front of the room. When the demonstration was complete, they should have been acknowledged and invited to return to their seats immediately. This would have made the two volunteers comfortable. It would also have avoided the issue of having the other students become distracted by their presence in front of the room.

The previous section discussed the idea of keeping audience members physically comfortable to maximize their ability to pay attention. A parallel issue is that of completing actions that have been started. Without this sense of completion, audiences may become distracted from important information while waiting for directions to complete an unfinished task. They also may be left in a physically awkward position, creating a sense of unease. That feeling of uncertainty could easily interfere with their ability to focus on the content. Completing each action that has been started allows students to leave behind what they have been doing and fully focus on the next section of information.

Examples

Following are a series of situations that involve a student initiating some type of action. The key is that if the action has been started, it is important to make certain it is completed at the appropriate moment.

- A teacher asks students a question that invites them to raise their hands. For example, "Raise your hand if you've ever been in a similar situation." When the question has been completed, it's important to remember to tell them to put their hands *down*. Otherwise they will be left with their hands raised high, dangling in the air as the instruction continues, definitely an uncomfortable feeling. This action can be completed by either saying, "Thank you, please put your hands down" or "Thank you," as you lower your own hand. Clearly modeled, this action serves the same purpose with fewer words.
- When asking audiences to relax, teachers may say, "Please take a deep breath." However, if people are asked to breathe in, *it's nice to tell them to breathe out!* While this may seem obvious, it is amazing how many times I have observed teachers only do the first half of this action. Yes, as we all know, breathing is useful in the classroom. However, if you ask them to inhale, be certain to complete this action by specifically telling them to exhale.
- If students have been asked to learn a new activity, be certain to bring them through to the point of success. Otherwise, they might be left in a state of mild frustration that will distract them from learning. For example, there is a brief activity which has students take a pen and rotate it from the top of their hands to the bottom. It usually takes less than two minutes for all students to learn how to accomplish this task. However, once it has been introduced, *be certain everyone has learned how to complete the action successfully* before moving to the next section of instruction. Students who do not reach a point of success with the activity may very well end up continuing to attempt to master it, which of course means they aren't paying attention to the information any longer.
- A teacher needed to divide her room into two random groups. She used an unusual, although highly effective, technique to accomplish this. She held a box of pens, half of which were red, and half of which were green. Students each came forward and chose a pen. Those holding a green pen became one group, and those holding a red pen formed the other group. The two teams were then given a task to perform. However, while working on their task, *all of them continued to hold onto the pen*, because they hadn't been told to put it away. This hindered their ability to accomplish the task they had been given. In this case, the pens were introduced simply to serve the purpose of dividing the audience into two

groups. Once this purpose had been served, the pens should have been immediately returned to the box.

- The day was coming to an end. In one of the closure activities, groups of three to four students were formed. These groups worked together on a large sheet of paper creating a visual representation of what they had learned that day. When all groups had finished their posters, the entire class formed a circle so the teacher could make some final announcements. However, during these last few minutes the students were distracted by their desire to see what other groups had created on their paper. While the teacher spoke a few final words, most students were trying to casually glance at the other creations, ignoring the closing announcements. Instead, the teacher might have first said, "Please take thirty seconds to walk around and enjoy what other groups have created." This would have fulfilled their desire to look around so they could then focus their full attention on the final announcements.

- As mentioned in the section on acknowledgment, it is important to bring closure to each interaction students have with each other. This can be done by a simple thank you, a handshake, a high five, or some other form of acknowledgment. Because they have initiated an action by coming together, either in pairs or small groups, it is necessary to complete the action by acknowledging each other in some fashion.

- Young students were playing a game. One person stood in the middle of a circle of chairs and made a statement such as, "All my friends who are wearing shorts." If people were wearing shorts, they had to leave their seats and find new ones, a variation on the classic game of musical chairs. In this particular session, one individual made a mildly inappropriate statement, and the teacher felt a need to correct this behavior. She stepped to the middle of the circle, paused the action, and talked to the students about the use of appropriate language. Her comments took less than two minutes. However, during this entire time, the person who had been about to make the next statement was left in the middle, uncertain what to do with himself. It was apparent that he felt awkward standing there, and he fidgeted and twitched as he waited for his turn. The teacher could have asked him to have a seat on the floor, or in a chair, as she spoke, which would have made him more comfortable. Then, when she had completed her remarks, she could have invited him to return to the middle of the circle as the game continued.

Being Complete

According to scientific theory, each action produces an equal and opposite reaction. In learning, an identical principle applies. In this case, the "action" is the beginning of an instruction that requires involvement at some level by the student. The necessary "reaction" is the completion of the original movement and bringing the action to closure. This allows students to avoid potential distractions and fully focus their attention on the next piece of information.

CONTRAST

Black letters stand out when placed against a white background. In a field of green grass, a large red ball is easily found. In the blue-green ocean, a white ship is easy to spot. If a crowd of people are hurrying somewhere, it is a simple matter to isolate the one person standing still. When sanding a piece of wood, the areas yet to be smoothed out are readily identifiable to the hand. A car alarm going off in the middle of a quiet evening can be heard for a considerable distance.

The degree to which each of these sentences is true depends on the level of differentiation between the two factors included in the statement. That difference might be based on color, movement, texture, auditory cues, or on any number of other sorting parameters. The concept of *contrast* allows the human brain to isolate and highlight certain elements that are different from others in the immediate environment. This same concept can be applied directly to the process of effective teaching, assisting students in recalling key ideas and concepts from the plethora of information they receive during the natural process of learning.

Clarification

During the course of a single classroom session, a teacher will say many things from the front of the room. However, within all those words are certain key thoughts that may facilitate students' acquisition of the remainder of the material. Through the use of contrast, these central ideas can be highlighted for the students. Once memorized, these points become the building blocks on which all further information is based. The stronger they are encoded in memory, the more solid the entire knowledge structure becomes, and the sooner the information can be comprehended at a functional level (Driscoll 1994; Squire 1987).

Contrast can also be used to create a differentiated learning environment for students on a larger scale. If a quieter, more focused portion of instruction is followed by a more active session, both become unique in comparison to the other. This serves the dual purposes of simultaneously creating a mental state change for the students while contrasting these segments of learning from each other.

Examples

Following are a series of examples in which contrast either has been used, or *could have* been used. They are taken from a variety of learning contexts in order to demonstrate the wide-ranging applicability of this concept.

- The teacher intends to make an important point. He wants the audience to note how often people are mentally tied up in "knots" in their head, meaning they are unwilling to try new options. One way to accomplish this objective is to simply make that statement. While a straightforward approach works well in many circumstances, he wants to maximize the impact of this critical point through the use of contrast. So, he tells a story about how young people move through life gradually learning what they "can't" do, such as "I'm not a tennis player" or "I'm not a singer." He moves through the various examples, using comedy, physical humor, and fast action. Finally, when it is clear that the point has been made, he stands in the center of the room and stops moving. He pauses, carefully makes eye contact with all students, then, with a minimum of movement, makes the original statement. The contrast in his voice tone and the physical gestures, as well as the pause before speaking, now clearly makes his main point stand out for the audience.

- Suppose a brief lecture contains one central idea. Consider having all students stand and listen for one minute to this important point. Then have them remain standing while they spend a moment briefly discussing this point with people near them. This change of physical posture will serve to differentiate this piece from the rest of the information. Another option might be to simply have them stand and discuss this idea with each other *after* the point has been introduced.

- Similarly, imagine the teacher is teaching a thirty-minute segment. She wants to be certain that students remember the central idea, which she intends to illustrate through the use of one particular example. For dramatic emphasis, she takes the entire class outside into a courtyard. Once there, she guides them though her primary analogy. After they have briefly discussed this idea, everyone returns to the classroom. While the decision to physically relocate the class may appear at first glance to be a somewhat dramatic choice (too much like *The Dead Poet Society*?) it will certainly help ensure that the students will remember the information that was presented while they were outside in the courtyard.

- It is the beginning of the year. This particular course will be taught primarily through lectures. Testing will happen only twice, and is the sole means of determining students' grades. Given that such a high value has been placed on the content of the lectures, the teacher makes an announcement. He clearly states: "There's a strong chance that anything I repeat, slowly and distinctly, will appear on the test." He then repeats this statement to be sure they understand what he is saying. Subsequently, during the lectures, he *does* repeat these important pieces of information, which then do appear on the examination.

- The students had just completed an entire day spent on an outdoor ropes course. It was a physically challenging day, full of excitement, action, laughter, and fun. In the evening, the group has gathered together to discuss their experience of the day. The teacher wants to draw out two key points during the discussion that follows: (1) Everyone learned something from their day, and (2) everyone can transfer this learning back into their own lives. In this situation, they need an opportunity to talk before they can become effective listeners. They need a chance to express their excitement about their successes. So the teacher lets them do this, sharing with each other in small groups, then in the large group. Only when this has been accomplished will she move to the topic of applying any insights they may have gained from their experiences. It is only after having had the opportunity to express their excitement that the conversation will focus directly on the learning that can be taken from the day. The contrast between the joy of self-expression and the quieter moments of introspection will assist the students in understanding the significance of the ways in which this information can be transferred to their world outside of this course.

- When asked to stand up, students often grumble, mutter, or complain under their breath. If a teacher hears this reaction, he can turn it to his advantage by reacting appropriately to their response. Instead of ignoring it, he says, "Oh, no, that wasn't right at all! If you're going to do something in this world, always remember to do it *all the way!* Sit down again. OK, this time when you stand, mumble, groan, and complain as loudly as you can, I really want to hear it all!" As the students follow this direction, they can't help but laugh. With this instruction, the teacher has turned a potentially depressing moment into one filled with enjoyment and smiles. He has accomplished this objective through the simple application of contrast: taking what they expected and transforming it into something more useful. In addition, this is a much more effective learning state for the students to be in as the next session commences.

- When workbooks are first distributed, students usually have a strong need to look them over. In most classrooms teachers either ignore this desire or deliberately tell them not to look ahead. In some cases, that may be a necessary choice to make. However, in many situations there is no reason to prevent them from looking at the materials. When they receive their material, the teacher might simply tell them, "When I say go, you have one minute to see every page in this book. You don't have to *read* it, simply scan through it to get an idea of what's ahead of us." Then turn on fast music, if available, while they rapidly flip through the pages. That one minute brings action, humor, and music into the room. The contrast between that action and the subsequent instruction will make the learning stand out clearer than might otherwise be possible.

- In a seven-day summer accelerated learning program for teens, one late evening is spent on a very personal topic. Each student will have an opportunity to examine the current status of their relationship with their parents. The evening starts at 9:00 P.M. However, students are all arriving from a long day of academic study in other rooms. Before they can dive into a deep conversation, it's useful to give them a chance to release any pent-up energy they may have left. Therefore they are first given several activities to do that are brief, high energy, and very active. Once these have been completed, the teacher can gradually ease them into the conversation. Without some sense of contrast, the discussion may feel too much like what goes on in their academic rooms. Now, however, this important discussion will now stand out on its own merits.

- The scene was a one-hour briefing prior to the start of a physically challenging day for a group of teens. Many of the staff for the course were very experienced, and to ensure safety and consistency, it was necessary to cover the information again. The teacher in charge of this group chose to handle the meeting by reading the necessary information directly from the company manual for the entire hour. The staff was bored, restless, and not paying attention. In this situation the teacher might have provided contrast for the group by being more interactive. He could have asked several people from the group to share their experiences, given their knowledge levels. He then could have acknowledged their input and provided any further clarity he deemed appropriate. The staff could have even presented some of the sections themselves, or they might have at least been provided with an opportunity to ask questions. The element of contrast—different speakers, different voices, different stories—might have helped maintain a higher level of attention than was achieved using the chosen method.

- Humor, used appropriately, can provide a wonderful sense of contrast. Even in tense, critical moments during instruction humor can provide a different perspective on the information, one that might be useful to students. One-liners, jokes, humorous stories and examples, or even unusual facial movements may allow students to consider an issue from an unusual point of view. This differentiation could assist them in retaining these key points for a longer time (Gage & Berliner 1998; Jensen 1996; Larkins et al. 1985; Brigham, Scruggs, & Mastropier 1992).

- When using music in a classroom, there is a perfect opportunity to provide contrast between learning sessions. Suppose students have just completed a fairly upbeat session. The one that is scheduled to follow the break will be sedate, more focused on thinking and planning for an upcoming project. The teacher could begin the break with up-tempo music, matching the state of the students as they walk away from that session. Then, during the course of the break, the teacher could gradually bring the choice of music down to a more relaxed, gentler level. The contrast in musical selections will alert students that the next piece will be something different.

Too Much, Too Soon

At the same time that contrast can be a useful tool, used inappropriately it can also be abusive to an audience. Too much difference between the "norm" and the "new" can send shock waves through an audience. For example, when first introducing music into an already established classroom, it may be useful to keep the volume fairly low while people adapt to the presence of a stereo system. Or, if a teacher will be using many activities during a class, she might begin with one that requires a lower level of active input from the students, building later to those with higher levels of involvement or risk. Working at a gradient level appropriate to the audience's past experience, while still challenging them, can be instrumental in successfully applying contrast to learning environments. I recently observed an example of how this concept plays out in a very real, very physical sense.

> The scene was a location outside Melbourne, Australia, in the foothills of the Grampion mountains. A group of ten people was about to spend a day rappelling off cliffs (using a rope to walk backward down a cliff). In the group was one young woman who had never had the opportunity to experience this challenge previously. While excited about the adventure inherent in doing something new, she was also quite nervous.
>
> The first cliff chosen by the group that day was quite high, a full 35 meters from top to bottom. As the group anchored the ropes, this young woman's nervousness began to assert itself. She started talking rapidly and her

breathing became very quick. When her turn came, she allowed herself to be hooked up into the safety harness, even though she had begun to cry hysterically. The leader of the group talked her through her first few steps, but she soon froze, unable to move up or down. Finally he placed his body beneath hers, so she could feel his physical presence, in the hopes it would provided her with a sense of security. Together they continued their descent down the cliff face.

Still sobbing loudly, she gradually approached the base of the cliff. The rest of the group cheered her apparent success, but, on reaching the bottom she quickly unhooked herself and walked away. Despite repeated invitations to try again, she refused to take advantage of any other opportunities, preferring to sit apart from the group for the rest of the day. She was even unwilling to touch the ropes at the end of day when the others were wrapping them up and preparing to go home. It was clear that she would not be doing any more rappelling in the near future, if ever.

It was simply too much, too soon, for this young woman to handle. The contrast between her fear and what had been asked of her for this first time was simply too great. Perhaps, if she had been given the opportunity to begin rappelling off a much lower cliff, she could have completed it, celebrated her success, and rested for a while. Later, the contrast between that successful experience and the attempt to rappel from a slightly higher cliff might have felt more manageable, and she might have continued to try higher and higher cliffs throughout the remainder of the day. As teachers in the classroom, we need to take this lesson to heart. The last thing we want is for students to stop learning: Finding the appropriate level of contrast can be instrumental in assisting them to stay focused and engaged without scaring them away.

In Summary

In teaching, contrast is a powerful educational element, and it should be consciously and carefully used at specified moments during the process of instruction. In advance of each class, teachers would be well advised to identify what they believe are the key pieces of information. Specific steps should then be taken to clearly establish these concepts as unique and different from the remaining content. If these key concepts are easy for students to recall, related information should be equally memorable.

DISTRIBUTING RESOURCES

It was the first day of the class. Students had arrived and taken their seats. The teacher had introduced herself, and it was time to get the class underway. She picked up a stack of papers and turned to face the students. Holding the papers up so everyone could see them, she said:

"Here is the schedule for this class, the syllabus."

She then approached the first row of students and started to hand a few to them. In the middle of this motion she paused, then returned the papers to the general stack. Grabbing the entire pile in both hands she said:

> "Actually, if you're really interested in what's going to happen in this class, it's up to you to get one of these!"

Saying this she threw the entire stack up into the air in the middle of the room. The stunned students stared at her for a moment and then quickly moved to pick up one of the pages that were now strewn about the room.

Why did she engage in this seemingly bizarre behavior? Was it merely a random act of strangeness, was she close to suffering a nervous breakdown, or was there a larger purpose behind her actions? In fact, when preparing for this class, this teacher had decided it was important to let the students know that this was not going to be an ordinary class right from the start. She could have simply said that, but how many times have they heard that one in the past? Probably quite a few times. No, she wanted to *do* something different.

This teacher wanted to *demonstrate* to her students that this course was going to be a very special experience for them. In looking at how she was going to start this class she realized that a suitable circumstance for making this point was available right at the start of the first class session. Passing out the syllabi was a chance to do something ordinary, or a chance to do something *extra*ordinary. For this reason she chose this unique method of opening the course. And it worked. The students were startled into being fully awake, and she could now build on the energy generated by this creative jump start to her class. However, there was even more going on behind the scenes than just an unusual opening. In fact, this teacher was utilizing a very specific instructional strategy for creating a high-impact classroom. It was a strategy she was fully planning to repeat in future moments in her classroom. You may also find the unique idea of occasionally "throwing papers out" to be useful in your classroom at some point.

Clarification

Distributing resources, such as papers, packets, and pens, provides an excellent opportunity for making an impact on students, for keeping them energized and awake. In a more traditional classroom, the methods used to distribute resources tend to follow a few well-repeated patterns. For example, consider a situation where the teacher needs to provide each student with a worksheet. How would these papers normally reach the students? Perhaps the following methods will seem familiar to you:

- Walk around and give each student one.
- Give the worksheets to two or three students and have them pass them out.
- Pass the worksheets out to the people in the first row. Then have these people hand them to the people behind them, until everyone has one.

Even young students will have seen these methods used on a frequent basis. Repetition, while useful in some situations, does nothing for the students here. A teacher wishing to make an impact should seize this chance for inventiveness and find some unique method of accomplishing the task. Handled creatively, the same result will be achieved while bringing energy, humor, laughter, and excitement into the room. These are characteristics that most learning environments could have in greater quantities. Look at the following situations and consider the unique methods of achieving the required task.

Example 1:   *The Challenge: Distributing workbooks.* To do this in a creative manner, there are numerous possibilities. One approach might be to arrive early in the day and place them around the classroom so they are "semi-hidden" from view, such as under a table, behind a curtain, or beneath a ledge. When the moment comes for the students to need these workbooks, the teacher would say:

> "Located in a variety of places throughout the room are the workbooks we'll be using today. They look like this. [Hold one up.] When I say 'go' you have one minute to find one for yourself and then to make sure everyone around you has one also. Please, find yourself a workbook. Go!"

Now music can be put on while the students walk around the room in search of their materials. They will probably be laughing and talking to each other while locating the workbooks, perhaps passing them to each other as more and more are found. The scene is much like a variation on an Easter egg hunt. Soon everyone will have a book in their possession and the class can continue.

Compare this sequence of events to what might take place in a more low-impact setting. These workbooks were probably handed out one by one, usually in silence, or at most with some very quiet conversation. This would probably have taken at least a full minute, perhaps even longer. Instead, using the strategy discussed here, the room is filled with music, students are talking to each other, and they are waking their bodies up as they walk around the room. The tone of the room will have changed significantly, while the *same goal has been accomplished.*

Some of you may be concerned as to how this strategy might feel to the more "mature" students. Would it be weird to have teens engaging in a simulated Easter egg hunt? In fact, I have used this approach many times and seen it used by other high school teachers quite effectively. Strong testament can be given to the reality that most teens prefer movement and action, even if it is not something they are familiar with from their past experiences in school. But, if for some reason this idea sounds too outrageous, it could be modified to a tamer approach. For example, the workbooks could be set on various tables located at the sides of the room, in five or six different stacks. When it comes time to distribute them simply ask the students to stand and go to one of the tables and get themselves a workbook. In this simplified version, at least they would still be walking somewhere, so the movement aspect of the idea would remain intact.

Here's a final variation on this idea, one that is used quite extensively in some schools. To distribute the workbooks, designate four individuals to come to the front of the room. Give each one a stack of workbooks and ask them to choose a corner of the classroom and go stand there. When they are ready, tell the students:

> "Located in each corner of the room is someone who is holding your workbooks. If you would like to have one of these, your task is quite simple. Just approach one of these people and give them a compliment! If they like your compliment, they'll give you one. If not, you might have to go see someone else!"

The significant change from the first idea is the addition of having them compliment each other. Even though they may not know each other, people generally make something up, laugh and interact. This provides social contact, which again adds energy and excitement to the classroom.

Example 2: *The Challenge: Distributing colored pens to the students* that they can use to take notes during the class. Suppose the pens were all placed together in a basket at the front of the room. The simplest way to handle this situation might be to say:

> "Please look at me. In this basket are some colored pens that everyone is free to use at any time. There are a variety of colors that you can share with your neighbors. To get the ball rolling, let me share some of them with you. Please hold both hands up in the air, palms up, and place them over your head. Ready? Here they come!"

Then simply grab handfuls of pens and toss them out into the classroom! Having their hands up protects their faces, and allows them to snatch a pen or two out of the air. Could a teacher really do this with a secondary school classroom and have it work? Absolutely, as has been proven many times in the past.

Example 3: *The Challenge: Distributing work sheets.* This example was used to begin this section. However, there are numerous variations on the idea of throwing the papers out to the students that could be used by the teacher. In the example mentioned before, the scene was a high school classroom. Throughout the remainder of the year, perhaps the students could be given a chance to join in throwing the papers out. In fact students often enjoy being given this task to perform! Sometimes they could throw them from the back of the room. Other times perhaps only one person could be given this task; the challenge would be to get the papers evenly spread throughout the room with a single throw. Certainly, more ways could be invented to further add to the enjoyment of the act of throwing papers out, keeping this single idea fresh in the minds of the students.

In Summary

The examples shown above are but a few of the many ways in which a teacher might choose to distribute materials and papers to students. The key is to remember that distributing things to students is an excellent opportunity for creativity and individual expression on the part of the teacher. How else might this same task be accomplished? What would work best given the materials in question, the age of the students, the content of the class, and the personality of the teacher? Be selective when choosing a strategy and keep generating new approaches. Most importantly, beware of the belief that such variety and inventiveness is inappropriate for a particular age of student. Enjoyment of laughter, music, and human interaction is not a quality limited to students of a particular age group. Everyone can appreciate the benefits that emerge through the teacher's use of creative, energetic strategies for distributing resources.

DO IT STANDING

It is a typical classroom setting. The students come into the room and take a seat. They listen to a lecture, remaining seated. They move into circles and hold a small group discussion. As before, they remain in their chairs. A large group discussion ensues, and the students remain in their chairs. A video is put on, and the students watch from their chairs. Several overheads are shown, and once again students are left in their seats. As the class nears its conclusion, they are asked to spend five minutes preparing a brief presentation. They gather in a group and prepare their talk, *while sitting in their chairs*. Finally, as the various groups get up to speak, the others remain in their chairs and listen. When the bell rings to end the class, everyone is still seated.

An Observation

In an interactive environment, it is natural that students will be involved in a number of different forms of instruction. Several are perfectly suited for standing instead of sitting. Yet, in the minds of many teachers, learning seems to have become linked to sitting. A paradigm appears to exist that implies that no credible information could possibly be taught while students stand on their own two legs. But think about it for a moment. There are many learning objectives that could just as easily be accomplished while the students are upright!

Opportunities to Stand Tall

Most of the activities described below would last less than five minutes, a length of time that most students are easily able to remain standing. Consider having students stand up while doing any of the following:

- participating in opening activities or conversations;
- having small group discussions of less than five minutes;
- observing a short demonstration in the front of the room;
- viewing overheads;
- participating in any brief activity during the class session;
- gathering resources; or
- engaging in carousel activities—students write on papers hung on walls at different locations throughout a classroom.

In Summary

Is it any wonder that some students may come to dread the time they must spend in a learning environment? From a physical standpoint, the great majority of classrooms require that they stay seated. In this posture it is sometimes difficult enough merely to remain awake! It is clear that, during certain moments in the course of instruction, it is useful for students to be in their seats, such as when they are taking written notes. However, there are numerous other moments during most lessons when remaining seated is not necessary for the learning to occur. At these times, students should be invited to stand, stretch their legs, and energize themselves. There are usually many of these opportunities available in every learning session, and teachers should take the fullest advantage of each one of them. Giving students the chance to stand, stretch, and get their circulation going can only benefit them in the long run.

HONORING WRITTEN NOTES

When a teacher is giving a lecture, there is usually an unspoken expectation that students should be writing down notes. This seems to be such an accepted form of behavior in the classroom that there is no need to even mention it. However, when students are writing notes, much more is happening than most teachers realize. The process of taking in, analyzing, and recording new information is a challenging enterprise for most students, the complexity of which is far too often overlooked. Those teachers who learn to successfully handle these note-taking situations in the classroom can greatly contribute to the long-term learning of their students.

An Example

I first became fully aware of the magnitude of this issue as the result of a personal experience. The setting was a four-day personal and professional development seminar that has been run extensively throughout the United States, Asia, New Zealand, and Australia. I was a student in a program being presented in Brisbane. Over the course of the first two days, the teacher had established an unusual pattern of speech when delivering content. He would pause just before the last word of many of his sentences, waiting for the audience to fill in the necessary word. For example, he might say:

"Hopefully it's now clear what I've been trying to . . . *explain*."

 He would not actually say the word *explain* until the audience had said it, and sometimes he would not say it at all, but just continue with the next sentence.

It was a curious approach to content delivery. In a conversation over one of the meal breaks someone asked the presenter the purpose behind it. He explained that the approach was predicated on the belief that students would stay more in tune if they were interacting with him in this manner while he was presenting. From a theoretical perspective, the idea did make some sense. From a personal perspective, however, I confess that I found it mildly irritating, although not enough to significantly impact my experience of the program in general.

Early on the third day, however, I had occasion to witness a moment in which the approach was definitely *not* used successfully. As I observed this interaction, I learned something critical to my future teaching endeavors. The teacher had been lecturing on a topic that was of considerable interest to the rest of the group: how to make lots of money! He had just finished speaking about one idea in particular that seemed to capture the imagination of many of the students. All were furiously scribbling in their workbooks.

At that exact moment, the teacher paused at the end of a sentence, waiting for the audience to fill in the blank. This time, however, no one responded to his prompting. He had been writing at the flip chart when this occurred. When his pause was greeted with silence, he whipped his head around, glared intensely at the audience, and yelled:

> "Come on, people! You've got to do better than that! This is important information, and the only way you're going to get it is to stay awake, stay present, stay with me! Come on, now, get focused and stick with the program!"

Strong words, yet I was chuckling inside. As a teacher he had seriously miscalculated. He had failed to recognize *why* people had not responded, and was reacting simply to the fact that they had not verbally completed his sentence. Why did the students not answer in that moment? Simply because they were actively engaged in taking notes! By asking them to respond to his pause at that point, he was effectively *interfering* with the learning process by pulling people away from taking their notes.

Generalizing the Idea

The learning from that experience was deeply impressed on me. I still see the applicability of this lesson in almost every teaching situation in which I find myself. If I'm speaking, and suddenly realize that many students are taking notes at a certain moment, then I have this radical thought: *Perhaps I've actually said something worth remembering*! If that's true, the last thing I want to do is interfere with them while they are gathering that gem, writing it down, and storing it away for future reference.

I've learned to recognize these precious learning moments and I do my best to respond to them by pausing, even if I'm in the middle of a sentence. When students have written whatever it was that caught their attention, they generally tend to look back up at me. When the majority of them have looked up, I know it is time to continue and I resume speaking.

A Second Issue with Written Notes

There's another way teachers can honor individuals who take notes. Most often, students experience a sensation of panicked energy when trying to take down what the teacher is saying during a lecture. When they are in this frantic state of mind, it is understandable that they rarely take the time to glance *back over* what they have just scribbled on their paper. They are rushing to get the next name, date, or statistic written down correctly. They may not look back over what they have written until that night, the next day, or perhaps even the following week.

But if they return to the information at a much later time, they have missed a golden opportunity for long-term learning. The images, ideas, or stories that were connected to the few words they had time to jot down will quickly fade from their memory. Teachers can take specific action to help increase student recall during times when they have taken notes.

Quite simply, provide them with classroom time that is specifically designated for a brief review of what they have just written in their notebooks. This could be handled in a variety of ways. Perhaps the teacher could pause every ten or fifteen minutes and give them two minutes to look over what they have written so far. During this time students could be encouraged to add any other words to the ones they already have that would help them remember the information. Perhaps they could even be encouraged to draw symbols, diagrams, or doodles that would help trigger their memories of the discussion through visual cues. Finally, after they have had a chance to do these things, they might even be given a minute to ask clarifying questions about the information presented up to this point.

Taking the time to do things like this can help students avoid times later when they are studying and stare at their notes in amazement, wondering "why did I write that down?" If this has ever happened to you as a student you'll be familiar with this frustrating, hair-pulling experience. Students' retention will increase immediately and dramatically if they are given even a brief period of time in the classroom to enhance their understanding of their notes through review and reflection.

Of course, to do this you will have resist one of the most dangerous beliefs in education. Teachers sometimes get trapped into thinking, "If I say it, they'll remember it." They end up filling every moment of the class with verbal input. If there's an extra minute or two available they'll leap into the gap and repeat themselves, in the hopes it will increase student learning. Avoid falling into this trap. We know this is not how people learn best. Help your students learn easily and naturally by allowing them to consolidate their notes while in the classroom.

In Summary

The important thing is to honor students when they take written notes. Help them learn the material faster and easier by giving them time in the classroom to pause and reflect on the ideas they are learning. Encourage the natural learning process by making sure they have sufficient time to build the mental connections between the information they are hearing and the notes they are taking. Learning to use this idea in your classroom can remove some of the panic and alarm students often experience in class and fill them, instead, with increased levels of confidence and optimism.

LAYERING

It was early in the day. Students were about to engage in a physical challenge that would demonstrate an important concept. The teacher wanted to give them a chance to warm up before moving into the activity, because he knew this would assist them in getting the most out of the activity (Ormond 2000; Vygotsky 1987). To accomplish this objective he used a three-step sequence.

- First, the students organized themselves into groups of approximately four or five. Each group received a hacky sack, a small round object that people pass around using only their feet. In this case, however, the teacher invited them to try *hand hacky*, meaning they were to pass the ball to each other by using their hands to bat it in the air. Music came on, and the members of each group began passing the ball to each other by batting it with the palms of their hands.
- After the groups had done this for about one minute, the teacher stopped the music and asked them to pause for a moment. He then introduced the next element in the activity. Each time the hacky sack hit the ground, the group was to vigorously applaud their efforts before they could pick it up and continue passing it to each other. The groups added this component and the activity continued.
- After another minute had passed, the third aspect of this activity was presented to the groups. They were told that from this point forward each time a person hit the hacky sack they were to count out loud. The objective was to see how long the group could keep it in the air before it hit the ground, at which time they would applaud their efforts, pick it up again, and start back at the number "one." The groups reformed, began again, and added counting to the activity. After another minute had passed, they acknowledged each of their group members with a "high-five" or a "thank you" and were ready to engage in the primary activity.

The entire sequence lasted less than four minutes, including time spent giving instructions. At the conclusion of this activity students were alive, energized, and ready for whatever was coming next that morning. Part of the reason for the success of the activity was that in leading it the teacher had used a teaching technique known as *layering*.

Defining the Term

Layering refers to the structure a teacher uses in order to communicate a specific sequence of steps in a lesson. It is a technique for subdividing activities, learning sessions, or instruction periods. Its purpose is to assist in the development of a central idea through the sequential, deliberate addition of new elements to what is already known.

Clarification

In the previous example, it's important to note that the same exercise could have been led using a completely different approach. The teacher might have given all the directions at once, including batting the object with one's hands, applauding when it hit the ground, and counting each hit. At first glance this may appear to be a simpler method of leading the activity. However, the teacher had a specific reason for presenting the activity in the manner described.

The primary reason for layering the activity—presenting it in three separate components—concerns the ability of a group to fully remember each component of the exercise. For example, if the entire activity were presented at once, in some cases groups may forget one of those three instructions, such as the need to applaud each time the object hits the ground. They may be caught up in the excitement of seeing how many consecutive hits they can attain and overlook this direction entirely. To have the activity achieve its full potential, layering was used.

Layering occurs when, within a single activity or instruction, there are a series of small changes and adjustments that build on each other. Each time a new element is introduced, students must pay careful attention to this instruction, which helps keep them focused. Layering can maximize both the ability of a group to pay attention and the effect that is ultimately created.

Examples

Layering can be applied to a variety of teaching situations. Teachers may choose to use it at any point during a lesson, including moments when there is an activity, a learning exercise, a demonstration, or a lecture. Here are several situations in which it may be utilized. Note the broad scope of applications for this concept.

- At the start of a seminar, a class, or a speech, a presenter may want to ask a series of "enrolling questions." (This concept is further detailed in Chapter 6.) Layering can be applied to this situation in the following three steps: (1) the presenter asks the audience several questions; (2) the presenter chooses members of the audience to ask the group questions; and (3) it is open season: anyone can ask a question without being invited or prompted. These three phases are distinct from each other, and members of the audience will be alert to the switches, wanting to be ready in case they are the person asking the next question.
- An energizer known as "Questions" is similar to the previous example, although it occurs in a different context, and frequently with smaller audiences. In this unusual interpersonal interaction—a "get to know people" activity—the group forms a circle. The teacher asks a question that everyone answers, for example, "How many brothers or sisters do you have?" or "What's your favorite color?" The layers commonly used here are: (1) the teacher asks the first few questions, then (2) the opportunity is given to the group members to question the group.
- Another energizer goes by the name of "All My Neighbors Who." In this activity, a circle of chairs is used. One person, however, does not have a seat, and he or she is instructed to stand in the middle of the group. This person makes a statement beginning with the words "All my neighbors who . . ." and completes it with anything, such as ". . . are wearing tennis shoes" or ". . . have something blue on" or ". . . ate breakfast this morning." Those people who fit the stated category must leave their chair and find a new place to sit. At the same time, the person in the middle finds a seat, meaning that someone new will not have a chair. That person now comes to the center of the group and makes a new statement beginning with those same first four words. The three layers commonly used in this activity are: (1) exactly as it is described here, (2) adding the words ". . . have ever . . ." and making the original statement "All my neighbors who have ever . . . ," and (3) adding stealing, which occurs if two students can "steal" places, meaning they can exchange seats with another seated individual while the person in the middle is thinking of the next idea.

- Some interactive learning environments use a device known as a "ZeeBee," a Frisbee made of a soft material so it can be used safely indoors. It is excellent for children, teens, and adult students, and is frequently used as an energizer, perhaps immediately after lunch, when students may need to be "wakened up" a bit. Here are just three of the many possible layers that could be used to direct this activity: (1) throwing the ZeeBees to other people while standing in a circle, (2) adding "creativity," when they have the opportunity to toss or catch it in a creative manner, with others applauding the unusual ideas they see, and (3) "Star in the Middle," where several students are brought to the middle of the circle; if they intercept a ZeeBee thrown by someone else they can trade places with that person, who now becomes the "star" until he or she catches a ZeeBee and then trades places with someone else.
- In many environments, *physically* thanking each other is an appropriate form of acknowledgment. In cases where this is acceptable behavior, "high-fives" are one common form of expression. This occurs when two people each raise their hand and slap palms, the "five" referring to five fingers. Many layers can be used when first introducing this idea to the group, such as: (1) giving a regular high-five; (2) using the *opposite* hand, which may feel strange to some people; (3) giving "low-fives": instead of raising their hands they lower them; (4) giving high, low, and behind-the-back "tens," using both hands; (5) getting creative and doing high or low "sevens," "threes," or "nines"; or even (6) allowing thirty seconds for each student to give and receive as many different kinds of high fives or tens as possible from the other people in the group.

Layering can also be part of more extended learning activities. Consider the following two situations:

- The "Maze" is a popular training activity in which masking tape is using to create a $9' \times 6'$ grid of squares on the ground. Students must "solve" the maze by finding the path of correct squares from one side to the other. It is commonly used to start a conversation concerning people's willingness to take risks. This challenging task has been layered for the students by doing it once each day during a five-day training course. Each time it is done, a new element is added. Some of these additions include: (1) conducting the activity as described above, (2) having half the teams wear blindfolds, (3) having students start simultaneously at both ends of the grid, (4) changing which squares are the correct ones during the course of the activity, and (5) challenging students to realize that in order to solve it correctly they must step *off* of the maze at one point and *re-enter* it two squares forward. Each of these layers could be used to illustrate a different point.
- Another activity, which is currently popular in many outdoor classes, is one in which students are challenged to each break a wooden board. It is not a trick, it is an actual $12'' \times 12'' \times 1''$ pine board. To complete it successfully requires some degree of force, but mostly focus, concentration, and determination on the part of the student. This discussion of the activity is not meant to serve as a lesson plan

for the actual activity: I strongly advise against doing this activity unless you have been personally trained by an experienced person. The metaphor commonly attached to this powerful experience is about each individual's willingness to move past the "barriers," symbolized by the board, that might be holding them back in life. The experience might be layered for students by having them accomplish this task three different ways, once at the end of each day during a three-day training program. The three steps could include teaching them how to (1) break the board using a foot, (2) break it using a hand, and (3) break it using their hand in a way that requires significantly less force, yet substantially more focused energy. The principle taught through the three experiences could follow the lines of finding a multitude of methods for moving through personal barriers. If one approach does not work, perhaps another one can be found that will be successful to achieve the outcome.

Of course, the idea of layering can certainly be used during the course of direct instruction or lectures. Here are two examples of how this has been put into practice in programs I have taught.

- The concept to be learned by students is one of a series of memorization techniques. The particular method is know as "Linking": items are memorized through the process of creating a story, using them in the order in which they appear on a list. The first layer used to teach this piece is to simply tell the audience a story and have them tell the story to someone else. Then they are informed there are a certain number of items contained in the story, and are asked to see how many they can recall. This opening demonstration shows students the validity of the method, as in most cases they will be able to recall every item. In the second layer, the teacher gives them a different list of items, and they create their own story for the purposes of memorization. Finally, the third layer is to give them a list that has personal or professional relevance to them. They must then create a story for memorizing these items. For example, with teenagers, one list that could be used is the mineral hardness scale from science, which is a sequence of ten minerals from nature. These range from the softest mineral (talc) to the hardest one (diamonds). This final layer allows the relevance of the concept to be demonstrated to all students.
- The principle of Open Loops is presented in the third chapter of this book. When presented in a seminar session, I use a series of layers to develop this concept for the students. The steps used in this sequence are: (1) provide a definition of an open loop; (2) clarify it by giving several examples; (3) in small groups, have students discuss loops that have been used in that seminar; (4) provide more specific examples, which include some that are written for them in their workbook; and (5) discuss examples of open loops in everyday life. The use of layering in this instructional setting allows the central concept to move sequentially from a single, clear definition to widespread applications. At the conclusion of the session, students should be clear both on the meaning of "Open Loops" as well as how to apply them in a variety of settings.

In Summary

Not all aspects of instruction may lend themselves readily to this concept. As with many other ideas contained in this chapter, teachers should consciously choose whether it is appropriate to layer an energizer, an activity, or a lecture. However, when applied correctly, it can be a useful and powerful instructional tool.

MUSIC

Situation 1:   Two university summer courses were preparing to get underway. These sessions were being held in classrooms next door to each other. In the room on the left, background music was being played. In the room on the right, no music was being played. Standing in the hallway, looking into both rooms, an observer could easily notice a clear difference in the manner in which the students were interacting in each room. In the room with the music on, most students were engaged in conversation with each other, while in the other students were sitting quietly, staring forward, waiting for the class to begin.

Situation 2:   It was 10:30 in the morning. The teacher asked the students to assist him by moving the tables and chairs to the sides of the room. As the students stood up, the teacher turned on upbeat, lively music, with the volume fairly high. The students moved rapidly to accomplish the task, and energetically moved to the next activity. Later that day, the same task needed to be accomplished once again. This time, as the students stood to move, no music was turned on. While students still accomplished the task, their movements were sluggish and it took much longer to achieve the same objective. As the next activity began, the teacher struggled to get the students fully engaged.

Clarification

Music is a powerful tool that can be added to most, if not all, learning situations. It has a direct physical, emotional, and psychological effect on both the students *and* the teacher (Jensen 2000). Properly employed, it can create a heightened social learning context, motivate students to engage themselves more rapidly, and provide a sense of safety that might not otherwise be possible. Each of these factors adds considerably to the development of a powerful learning environment (Burko & Elliot 1997; Weinberger 1998). As far as this book is concerned, application is everything, so here are some distinct ways in which a teacher might consider adding music to enliven learning contexts.

Four Places for Music

Music before Class.   Imagine a silent room on the first day of a new course. Students might not know each other, so they are more reticent about saying hello to someone.

Even if they did decide to introduce themselves to someone else, there is a danger because the room is silent, so any words spoken would be heard by everyone. Suddenly, merely talking to one other person becomes an adventure in public speaking; everyone can hear what is being said. Also, because there is no other noise present in the room, speaking up almost feels out of place. Have music playing as students enter the classroom.

With music playing in the background, it is as if permission has unconsciously been given for people to speak to each other. Because there is already noise, it does not seem so threatening to simply "add to it"; subtly, students are invited to interact. With the music playing, when they engage in conversation, people across the room won't be able to hear. Thus, the internal feeling of risk is greatly reduced. Given these circumstances, it is not surprising that students in the first example described above, who had the benefit of music in their environment, were already talking to each other, building a social learning environment. Most teachers realize this is a useful component in any learning context. In a way the students have already begun the class, independently moving to achieve one important objective of this first session.

Music at the start of a session can also serve to set the tone, the atmosphere for the session. If the class is going to involve activity, or if lively group discussions are anticipated, it might be useful to have more "up-tempo" songs on, beginning to build the energy in the room. In this situation, music may act to subtly bring to mind a partying atmosphere, a useful mind-set for the delivery of certain lessons. However, if the lesson plan calls for a more quiet, contemplative, or perhaps even emotionally challenging session, the choice of music might be softer songs, or gentle classical and baroque selections.

There is one other good reason for teachers to have music playing at this point in the course of instruction. When it's time to begin the class, the music is simply turned off. Even in the few moments before instruction begins, students will already have been primed to having something auditory present in their environment. The loss of the music will cause them to turn their heads, knowing that something is happening. Seizing the moment, instruction now officially begins. This saves the teacher from having to start the class by using such phrases as "OK, could you all look at me?" or "Well, I guess it's time to begin," or "Everybody, could you please get quiet so we can start?" With the successful use of music in this manner, the teacher can move directly to the lesson with the first spoken words.

Music during Movement.   When students are moving, it is rarely necessary for them to be listening to any words from the teacher. Therefore, this is an excellent place to include faster-paced music. For example, as in the second situation illustrated in the beginning of this section, perhaps students are required to move their chairs. In other situations, they may be forming groups, or moving to get supplies. Whenever movement is introduced into the learning setting, music can be used to help motivate the students to accomplish the task more rapidly, and with a sense of animation and enjoyment (Jensen, 1996).

Upbeat, bright, energetic music is best in these situations. Because the overall goal is to move rapidly to the next direction or activity, music can auditorily stimulate the students' physical movement. The sense of energy brought into the learning setting by the inclusion of this type of music can be captured and built on by the teacher, used to segue into the next section of the lesson. It saves the teacher from having to expend precious energy to get the students up and motivated. Every time there is movement on the part of the students, turn on music that matches the mood you want to create. Use of music at these important moments is one of the keys to maintaining a successful learning environment over the long term.

Music *behind* Small Group Discussions.   Many times, students will be given the opportunity to discuss various aspects of the information they are learning with other students. Sometimes they will be talking with just one other person, other times it might be within a small group. In either case, with several different groups holding conversations in the same room, there is a chance that the volume level of the conversation from one group may intrude on the conversation of another group. Music played lightly in the background can lessen this sense of interference.

This effect is referred to as a musical "pad." Physical padding is used to sound-proof rooms in a home, walls in an apartment building, or a musical studio. In the classroom, the use of light background music effectively "pads" the room so that sound from one group will not interfere with sound from another group. In a silent room, if one group should break into laughter, the sudden intrusion of sound can be quite disruptive to other conversations. However, with a pad of music playing the effect of the interruption can be significantly diminished.

Similar to the discussion of the use of music at the start of a class, this pad can also *encourage* conversation within a group. In a silent room, it may be a bit intimidating for some students to speak up and voice their opinions even in a very small group, because they don't know if people from other groups will hear what they have to say. With the sense of protection and privacy that the use of a pad offers, students frequently feel freer to engage themselves in the interaction. This effect facilitates both the initiation and the continuation of the interaction.

There is one more aspect of using music behind group conversations that might be useful to consider. Because students will be talking during this time, decide whether to choose songs with or without lyrics. Sometimes, songs with words may prompt people to listen closely to the song, which in turn causes them to tune out of the conversation in which they are supposed to be participating. In most cases, this is definitely *not* the effect you are trying to create.

In general, there are three choices to consider regarding lyrics: none, unfamiliar, or familiar. First, music without words can sometimes provide a gentle pad that supports the conversation by providing a low level of background sound. Second, songs with lyrics they *don't* know may be useful in some cases, because the mere presence of words may encourage them to talk and interact. Personally, I occasionally use gentle Hawaiian music in these circumstances, partly because the melodies are a nice background choice, but mostly because people don't understand Hawaiian! Finally, in rare cases, songs with lyrics they do know may work, especially if the words somehow relate to the current lesson. Remember that it's always your choice of what to use; just make sure it helps create the atmosphere you feel is most useful in each learning situation.

Music after Class.   As the class ends, students gather their belongings and begin to file out of the room. This is a wonderful opportunity for music to be playing. The selections chosen at this time should leave students with a positive impression of the session that has just been completed. Because this is the final feeling they take away from your classroom, it will frequently be the first thing they think about when they begin to organize their thoughts for their next class with you. Obviously, it is much more useful for students to begin the subsequent session with a positive rather than a negative feeling about the last session they attended.

These four places are an excellent starting point when deciding how to use music in the classroom. However, if this is the first time you are considering the inclusion of this form of auditory stimulus in your lesson plans, organizing even these isolated moments might be an overwhelming experience, given everything else that is simultaneously happening in most classrooms. Give yourself time to learn, and feel free to experiment with a variety of musical choices while looking for what works best in the environment you are trying to create. Here are some other thoughts to consider when you are ready.

A Cornucopia of Useful Points regarding Music

Volume Level: One tricky aspect of the use of music is the volume at which it is played. Know in advance that *it will never be exactly right for every student in the room.* Some individuals will always want the music louder, while other people will want the music softer. Similarly, some people will like the song that is currently playing, while others will want it changed immediately. This is a natural by-product of any aspect of instruction when students have the opportunity to have input. Understanding that this is the case may help you maintain your sanity when these situations arise. As much as possible, aim for the middle. Adjust the volume so that it maximizes the desired effect, and minimizes the number of people who are distracted or feel a need to complain. Alternate song choices so all students get to hear something they prefer at some point in the lesson. Continue to stay focused on the changing needs of the group and adapt as necessary.

Type of Music: You might also want to consider what type of music to play. This should be based on the reaction sought from the students. For example, if working with teens, ask them beforehand which CDs are currently most popular, and have some of these on hand. If you don't personally own any of these, you might want to ask your students to bring in some from their own collection. This request saves you money, and it also brings a sense of student "ownership" into the room. It is important to note here that what the teacher prefers to listen to is much less important than what will create the desired effect for the learning setting.

Teachers of teen audiences may also have to cope with one very specific issue that other teachers may never encounter: Beware of most rap music. While its appeal as basic entertainment may be quite strong to some students, its usefulness to a teacher in a learning setting may be quite limited because it frequent relies on bass sounds. Heavy low tones are counterproductive for the needs of almost all aspects of learning and recall. Students who enjoy rap music may ask that it be used during class. In these situations it becomes quite important to explain the purposes behind the music that has been chosen for the classroom.

> "I think rap music is fine. I even own a few rap CDs myself. However, much of that form of music relies on heavy bass notes. The wavelengths these notes produce do not encourage learning or long-term memory, which is the only reason we're using music. When we're in class, that's the purpose of the music—to help everyone learn. So here's what we'll do. If you're willing to let the class use music that is useful for learning when we're studying, I'll be willing to have rap on during the breaks, provided, of course, that the lyrics are appropriate!"

Offering to allow them to listen to their music at breaks can be a significant aid in getting buy-in from them for the appropriate use of music during instructional periods. Teachers are free to borrow these words and adapt them to ones that will work for their environment and their students. Generally, however, it has been my experience that, with a clear enough explanation, the majority of students are willing to compromise and go with the program. Interestingly, many of these students—even rebellious teens—often come to enjoy the other forms of music fairly rapidly. Their understanding that the music is not there purely to entertain them is frequently the key to making it work.

Finally, consider choosing music that speaks directly to the current lesson. Earlier in this section, I mentioned that the choice of certain songs with certain lyrics should be deliberate so that the music fits the instructional moment. This might be music used to set up a conversation, such as having teenagers listen to "Father and Son" by Cat Stevens or "Cats Cradle" by Harry Chapin prior to initiating a conversation about their relationship with their parents. Or, after a discussion about their personal vision in life you might choose to play "I Can Do Anything" or "You're the Voice" by John Farnham while they spend a moment visualizing their own future.

Call-Back Songs: Teachers may want to add one element to something I mentioned earlier. One of the four times for beginning to use music is at the start of each class. To further clarify that the class is about to begin, a particular song could be played just before the scheduled time. This cue would let students know that the session is about to begin, and they could find their seats at that time. Experience shows that students of all ages quickly adapt to this approach to the start of a class. For courses of extended lengths, keep things fresh by changing to a new song as needed, perhaps once every week or two.

A junior high school in southern Texas has even chosen to use this approach on a school-wide basis. Instead of a bell to signify the start of each new period, a song is played over the speaker system. Students must be ready for the class to begin when the song reaches its last note. Of course, this means everyone is hearing the same song six times a day, so the song is changed at the beginning of each week. Students have further ownership in this process because they are the ones who nominate the songs, and a committee of their peers decides which one will be used the following week. As a final bonus, the name of the person who nominated each new song is announced when the song is used for the first time on Monday morning.

Music in the classroom can also benefit the teacher beyond anything discussed so far in this section. If the teacher decides its appropriate, it may be useful to allow students to be involved in playing the music. Before rejecting this idea as completely insane, you should know that many people can focus quite well on two things at once. Also, in a situation such as a year-long class, the teacher may play the music for the first few weeks. Then, once students have understood the role of the music, they could take charge of this aspect of the classroom. Finally, if there is one person—at any age level—who just can't seem to pay attention, watch what happens if he or she agrees to play the music. While some people may argue that this student is no longer paying attention, think about it more. In order to run music properly, and get the timing right, this person must *follow your instruction very closely*. Perhaps, because he or she is now actually paying attention, he or she will pick up more of the information you are teaching. If other motivational strategies you've tried have not been successful, why not give this unique approach a try?

Starting a CD Collection: If you are only now beginning to build a collection of music to use in the classroom, here are several ideas to consider. First, if possible, focus primarily on buying CDs. They are far easier to use in the classroom than cassettes. It's very simple to locate a certain song on a CD, whereas with a tape it may be necessary to rewind or forward to the appropriate spot. CDs also tend to last longer. Finally, consider buying mostly CDs that are compilations. These could be the best of a certain time period, such as the 1960s, the best of a certain group, such as the Eagles, or the best of a certain type of music, such as jazz. Usually, these will have a high percentage of songs that are usable for instruction. Individual albums by individual artists frequently (although not always) feature only two to three songs that will fit your needs. Conversely, the majority of selections on many compilations will be applicable to one learning situation or another.

Which Stereo Is Best?   When considering what kind of stereo system to use in the classroom, it might be necessary to consider the following parameters. What level of sound can the unit produce? Will it be loud enough to fill the room when a high volume level is required? (Remember that the more people present, the more sound usually needed.) Does the unit come with a remote control? If so, how easy is it to use? Some teachers find that ease of use of the remote is one of the most important decisions to make when selecting a stereo, as they come to spend a considerable amount of time with it in their hands. Is the unit capable of handling just CDs, just cassettes, or both? Is having the opportunity to use both an important consideration?

Also, if the teacher will primarily be using CDs, *how many* will the unit hold at one time? There are a variety of opinions on this matter as to whether a single- or multiple-loading unit is preferable. Some teachers enjoy preloading three or five disks at a time, and simply alternate between these during the course of an hour-long lesson. Other individuals prefer to use a single-loading unit because they find that disks for single-loading units can usually be switched more rapidly than those that hold more than one. It's mostly a matter of personal preference, so you choose.

In Summary

Music is a powerful force that can be used to great effect in a learning setting. Handled correctly, it can unleash the energy of any class and help guide it in a useful direction. Interestingly, teachers who use music in the classroom actually need to expend less of their own valuable energy to build a dynamic, interactive, engaging experience for the students (Bucko 1997; Jensen 1996).

The intention of this section has been to examine several pragmatic methods for the use of music in the classroom. If you are interested in the more technical aspects of music (for example, its effect on the brain's wave patterns) I recommend that you explore other resources. If you have a yen for knowing the research that supports the statements I'm making here, it's definitely out there and I encourage you to learn more about it. However, such discussions are beyond the scope and intention of this book. For more detailed theoretical and physiological background information, consider browsing through some of the brain research volumes mentioned in the reference section.

On a final, more prosaic note, it is amusing to mention that all the good things that can come from the proper use of music are frequently undone by a very simple logistical issue. Teachers whose situations require them to be mobile may not want to "go to all the trouble" of lugging a heavy CD player around with them as they move from location to location. For these people, remember that the focus of most instruction is to add value to the lives of the students. Music is invaluable in helping achieve this objective. Therefore, find a way to make it work. Have a student carry the equipment from room to room if needed. If you don't have your own classroom, have someone from the class come to your office and haul the stereo for you. Hire an assistant. Buy a more compact, powerful system that's lighter to carry. Or buckle down, carry it yourself, and simply enjoy the idea of bringing music into students' lives. Most of all, find a way to use music. It works.

OWNERSHIP

When a teacher begins the school year with a new class, it is common to take a moment and do some form of self-introduction. There are several purposes for providing students with this information, including establishing the teacher's credibility and building rapport with the students. Frequently these objectives will be accomplished by providing background information relevant to the class, perhaps with a humorous anecdote or two thrown into the mix. However, achieving this objective also opens the door for a unique opportunity to engage the students in a manner that simultaneously fulfills another important, although less evident, teaching objective.

Recently, I observed a teacher introduce herself in the following way.

"I'd like to take a moment and introduce myself. However, rather than do it in the usual fashion, let's do it the following way. Instead of me telling you about myself, I'd like to know what you're interested in knowing. Please take a moment and discuss with some people near you what you would like to know about me. What would give me some credibility? What might be something that would help you feel like you know me a bit better?"

The students then have a moment to talk with others near them and generate some appropriate questions. These are asked, and the answers are given.

In using this introduction sequence, one key difference emerges when compared to the more traditional approach. This difference is that the *students* are briefly in charge of what happens in the room, rather than the teacher. They have been given ownership of their experience. When the students have control of the environment, a subtle, although important, shift in their perspective toward the classroom occurs. No longer are they simply sitting back and receiving information. Now they are involved in the very creation of the content! While the moment may be brief, it serves the deeper purpose of giving them a new orientation toward the class, one of involvement, responsibility, and ownership.

Clarification

When students first enter a classroom, there may be a perception that the teacher is the one with all the ownership of the class. It is easy to see how this idea is formed. After all, students assume the teacher has a strong knowledge base regarding the content, or else he or she would not have been hired to be the teacher in the first place. It is clear that the teacher will be in charge of many important details, such as the speed at which the class will progress, the materials that will be used, and when breaks will be taken. It is even probable that the teacher has been the one responsible for the physical arrangement of the classroom. Even on an unconscious level, students will be aware that this person will have a significant impact on their experience.

Taken together, all of these factors immediately place the teacher in the dominant, controlling position. As a natural by-product of this impression, students may feel positioned in the less responsible, less involved role. Creating an environment where students have greater ownership will necessitate that the teacher reverse this trend at all possible times. Not only could this occur at the start of a course, but it could also be necessary to continue to bring this back into the consciousness of students frequently throughout the year.

In one way, primary school teachers probably already use this technique to a great extent. For example, many classrooms of younger students proudly display the product of their endeavors, from cutout silhouettes to drawings, finger paintings, and even examples of well-written paragraphs. However, as students grow older, it appears that upper-grade level teachers think that it loses its applicability. It is the purpose of this discussion to remind all of us of the fundamental validity of this approach to learning for groups of all ages, and to extend the idea into some new directions. The following statement will serve to guide the development of this idea:

Definition: Giving *ownership* to the students means looking for as many ways as possible for them to be intimately involved in the creation, the presentation, and the evaluation of the relevant information.

Benefits of Student Ownership

At the center of this issue of student ownership lies an important question: Why bother? What gains can teachers expect from the efforts they expend in seeing that students develop a perspective of responsibility and accountability? There are two primary benefits. The first is an avoidance of negative or potentially destructive behavior patterns. The second is the development of an attitude on the part of the students regarding the content, and how this will enhance their learning and long-term retention of the material. Both of these issues are important for teachers to address many times during the school year.

Each student comes into the classroom with a personal history of school experiences, some positive and some negative. Each student's history is an internal chronicle of how he or she has behaved in similar situations in the past. Over time, these patterns of behavior become deeply ingrained, and can be triggered by associations with anything that is recognized from those previous scenarios. Now, imagine teenagers walking into class at the beginning of the year. As they sit in their chair or desk, they look around the room. Everything seems familiar. They remember being seated at a desk, looking at a chalkboard, raising their hand to ask questions, and listening to someone else speak. It all seems so familiar, and suddenly, they are flooded with memories of being in other classrooms. Even though they may have been out of school for the summer, given the confluence of these readily identifiable stimuli, those memories may exert a powerful influence on their behavior at this moment.

This quick stroll down memory lane can have potentially adverse consequences. While it is sincerely hoped that older students will one day, as adults, remember school as a productive, exciting time in their lives, this is all too often not their current reality. As teens, they are more likely to access memories of boring lectures, information overload, and utter apathy, although this has nothing to do with the teacher in front of the room at the present time. Before that teacher utters a single word, students may be mentally moving themselves into a resistant frame of mind. Most importantly, *this may not be evident on a conscious level*! Students may not even be aware of this dynamic themselves, but simply find themselves uninterested in the current class.

For these students, it is vital to engage them in the learning process, hold them as responsible as possible for the interaction that occurs in the room, and invite them to share in the process of assessing the applicability of the ideas to other parts of their lives. This idea holds true for students in middle school, and even those who are much younger. Behavioral habits can develop quite rapidly, although we have known for a long time that they are much more difficult to change in later years (e.g., see Yerks & Dodson 1908). The idea of student ownership may be one of the most powerful tools teachers have available to counteract these potentially destructive feelings.

A second benefit comes from providing students with a sense of ownership. Done consistently, it helps all students feel as if it is *their* learning environment, rather than the sole domain of the teacher. This distinction can create a powerful shift in how students view their environment and as a side effect, how they perceive and encode the information. When students feel personally involved in material, they tend to look harder to find the value in the information, and how it might apply to them. This attitude toward learning in general, and specifically toward the broader applicability of content, will enhance students' overall ability to remember the information.

Opportunities for Student Ownership

Example 1: What if students had freedom of choice when deciding where to sit in the classroom? Handled appropriately students can easily begin on the path toward a sense of ownership with this simple gesture on the part of the teacher. While this may seem like a fairly easy means of giving students some sense of choice, it useful to have several strategies for conveying the idea of student ownership on a physical, kinesthetic level. This may be an excellent starting point.

Example 2: Again, concerning the issue of physical involvement, consider the arrangement of the room, the position of the chairs, desks, and tables. Many teachers prefer to have the room carefully arranged before students arrive each day. However, what if students occasionally walked into an unprepared room? On the board the teacher has drawn a picture showing how the room is to be arranged for the next session, and asks everyone to help make this happen. Now students are physically involved in the creation and organization of their learning environment.

Example 3: Suppose that the objective of a particular session was to clearly define ten terms for students. They are given a work sheet showing these words and phrases. A more traditional approach might be to start with the one at the top of the page, and then go straight down the list. Instead, consider asking one of the students which term to discuss first. When that is complete, ask another student to choose another term, and continue until all ten have been completed.

Example 4: Imagine that one class period has been set aside to cover the issue of communication skills. Yet there were three different aspects of communication that the teacher felt could all equally benefit this group. Why not explain the three different topics and ask the students which idea appeals most to them? The teacher would have to make a decision anyway, so they might as well consider including the students in the process. As long as the decision is made rapidly and the focus moves quickly to the lesson, the time spent in getting their input could be quite valuable. Now, the students have a higher level of investment in the information which is presented.

Example 5: Consider a high school course that is scheduled to cover a very broad topic; even the entire year will not be sufficient to cover all aspects of the material. If this were clear from the start, the teacher could create a list of the twenty key ideas. On the first day of class she could then note that, of these major themes, there would be no way to spend time effectively on all of them. Instead, the class will only cover ten of them in depth. She has chosen the five she feels should definitely be a part of the course, and now it is up to the students as a class to decide which other five they would like to address at some point.

Example 6: Suppose students have engaged in a brief discussion and groups have generated answers to a question posed by the teacher. The next step in the lesson will be to have each group call out their responses and have these written on the board for later discussion. The standard approach would be for the teacher to stand in front of the room, ask students to call out the answers, and simultaneously write them on the board. To accomplish the same objective with more student ownership, have three students come to the front of the room. One student is responsible for calling on each group to give their responses. The other two are responsible for writing the responses on the chalkboard. The teacher, meanwhile, stands to the side and steps in only when the process has been completed and all groups have given their responses.

Example 7: Teachers normally present most, if not all, of the content in a classroom. Yet, frequently there are advanced students in the class, or students who have familiarity with a particular idea from some other class. These students could be invited to teach at least a portion of that particular segment of the class. This could be anything from a simple one-minute comment to taking over the entire lesson, with the teacher providing details as needed either during or at the end of the presentation. I personally used this approach quite successfully in teaching a precalculus course for high school seniors. Over the course of the school year, students ended up teaching over 70 percent of the text material. Some even went as far as writing work sheets and creating the chapter exam.

Example 8: If students are given resources that are theirs to keep, have them "own" it in some manner. If they have a packet of materials, give them thirty seconds to decorate the cover with some doodles. If they have a text, have them cover it and then put some unique design on the cover. If the room is arranged so that young students have their desks in groups of four, have them create name markers for each other's desks. If a class topic begins with flip charts and signs posted on the walls, create places for the students to develop other visual reminders of the information. The investment of just a few moments to accomplish these tasks can reap long-term benefits by generating a sense of pride in their environment.

Example 9: When breaks are scheduled that are not governed by the needs of other classes (such as the school bell), how long should they be? Why not ask the students how much time they need to be fully ready for the next class session? In this circumstance, they usually make a quick joke about taking the whole day off. Yet the joke is simply a need for them to express their independence, and they will soon make an appropriate decision. Do the same thing for longer breaks, such as lunch. How long will they reasonably need in order to walk to the place they'll eat, get their food, and returns. It's more effective to ask them what they feel would work best than to guess and impose a decision on them. The fact that they were given an opportunity to help decide how long the break is going to be firmly establishes that they are an integral part of the learning community and helps confirm their commitment to return on time.

Example 10: Suppose two students in a group of twenty-eight were unable to be present for a particular class. Now it is the next day, and the teacher wants these two students to at least have an idea of what happened. It was such an important class that he was planning on having a review session anyway. He first invites the two students to come to the front of the room. Then, the rest of the class is instructed to tell, to the best of their ability, what they learned yesterday. When they have finished, the teacher asks the two students to repeat what they think they have heard. Finally, the class has a chance to fill in anything that was missing from what the two students have just said. This approach accomplishes the dual objectives of providing an overview for the students who were absent the previous day, while simultaneously having the other students actively process and review the material.

Example 11: The teacher plans on using charts posted on the walls as part of his presentation of the lesson. He has many of these placed around the room as students arrive, covering approximately half of the available space. As the course progresses, there are several places where students can create flip charts based on the information they are learning. These are placed on the walls alongside the teacher's charts. As more and more of the students' charts are placed on the walls, the classroom can begin to feel quite distinctly as if it belongs to the students.

In Summary

Everyone appreciates feeling valued for what they can contribute. Students enjoy feeling as if they are an important part of the learning process. Teachers should continue to find ways in which they can communicate this message to their students. This communication can be blatant, such as asking students to help in arranging a room, or less obvious, such as giving them the opportunity to generate questions for a speaker about her background. An increased sense of ownership and responsibility is created when students are invited to be a part of their education, growth, and development.

PAUSE FOR VISUALS

Examine the following situation. There's a potential problem with how the information is being presented to the students. What's the challenge that individuals in this classroom must overcome to be effective students?

The teacher is busy delivering a lesson using an overhead projector. The students are busy copying the information down in their notebooks. When the teacher is ready to move on to the next overhead, she pulls off the one that had been showing previously and replaces it with a new one. She continues teaching.

Think carefully here. What's the first thing students do when they see the new overhead? Naturally, they'll want to understand it, so they take a moment to study it. Can you spot the problem? If they are concentrating on the visual, what are they *not* concentrating on? What the teacher is saying, of course! Or, if they are furiously trying to *copy* the information, they are more focused on getting it all down than on *understanding* what it means, and paying no attention at all to anything the teacher might be babbling about.

However, the teacher in this situation does not appreciate the difficulty her students are having, and she plows full-steam ahead. She is blissfully unaware that she has just left most of them bobbing helplessly behind in her enthusiastic wake. She is then amazed to discover that the students failed to remember most of what she was talking about! She is shocked that they don't remember the material, because she *knows* she said it! She reprimands them for not paying close enough attention to the material.

Did anything like this ever happen to you as a student? Once? Or hundreds of times? If you're like most people, scenes like these probably sound all too familiar. It's simply not a situation that is conducive to effective learning, and as students we fully understood the problem. Now that you've recognized this problem, what can you, as a teacher, do differently in the future when you encounter a similar situation,? Here's one answer to consider.

Clarification

When new information is visually presented to students, they must be given time to familiarize themselves with it. Depending on the complexity of the content, this may take only a few seconds, or as much as a minute. Sufficient time should be allowed for students to mentally organize an image of the material and become comfortable with it. Other content can be introduced only after this has been completed, *even clarifying information regarding the visual.* The key is for teachers to allow students to become fully comfortable with the image that has been shown before moving ahead with the presentation.

The primary goal in these situations is to avoid splitting the students' focus. If the teacher simultaneously shows a new visual while continuing to speak, he is asking that students pay full attention to both what is being shown *and* to what is being said. What happens? The students ends up putting only half of their focus in each direction, with an obvious reduction in understanding of both things. It's more productive for everyone involved if the teacher keeps students' attention focused in only one direction at a time.

There's a simple solution. *Pause whenever an important new piece of information is visually presented.* Don't talk for a moment and give students a chance to put all their attention on understanding the visual. It's that easy. Stop speaking every time a new visual is introduced during a lesson. Continue speaking only when it appears that everyone has seen and feels comfortable with the new information. After they have had time to construct a mental picture, they will be able to concentrate more fully on what is being said.

Situations

There are a number of places in the natural course of teaching in which pausing for a new visual might come in handy. Here are a few of the many situations where you might apply this idea:

- When showing a new overhead: As mentioned in the introductory example, overheads provide at least two challenges to students: Copying the information and understanding it. Sufficient time should be allowed for both things before the lesson continues.
- When distributing handouts: Even though each person will have his or her own copy of the "visual," the same idea applies. Give students a moment to glance completely through the handout before providing any comments or explanations about what they have received.
- When demonstrating the solution to a math problem on the chalkboard: Because the teacher's back may be turned to the students, part of the information may be obscured from their view. Once the solution is complete, turn around and step aside so everyone can clearly view it. Remain silent while the students study the steps in the solution.
- Writing ideas on a chalkboard: In addition to math problems and numbers, teachers may write information related to the lesson on the board in words or symbols. These might include dates, names, quotes, or diagrams. In each case, the same idea applies. Depending on the complexity of the information, students might find it useful to have a moment to process and organize the information in their own minds.
- When using flip charts: Some teachers will prepare paper flip charts in advance for certain lessons, then tape these on the wall for use during the lesson. If there are more than a few flip charts, consider asking students to stand and walk around, reviewing them in preparation for the upcoming discussion. Perhaps it might even be useful to have them find a partner. As they walk, they are to discuss what they think each chart means.
- When showing slides: Slide presentations are quite useful to incorporate during some lessons. Which slides might the students need a few moments to study before the teacher makes any comments? Which ones are easy to understand and will not interfere with their concentration on what the teacher is saying? These are important ideas to consider prior to presenting the lesson.
- PowerPoint presentations: The use of PowerPoint or similar programs as a visual aid is becoming increasingly popular in classrooms. Despite the useful advances in technology, the underlying ideas of learning still apply. Each new visual shown is similar to a new slide, flip chart, or overhead. As dictated by the density of the information displayed, teachers will need to pause long enough to allow students to gain a mental understanding of the image before proceeding.

In Summary

The first time you use this approach to introduce a new piece of visual information into the classroom, it may feel awkward. It might not seem natural to simply stop speaking while you're in the flow of teaching. (As you may have learned from personal experience, for some teachers even the notion of taking a *breath* while teaching may seem beyond their comprehension.) Yet the longer you use this technique for introducing new visuals, the clearer it will become how effective it is for the students. That feeling of "note-taking panic" in the classroom can be significantly reduced, because students now do not have to try to capture everything simultaneously. They are free to focus on only one thing at a time. Given that they are in a more relaxed, stress-free learning environment, it should come as no surprise to you that their ability to retain information increases immediately.

It's important to realize that in many situations students *can* have their attention divided and still be able to learn effectively. It would be silly to say that they can only focus on one thing at any given point in a lesson. It's simply not true. One of the most common examples occurs when students are listening and taking notes about what they are hearing at the same time. The key to the idea explained in this section is that its usefulness is based entirely on the complexity of the visual being shown. If students' attention is going to be so distracted that it causes a reduction in their ability to concentrate simultaneously on other relevant information, then perhaps a pause by the teacher would be useful.

Finally, of course, teachers are advised not to get carried away with this idea and pause *too long, too frequently* during a lesson! One can only imagine the tedium of visiting a classroom where a lesson was being presented with the constant interruption of lengthy, unnecessary silences. Doubtless the students may be left questioning the teacher's sanity in such a case. Pause only when necessary to assist the students.

PRESS AND RELEASE

In science, it is said that every action has an equal and opposite reaction. The concept of "press and release" could be summarized in much the same way. For every press situation that students experience, an equal opportunity for releasing should follow. This allows them to return to a more natural, balanced state. In this position they will be able more clearly focus their attention on the subsequent section of instruction. When students experience a solid sense of balance they can be their most effective as learners. Consider the following situation:

> The students had just completed an activity that required them to work together as a team to solve a puzzle. The activity had lasted for approximately ten minutes. During the activity everyone had to remain silent. At the completion of the exercise, the teacher intended to spend a few moments discussing what had taken place, developing the ideas of teamwork and communication. However, before beginning to facilitate this discussion in the large group setting, he gave everyone an opportunity to spend a few moments discussing these ideas in small groups of three or four people.

Why did he choose to spend several precious minutes of classroom time in this manner? In this case, the answer comes from previous experiences this teacher had gone through in similar teaching situations. He had discovered that if he did not allow the students time for *everyone* to talk for a few moments immediately after the activity, their ability to pay attention during the large group discussion was greatly reduced. It had become apparent to him that, if the students were silent for an extended period, they would need at least a few moments to verbalize their own thoughts and feelings before they could fully participate in a general discussion. Without realizing it, he had stumbled across a critical component in creating a successful, dynamic, safe learning environment.

Clarification

When students are mentally "balanced," they are in the optimum state for learning. However, there are times when students are asked to concentrate fully, such as when taking in new information and making meaning of it for themselves. These are known as "press" situations. Pressing situations in learning environments are perfectly normal. Used properly they create minor levels of stress that are actually quite useful for learning and retention of new information (Sapolsky 1999). However, extended periods of *pressing* will cause students to become unbalanced. This naturally results in a need for "release," some activity or event to bring them back to center.

In the example described above, the *press* aspect of the situation was the need for the students to work together in *silence* for an extended period of time. What the teacher discovered was that everyone started talking in the small groups. The opportunity to *talk* was the balance they needed at that point, the necessary *release* mechanism in the situation.

Viewed from this perspective, it is understandable how these groups reacted before he added the small group discussion time. Without it, the need for release was powerful enough to cause them to whisper to each other, fidget, or make silly remarks, anything to release that "pent-up" feeling in their body. By adding the release component to the learning situation, the teacher allowed the students a chance to regain a more useful learning state. Now they could easily turn their full attention to the large group discussion, which was the primary intention of the teacher.

Examples

Following are a series of situations in which students are involved in some type of activity in a learning environment. Both sides of the press-and-release equation are shown to demonstrate how integral this idea is to all aspects of teaching and training.

- In a creative writing class, students experience *pressing* as they create a short story or poem. They could *release* after they write by taking time to share their stories aloud, or to exchange their papers with each other and read them in silence, or even to have their papers posted on a wall where they can be read by everyone.
- While doing any type of visualization, students are *pressing* by keeping their eyes closed and concentrating. Afterward, they will need an opportunity to *release* by expressing what they have felt or seen, such as writing about it, discussing it, or drawing a visual representation of it.
- Any team activity is a *press* as people concentrate on working together. After the activity they can *release* by taking a moment to thank and acknowledge the other team members.

- During a team-building activity known as a "Blind Trust Walk," one partner is blindfolded and led on a walk by the other person. Doing this exercise is definitely a *press* for most people. Before they switch roles, they could *release* by spending a moment talking to their partner about what they felt or experienced. This might assist them in coming back to a more relaxed state before they begin the second part.
- The situation is an introduction to public speaking class. In this particular activity, the students are practicing their skills by introducing themselves to each other. After this occurs, they *press* by having small group discussions concerning some of the basic keys to remember when giving an effective presentation. They then *release* by moving back into a large group discussion where each small group recounts two or three of the main ideas they focused on during their discussion.
- When teaching in an environment where English is not the first language for many of the students, it is a *press* for them to concentrate on what the speaker is saying in this language. A *release* could be introduced by giving them several opportunities throughout the day to discuss what they have heard and how they might apply it, in their native language.
- An energizer used by many teachers has students organized into pairs. One partner is the "Artist" while the other is the "Blob." The artist takes one minute to mold their partner into a unique statue. This is the *press* moment. The *release* occurs when the statues stay as they are, while the artists "go to the art show." They walk around and compliment the other statues on how nice they look. Another *release* occurs when they reverse roles.

- It was a course for beginning classroom teachers. The project they were working on was learning to create a lesson plan, which was the *press*. The *release* occurred every ten to fifteen minutes, when the teacher asked them to pause in their work and briefly share what they had done so far with people around them. At the end of the class session a larger release took place when everyone walked around sharing with each other the lesson plan they had finally created.

Summary

Effective use of the idea of *press and release* creates a sense of motion in a learning environment. It introduces a feeling of dynamic movement. In traditional classrooms, students may primarily experience a sense of being pressed. If this is their only expectation for the learning environments in which they are involved, it should come as no surprise that they would seek to avoid this unpleasant sensation. They may create that avoidance by spacing out during the lecture, or by acting out undesirable behaviors. Or, they may simply choose not to attend school. The more appropriate opportunities for releasing they experience within the context of the class, the less threatening the classroom becomes.

PRIMING

The students had been vigorously taking notes as the guest lecturer spoke. At the conclusion of her remarks, the regular teacher stood and said:

"Wonderful. Please give our speaker a nice hand for taking the time to be here today."

However, the response from the students was somewhat muted. The teacher was disappointed by this minimal reaction, so he turned to them and said:

"Wait a minute. Is that any way to thank someone for coming here today and talking with us? Please, give her a really big round of applause. Let's hear it for all these wonderful ideas she has shared."

This time the students applauded with more enthusiasm and increased volume. The guest lecturer departed, and the class continued.

Now comes the critical question. Why had the students not responded immediately and with more energy the first time they were asked to acknowledge the speaker? A closer examination of the reasons behind their behavior reveals an important concept for teachers to consider.

Understanding the Dilemma

The first time the students were asked to acknowledge the guest speaker, something was physically obstructing them from completing the request. Remember what they had just been doing—jotting down written notes. Taking notes requires holding a pen. Applauding, however, requires two free hands. When they tried to applaud, they were still holding their pens, so it was *nearly impossible for them to do what was asked of them.* They were forced to do the best they could, so they clapped while still clutching their pens. The second time, however, as the teacher was speaking, they could see what was coming, so as he was repeating the request they were placing their pens on the desk so they could fully acknowledge the guest speaker.

Having an audience poised for the next thing that will be asked of them is called *priming.* This concept addresses the following central issue in effective teaching:

"Are students fully ready and able to follow the instruction that is about to be given to them?"

In this case, it is apparent that they had not been properly physically *primed* for the next request, and the result was, quite predictably, a reduced response.

How could the teacher have primed the students so they could provide applause successfully the first time they were asked? He may have said:

"Please, place your pen on your notes."

When it was clear that everyone had completed their last note and set down their pen, he could say:

"Now, please thank our speaker by giving her a big hand!"

With their hands now free, there is a much greater chance that the students will be able to fully complete this request the first time it is asked of them. Another way of wording this might have been to say:

"Please pause for a moment. Make sure your hands are free."

Now once again they are ready to applaud the speaker. Whichever wording is used, the key is to make sure that students have been properly primed so they can easily follow the coming instruction.

Prime Examples

There are numerous places where verifying that the students are properly primed to succeed is a useful idea. Expanding on the concept presented in the opening example, remember that in most active learning environments students are going to be physically involved in the learning on a frequent basis. Each time they are given an opportunity to engage in an activity, however brief, it may be important to consider whether there is anything that might physically interfere with their easily completing the instruction. Here are a few situations in which this consideration might come in handy:

- It is the beginning of class. For this session, the teacher knows that students will not be needing anything at this time, such as books or pens. He begins the class by saying, "Please place all your things on the tables located at the sides of the room." When this has been successfully completed, the potential encumbrance of those extraneous objects has been eliminated, and the students are primed for the physical movement that will be asked of them shortly.
- Occasionally, students may walk into the classroom carrying a can of soda, a cup of coffee, a sports bottle full of water, or perhaps a snack. If they are about to do something that involves interaction with other people, it may be useful to begin the class with a priming direction. For example, the teacher's first words might be, "Please set down anything you are holding, so your hands are free." When everyone has accomplished this he can continue by saying "Thank you. At this point, please shake hands with at least three people and tell them you're glad they came to school today!" Because they were properly primed, their hands are free and they can easily complete this direction. This avoids the potentially awkward moment of trying to shake hands with someone while balancing a cup of coffee in the other hand, or having their drink spill when they are jostled by the movement of the crowd. Priming alleviates these concerns.
- The physical set-up of an active learning environment may change on a frequent basis. Perhaps the chairs are turned to face in a different direction. Perhaps tables are moved so only chairs remain. Perhaps both tables and chairs are being removed to clear an open space for an upcoming activity. In any situation where a major shift in the physical arrangement of the room is about to occur, it is frequently wise to prime the audience by having them first glance around and pick up any glasses, purses, books, or other objects that may either interfere with the

movement or possibly be damaged. A priming direction allows the movement to happen with a minimum of potential interruptions.

- Before movement of any kind, whether shifting furniture or simply stepping outside for a break, consider priming the students by first asking them to stand up. From this position, they can more easily put their bodies into motion than if they were given the direction while still seated. It can increase the likelihood they will immediately follow the direction when it is given.

- Suppose students are completing a section during which they have been standing. The teacher should be aware of the potential danger implicit in making a statement such as, "Please take a seat and give yourself a hand for doing that activity so well." The problem is that *most people use their hands when sitting.* They either use them to balance or guide themselves into their seats. Asking people to both sit and applaud simultaneously makes it unlikely they'll be able to comply. Instead, divide this statement into two components. First ask them to sit down. Only when everyone has been seated should they be asked to give themselves a hand. At this point it should be an easy direction to follow. Or, do the applause first, and then have them take a seat.

- The conclusion of small group discussions illustrates another time when priming may be useful. Imagine that a group of students have been talking with each other for several minutes. The teacher could move forward in the instruction by simply saying, "Please thank your group, and let's continue." However, if this is done with no warning, there's a chance some groups may be caught by surprise, still deep in the midst of their discussion. It might be more useful to the students in this situation to prime them by announcing "You have thirty seconds more. Please try to bring your conversation to a close within that time." This announcement would allow them to make a few last remarks to each other and complete their conversation. When the thirty seconds have passed, then have them thank their group and continue with the class.

- A brief, but very important form of priming can also occur during direct instruction. If students are busy taking notes, there is a strong chance they will be looking down at their papers so they can see what they are writing. Occasionally it may be useful to prime them for the next piece of information by saying, "When you are finished, please look at me." Then wait in silence until everyone is looking up. It is important to honor the fact that they are taking notes by giving them sufficient time to complete their thoughts before speaking again. To keep this form of priming successful, however, it should be done on an infrequent basis, and only when it will serve a useful purpose during the course of instruction.

A Concluding Thought

Priming allows students to be prepared for the next instruction from the teacher. It helps avoid those brief but awkward moments during instruction when learners fully intend to respond, yet find themselves hindered in their efforts for a variety of reasons. You, as the teacher, know what is coming up next. If you correctly prepare students for each subsequent direction, they should be able to transition smoothly from one activity to the next.

STEP DOWN

Group management is always an important classroom issue, whether working with young children, middle school students, or teens. In an active learning classroom this may be even more true. Students are encouraged to talk openly about important issues, to share their beliefs, and to interact with each other through small and large group discussions. There is movement, action, and interaction interspersed throughout the learning session. In these situations, the teacher's ability to recapture students' attention becomes a critical element in generating high levels of instructional effectiveness.

Several methods for gaining and maintaining attention are mentioned in this book. For example, the use of consistent musical cues can build automatic response patterns in students that will help prepare them for the next piece of information. The utilization of the "see me" approach to giving effective directions (discussed in Chapter 5) can decrease the number of times instructions need to be repeated, helping students maintain their focus. And the inclusion of "state changes," as discussed in more depth in Chapter 3, can play a critical role in classroom management. Each of these techniques is useful for directing students' attention in an appropriate direction.

This section offers another option for focusing students' attention that teachers might want to add to their instructional tool kit. It's especially useful in situations where there is a low level of conversation in the room. Perhaps students are chatting with each other, and the teacher would like to move forward to the next section of information. At this time it might be appropriate to say:

"OK, everybody, would you please be quiet so we may continue?"

However, phrases similar to this one, used on a frequent basis, may become intrusive and disruptive to the learning process. They create a feeling similar to the "stop and go" sensation drivers experience in heavy traffic. On the highway, this experience is both frustrating and dangerous. In learning environments, the experience of students may be similar, making them increasingly hesitant to participate knowing they will be soon be "stopped."

For those moments when teachers would prefer to move gently into the next section without appearing to be a disciplinarian, they might consider employing a control technique known as "step down." Used properly, this approach to group management allows the teacher to simultaneously bring the students to silence while seamlessly moving the class forward into the next section.

Definition

The term *step down* refers to the process of gradually reducing one's volume of speech over the course of a single sentence. The teacher can begin speaking at a volume that is slightly higher than the audience's volume level, and gradually "step down" the volume level until, by the final few words, he or she is talking at a normal conversation level.

In Practice

Here's how the idea of Step Down works in a classroom. Imagine a moment during instruction when students are chatting with each other. Suppose, for the purposes of this example, they are expressing their ideas about the topic of effective interpersonal communication. The teacher recognizes that it is time to move the students forward and says:

> "Perhaps the most important aspect of this entire issue is the concern over whether or not people are willing to respect another person's opinion."

As he says this sentence, he uses the step-down technique to get the attention of the class. He does this by saying the first few words in a fairly loud voice, slightly louder than the overall volume level of the group.

Examine in slow motion what occurs next. Some students in the room immediately realize the teacher is speaking again. They know they should be listening, so they cease their conversation and turn to face him. As these people become quiet, the level of sound in the room is reduced. Here is the key. As the sound level in the room drops, *the teacher also lowers the volume of his voice.* He vocally steps down along with them. While his volume of speech always remains slightly above that of the class, it follows their cue and gradually decreases.

Because the sound level in the room has dropped, the teacher's voice becomes more obvious. Other students realize he is speaking. As they become quiet the situation repeats itself. Each time the level of sound in the room goes down, the teacher's voice steps down with it. By the end of the sentence, the room has fallen quiet and he is speaking at a level that is consistent with normal speech. He has accomplished the objective of prompting the group forward into the next section of conversation without having to be conspicuous about interrupting their discussions.

Further Details

Within the single sentence used to illustrate this idea are several distinctions that should be noted. This technique can be utilized in a wide variety of circumstances provided there is clarity on some of its more subtle aspects. One of these is the belief that teaching in a normal tone of voice is both desirable as well as effective for a number of reasons. Primarily, this form of instruction creates the sense of having an extended conversation that moves easily between teacher and students as well as among students.

Perhaps the most important key to the effective application of this tool is in the structure of the sentences that are used. In this example, note that the most important part of the entire communication has been deliberately placed at the *end* of the sentence. The first few words are sometimes called "throw-away" words because it does not matter if the audience actually hears and understands them. They serve primarily as auditory cues for the students that something new is happening. In this case, the next segment of instruction was going to cover *respect for other people's opinions.* Most, if not all, of the students will clearly hear this phrase because it is at the end of the sentence. When using step down, it is important to consider the structure of the sentence, and to have the critical information occur at the end conclusion of the statement, when the majority of the audience has tuned in to the teacher's words.

Teaching in this manner also may help some teachers save their voices during those days when they are teaching for an extended period of time, because the majority of their instruction will occur at the level of a normal conversation. With the goal of a normal conversational volume level as a "baseline," adjustments in pitch, tone, and pacing will serve to help students more easily pay attention.

Frequent use of the step-down approach may help teachers avoid common disciplinarian phrases such as "Would you all please stop talking now?" or "OK, it's time to be quiet." These expressions are certainly appropriate to use on an occasional basis. However, over an extended period of time, they can give the impression that the teacher is constantly disciplining the students, although in a somewhat gentle manner. Of course, that is *exactly* what occurs in most classrooms. However, the more this aspect of teaching can be handled in a gentle, unobtrusive manner, the less chance there is that some students in the class might react negatively to the feeling of having someone else "control" their behaviors.

To maximize the effect of the step-down technique, audiences should be alerted to what is expected of them when they first come together as a group. For teachers this would be at the start of the year, or whenever beginning with a new class. The key is for the teacher to be deliberate and measured when initially implementing this approach to classroom management, making certain each time that he or she is achieving the desired result. Even though it is best done subtly, students will quickly pick up on this unique pattern of speech. Once they become accustomed to this style of delivery, it can become a powerful tool for moving them rapidly toward the instructional goals cleanly, quickly, and effectively.

Summary

The step-down approach to managing a group is simply one of many methods that can be utilized in certain teaching situations. The effectiveness of this tool is based firmly on the teacher's ability to prime the class for this form of interaction, and to structure sentences with deliberate care. With time and practice, this technique will become a natural component within one's instructional style. Used properly, it serves to put both teachers and students on the fast road to high-impact learning.

VISUAL FIELD

Consider the seating arrangement in many typical classrooms. In some situations students are assigned a place to sit. In others they may have free choice, but even in these rooms they usually return each day to the same location on a regular basis. However seating is handled, students tend to view the class from the exact same desk or chair for every class session. They sit facing the teacher, who is standing at the predetermined front of the room. This physical and visual arrangement is how the majority, if not all, of the remaining classes are held.

Interestingly, the same situation holds true in classrooms where there is no assigned seating. Students arrive on the first day and randomly select a seat. Almost always, this becomes their seat throughout the remainder of the school year. At the start of each day they hurry back to the seat they vacated the day before. Of course, it's easy to understand why this happens. If they sit in the same location each time they enter a room, they begin to feel as if it is their own, and they become comfortable with it. People *like* to feel comfortable in a learning environment.

However, as with many aspects of effective instruction, comfort in learning environments can be a double-edged sword. At times it may serve a useful purpose. Perhaps by allowing them to choose their own place to sit, teachers are assisting students by adding to their sense of ownership for the experience. At other times, however, comfort may work directly against what the teacher is attempting to accomplish. For example, if students become *too* comfortable, they might become bored. It could create a feeling of "been there, done that." If this happens, students may mentally shut down or tune out the teacher.

Where possible, and at appropriate intervals, physical as well as visual change can be introduced into the learning environment. This helps students stay alert and focused on new information. For example, one way to accomplish this objective would be to occasionally switch the arrangement of chairs in the room, or the direction from which the teacher is presenting might be adjusted, or visual support items on the walls might be relocated. In whatever manner the objective is achieved, allowing the students to see and experience something different will provide them with a feeling of being in a new environment.

Defining a Term

By changing the arrangement of the classroom, teachers are also changing what students are seeing in their *visual field*, which includes all those items within their normal range of vision, given how they are arranged.

Adjusting the Visual Field

Regardless of how dynamic, interesting, and motivating each person is as a teacher, there are times when students' attention will move away from looking directly at her or him. It is a natural dynamic for all students. Once they shift their attention from the teacher, their vision will shift to anything around them. Because of the obvious importance of the visual field in these situations, conscious thought should be given to what is visible to students. Rather than trying to be *more* entertaining, in an attempt to keep the students looking in their direction, teachers should understand and work with this powerful dynamic.

If we accept that students' attention will occasionally shift away from the teacher, then perhaps it would be useful to provide students with things to see that will *support the learning*. Primary school learning environments typically do this quite effectively, such as having the letters of the alphabet posted around the room. Middle and secondary school classrooms, however, may tend to pay less attention to this potent opportunity for reinforcing the primary information. Teachers in these environments might want to consider how to take advantage of this natural phenomenon.

For example, one choice might be to have posters relating to the information covering the walls from the very first moment students arrive. Then, when their attention shifts, as it naturally will, they will be looking at material *related to the class.* Even a few seconds are enough to make a lasting impact on what is known as *implicit memory*, the process of encoding information without directly focusing on it (Ormond 2000). This ultimately supports the teacher's goal of long-term retention.

Another approach might involve the use of overheads. If there is a central focus to an upcoming session, consider having it showing on the screen even before students arrive. As they walk into the room, they will notice it and begin to register its importance. This technique might also be used during breaks, perhaps having an idea from an upcoming session visible to the students. Some teachers may want to take this idea one step further and have a video playing before the session, during breaks, or even in the background while they are instructing. Provided it is supporting the learning and not distracting from it, this may be a perfectly valid choice.

Additional Choices

What other choices are available to a teacher who wishes to change the visual field of the students? Each situation will naturally be different, given the dynamics of the physical environment. However, here are three options you can consider.

- Change the location in the room from which you are presenting. This could be a dramatic switch, such as rotating student' desks and tables to what was previously the back or a side of the room, and teach from there for a period of time. Or it could be a more subtle switch, such as bringing the chairs from the center of the room and moving them closer to the left or right side of the room. You can then present from that location, perhaps using a particular visual that has been placed on a wall in that part of the room.
- Find places in the instruction where students have the opportunity to come to the front. This can be done in a wide variety of ways. Perhaps they are simply writing things on the blackboard or white board. Perhaps two people write, while another student is responsible for eliciting ideas from the audience. Perhaps a student could facilitate a brief conversation with the rest of the class. For example, invite a student to the front to elicit responses to a question, such as, "What experience have some of you had with computers?" In a case such as this it is not necessary that this student know any actual information; he or she is there merely for the purpose of gathering ideas from the other students.
- Consider opportunities to leave the confines of the four walls and go outside. Certainly weather, available space, and potential distractions will all be considerations in these situations. However, it may be surprising how frequently it is possible to engage students in effective instruction inside once they have had a short session outside.

Meeting the Challenge

For some teachers, changing the visual field may be easy, given the content of the course, a particular group of students, or their own personality. Others may encounter problems when they first attempt to make these adjustments. For example, some teachers might feel trapped by some of the physical aspects of the room in which they are working. The location of power outlets, the placement of windows and doors, and the availability of equipment are all important factors. Each may have an influence on what locations seems to be the most appropriate places from which to teach. If an overhead projector and screen have been placed at a certain point in the room, it would require considerable effort to move them somewhere else. Teachers may be hesitant to teach with their backs to a wall that has a door in it, in case someone walks in late and distracts the other people. Or there might be only one blackboard available, and it is bolted to the wall.

The trick is remembering that all problems are simply challenges to be overcome. If it is a hassle to relocate an overhead projector and screen, ask for the assistance of several students. If there are no available power outlets, find a long extension cord. If someone does walk in through a door that is directly behind the teacher, he or she can be acknowledged before the class continues. Or a sign could be placed outside asking late arrivals to use another door. If there is only one blackboard available, teach from a different location *when the blackboard is not necessary.* Occasional changes in the visual field are an integral part of student success. It is up to each teacher to find ways to make this effective within particular circumstances.

In Summary

One of the advantages of changing the visual field is that it acts as a wake-up call to the students. When they shift to a new position, there will be a view in front of them that is different than the one they were previously enjoying. This change in scenery will cause them to be more mentally alert as they adjust to this new situation.

Occasional changes in the visual field help students stay focused and remain fully attentive to the content (Bernstein 1994). It can also enhance the effect of the instruction by having students consistently view materials that support the primary information. Timing is always an important factor, as you will need to decide when to make these changes. The key is maintaining an awareness of the importance of the visual field as an integral component in maximizing student learning.

WALK AWAY

The Challenge

An interactive learning environment will naturally have many exchanges between the teacher and the students. If the teacher is standing during those times, there is a tendency for them to move *toward* the person speaking. In the course of a personal conversation with one other person, this makes sense. If people are separated by more than a few feet from the person with whom they are speaking, it is natural to draw closer to them so that both people can be heard more clearly. Their proximity to each other allows the communication to proceed more smoothly.

In a teaching context, however, this instinctive reflex may work against the needs of the class as a whole. In the majority of cases, it is critical that all other students be able to hear what the speaker is saying. Yet, as the teacher draws closer to a student who is speaking, she will tend to respond to the approach of another person in an instinctive manner by lowering the volume of her voice and reducing the general scope of her gestures. If she does this in a large group setting, those individuals farthest from the student may not be able to hear what is being said. To keep everyone involved in the exchanges between teachers and students, it is important that each person be able to hear everything. Missing out on even a few words may cause people to become frustrated and lose their concentration on the discussion.

The challenge lies in getting all students to speak at a volume level sufficient for everyone to remain involved in the interaction. To accomplish this, it is necessary to understand that there is a difference between interactions that take place between two people in a normal conversation and the interactions that occur in a learning context. In personal interactions, it is only necessary that the other person hear what is being said. In a learning situation, however, while it is certainly important for the teacher to hear what is being said, it is equally important that the other people also be able to hear.

The Response

In many teaching situations, making certain everyone can hear is easy, and no adjustment on the part of the teacher is necessary. However, other circumstances may require that action be taken so that this objective can be met. For example, the class size may be fairly large, the acoustics in the room may be less than optimal, or a particular student may have a naturally quiet voice. In these cases, the teacher will want to avoid the natural tendency to move toward the person speaking.

Instead, he or she should remain focused on the person speaking and take several steps *in the opposite direction*. This can be done subtly, without distracting anyone from the person speaking. When the teacher moves away, the student speaking will frequently respond as he or she would if this happened while talking to another person in a normal setting by instinctively talking louder. This increase in volume enables other people to more clearly hear what is being said. Additionally, if a person is using hand gestures of any kind, he or she will also tend to increase their size thereby including more people in the communication.

Details

Creating the desired effect through the use of this technique requires that the teacher pay attention to a few small, though critical, key points. One important detail is keeping the attention focused on the speaker while moving away. The teacher should maintain constant eye contact while taking the necessary few steps, perhaps even nod his or her head a few times. Looking away could be interpreted by the speaker, or even the other students, as a lack of interest on the part of the teacher. Additionally, note that, in most cases, *only a few steps* need to be taken to create the result. The larger the room, the more steps that may need to be taken by the teacher. However, it is usually not necessary to completely cross to the other side of the room. After moving, come to a complete stop and maintain focus on the speaker.

Knowing *when* to initiate the movement is also useful. The most natural time to move is at the start of the student's comments. This works for several reasons. It is a transitional moment because someone else is now speaking, and movement at this point supports the fact that this is a transition. It seems more natural than if it were to happen in the middle of the student's comments. Also, if done at the start of these remarks, more of what he or she is saying will be heard by the entire group, and, consequently, less repetition will be required.

By walking several steps away, the teacher will less often have to say something like:

"Could you please speak a little louder?"

Such a request can be annoying if it is repeated too frequently. This is especially true because it most often needs to be interjected in the middle of a student's response, and runs the risk of interrupting the student's train of thought. If, instead, the teacher uses the walk-away strategy to get students to speak louder, it can be done without the students' conscious realization that it is happening, and without interrupting them in the middle of their comments.

In Summary

When students speak in group settings, such as when asking a question or giving an answer, it is important that everyone be able to hear clearly. Moving closer to the speaker will cause them to lower the volume of their voice. Moving in the opposite direction will have the opposite effect. Moving away causes speakers to raise the volume of their voice. The teacher should make a determination as to whether the rest of the group can hear the speaker, and respond by changing position to create the desired result.

CHAPTER FIVE

THE ART OF EFFECTIVE DIRECTIONS

> In an interactive learning environment, teachers need to provide directions on a frequent basis, as they explain to the students what they will be doing in each subsequent activity. This chapter looks closely at this crucial element in the development of an effective educator.

One of the least appreciated concepts in all of teaching is the "art" of giving effective directions. The choice of the word *art* in this phrase is deliberate. Effective directions are truly an art form. They require the artist's gift of personal expression, built on a strong foundation of technical expertise. And, much like a seemingly simplistic work of art, effective directions may be more difficult to create than they first appear. The teacher seeking to ensure maximum efficiency when giving directions must follow the same path as the budding artist. Mastery of the underlying principles is the most critical element to consistent success.

Presenting a lecture, telling a story or metaphor, facilitating a question-and-answer session, and giving effective directions are all unique aspects of instruction. The contrast between directions and these other modes of teaching should be as sharp as the contrast between the English and Russian languages. When moving into direction-giving mode, the words teachers use and their tone of voice will change. Sentence structure and pauses between sentences will be different. Even the teacher's proximity to the audience must be considered. The technical aspects of each of these components are critical for the teacher who wishes to be successful to understand and to incorporate into his or her unique teaching style.

Even in a fairly conventional learning situation, it is surprising how many directions are needed within a single session. Taking out a pen, locating a page of text, or talking in a small group are examples of simple student tasks that require directions. If a teacher chooses to take a more interactive approach to teaching, an even greater number of directions will be necessary. Students will be shifting from activity to activity, each preceded by a new explanation. Some of these instructions will be short, others will be long, but all share a common objective. In every case, the desire is to move as efficiently and rapidly as possible to the next task at hand, with a minimum amount of repetition on the part of the teacher.

However, to my personal amazement, the topic of giving effective directions is rarely addressed in most teacher-training programs. Teacher candidates emerge from college proficient in learning theory, child development theory, content knowledge, and, perhaps even in behavior management techniques, in the more fortunate cases. Yet, in terms of importance, giving effective directions is certainly on a par with these other topics. In some cases it may even be the most important issue, given the potential for success or failure that depends on the teacher's skill level in this aspect of instruction.

A lack of clarity in directions presents a variety of problems. Students who are unclear about what is required of them in a given situation may hesitate to involve themselves for fear of doing something wrong. They may quickly wander off-task, or, worse yet, they may *believe* they are on task, but end up spending precious classroom time on an inconsequential tangent.

Few teachers enjoy the moment when a student raises a hand and utters the dreaded phrase:

"Could you repeat that, please?"

When repetition is required, instead of placing the blame on the students for not listening more carefully, the fact that the question was raised suggests the possibility that the instructions might not have been delivered properly in the first place.

Lack of clarity in an instruction can also have a devastating, unconscious effect on the credibility of the teacher. Consider the following situation. It is early in the year and the teacher wants to warm up the students by having them get to know a few of the other people in the room. Attempting to accomplish this objective, he says:

"Please turn to the person on your left and introduce yourself!"

Pause and think about those words for a moment. Can you see it coming? Imagine what would happen if everyone actually did follow this instruction. If each person turns to his or her left, every student would end up facing the back of someone's head. Additionally, the people at the left end of each row would be facing a wall!

In practice, most students would probably laugh when they realized the absurdity of the instruction, and adjust by finding someone near them to meet. Yet, at the same time, the teacher may have unintentionally communicated a powerful message. If this simple instruction doesn't make sense, what else in the presentation won't be clear? Does this teacher know his content? Does he know how to teach? Obviously, no teacher wants students to entertain such ideas. Yet, if unclear directions continue to be a problem in the teacher's presentation, this may be exactly the effect produced. The key is learning how to mobilize students by giving clear, concise, and meaningful directions. In this case, the teacher might have said:

"Say hello to two or three people *near* you."

Now the instruction is easy for everyone to accomplish. The activity is successfully accomplished, and the class moves forward.

Perhaps it is an overstatement to say that the ability to deliver effective directions may be the golden key to instruction, but then again, perhaps not. It will certainly make a teacher's professional life easier; who could ask for more than that?

ONE AT A TIME

How many directions can students remember? Some primary and secondary teachers assert that even young audiences can easily manage four or five directions. Others believe that three is the maximum number possible for students to remember, regardless of age. For the purposes of this discussion, it is suggested that, where possible, teachers will achieve the maximum level of success with directions if they give *one at a time*. They should then wait until it has been completed before moving to the next direction. The examples provided below demonstrate how this concept can apply to a surprisingly wide range of teaching moments.

Example 1: Initiating Group Activity

I had been observing a number of beginning teachers. On this particular morning, I had been invited to watch a secondary-level creative writing class. The session began when, in a cheerful tone, the teacher spoke her first words to the class:

> "Good morning everyone. Today we'll be continuing the discussion from the last class. To start off, here's what we're going to do. In a few moments, we'll be getting into groups of about five or six. Each group will appoint a discussion leader. This person will facilitate a conversation about the topic so the group can remind itself of some of the key issues we were looking at last time, specifically concerning challenges in creative writing. After four or five minutes, each group will need to decide which two potential solutions to these issues they believe will generate the most success. Then select someone to write your two ideas on the board so we can see which are similar to those that other groups have come up with. Oh, and let's make sure that each group's ideas are written on a separate part of the board, so we can make notes near them. OK, let's begin!"

Knowing full well the dangers inherent in giving too many directions at one time, I inwardly sighed. I felt I had a pretty good idea of what was coming. Even with a class composed of juniors and seniors, it was doubtful that any of them were going to remember all of the instructions that had just been provided. When the teacher said, "Let's begin," there was general chaos in the room as students moved to organize themselves into groups of the appropriate number. In a short while this was accomplished. However, not surprisingly, they were uncertain how to proceed from this point.

What were they supposed to do now? There was a general murmur of conversation as each group spent several minutes debating what they were supposed to do.

The teacher had been looking down at some papers. Soon, however, she realized the students were not on-task. She reminded them to choose a discussion leader and get the conversation under way. Reminded, they could now accomplish this and were soon talking animatedly to each other. However, after five minutes, no one had approached the blackboard to write their answers to the original question. The teacher again reminded them of their assignment. This time, it was apparent in the tone of her voice that she was rapidly becoming exasperated with the need to repeat what she had already said. Then, as various members of each group began to write on the board, she had to remind them to spread their responses out so that other notes could be added later. This appeared to annoy her even further, although she made an effort not to show it. However, at one point during this process she turned toward me and rolled her eyes as if to say, "Why did I get the class of slow students?" Finally, all answers were on the board, and she began the large group discussion on the topic. Clearly, however, her earlier buoyant mood had been somewhat dampened, both by the need to repeat herself as well as the time that had been wasted each time she had been required to get the students back on-task.

It's important to note that neither the students nor the lecturer are necessarily at fault in this type situation (Smorginsky 1998). In this particular case, it was apparent that the students were *not* intentionally trying to waste time, but rather were processing the information that was given to them. In general, students simply respond to the situation in which they find themselves. As for the lecturer, she was probably replicating a scene she had personally witnessed many times during her past school experiences. This example is not the exception; rather, it is too often the rule when giving directions. If this teacher knew a better way of giving effective directions, she would doubtless have used it. It is the intention of this discussion to demonstrate another method for delivering instructions that may be more effective than what she had previously experienced.

Why did the students not recall all the directions in the order in which they were given? While it may be obvious that too many were given at once, understanding the process students go through may provide a useful platform for explaining how to proceed more effectively in the future. First, note that if the expectation is for the class to be able to follow a given direction, it is important to have their undivided attention. In this light, consider again, in slow motion, what happens when students hear the teachers' words.

The first direction that registers is the fact that they will need to organize themselves into groups. Instantly, where does their attention go? Naturally, they will look around as they mentally decide whom they want to have in their group. While they are glancing at other people, their attention has been diverted from the teacher, who is continuing to provide instructions, *important information to which they are now not listening*. Once students have missed a link in a series of connected directions, it is virtually impossible for them to get back on track and figure out what they are supposed to be doing.

What does this mean to the lecturer?

If an instruction is given that directs the audience's attention away from the lecturer, students need to be allowed to complete the task. When they have accomplished this instruction, they may then return their attention to the teacher for further information.

A critical issue concerning effective directions emerged in the feedback session with this lecturer. When asked about why she thought the class hadn't understood and acted successfully on the directions, she was confused. She was certain that the directions had been clear, sequential, and easy to follow. So certain was she, that, even though this feedback took place nearly two hours after the opening of the class, she was able to repeat what she had said *almost verbatim!* The reason quickly became apparent.

The directions she had given felt perfectly clear to her because *she had been mentally practicing them for some time.* Ever since she had begun to prepare for this class, she had been thinking about these directions, and how she would structure the sequence of instruction. As she prepared her lesson plan, she had actually written the directions out word for word. In fact, by the time the start of the class had arrived, she had completely memorized them. While preparing for her class, she had mentally rehearsed these directions at least ten times. Clarity came when she realized that, just because they were clear to *her*, it did not mean that they would necessarily be clear to the *students*. The students did not have the benefit of having considered the directions many times during class preparation. They were hearing them for the *first time*.

The first time we hear things our ability to recall them is vastly different from our ability to recall them after they have been repeated. In addition, a distraction was created when they turned to look at other class members and considered how to select their group. Therefore, the teacher needs to realize that how she presents the directions to students will likely be quite different from how she herself would need to hear them. Directions need to be considered in the light of how they will be heard and processed by the students.

Given all this, how could these directions be adjusted so they are accomplished with a minimum of repetition? In the original example, the first direction was for the students to arrange themselves into groups. The lecturer could have begun the class by saying:

> "Good morning, everyone. Today we'll be starting with some group work, so you'll need to organize yourselves into groups of five or six. Please do that now."

She then waits until the groups have been organized before speaking again. When everyone has found a group, she continues:

> "Thank you. Next, please select someone to be your discussion leader."

Again, she pauses while each group completes this task. When every group has a discussion leader, she explains the topic of this discussion, and tells them to begin. After several moments have passed and when she feels confident that the groups have had enough time and are aware of the important issues, she asks them to pause in their conversation for a moment. Then she provides the next direction:

> "At this point, see if your group can come up with at least two potential solutions to these challenges."

After they have had sufficient time to generate these potential solutions, the lecturer says:

> "Now, please select someone to come to the blackboard and write your group's solutions to these challenges."

When each group has selected someone to write on the blackboard, the lecturer completes this sequence of directions by saying:

> "For those of you who will be writing on the board, please make sure there is plenty of space around your responses, so we can add some notes to them later. Let's get those ideas up on the board now."

The students move to the blackboard and begin to write. Now the teacher can easily segue into the next section of the class, and she begins a large group discussion. Here is a summary of the sequence of directions used in this particular example. Remember that after each one is given the teacher must *wait until it has been completed* before moving to the next one.

1. "Find a group."
2. "Select a discussion leader."
3. "Have the initial discussion concerning challenges."
4. "Have the second discussion concerning solutions."
5. "Select someone to write on the board."
6. "Write responses, leaving space around them."

There are six separate directions in this sequence, and each should be accomplished before the next one is given. With the directions being presented in this manner, there is rarely a need for repetition. The lecturer has avoided potential frustration in feeling that her directions were not heard, acknowledged, and acted on. From the students' point of view, they are now confident about what is expected of them at each step of the process, and can immediately act to achieve each short-term objective.

Example 2: The Field Trip

It was vocational day at the school. Eighteen high school seniors interested in becoming teachers had been invited to a local elementary school to observe a special class. The teacher of this class was going to present a lesson in a unique format. The students were told to convene in the hallway outside the teacher's classroom at a specified time.

All the students were on time, and the teacher who was to demonstrate the lesson stepped into the hallway to address them.

> "Thank you for coming. There are some name tags and pens located on the table behind you. Would you each please make yourself a name tag? After that, find a partner and come stand by the door next to your partner in a double line."

The students moved to the table and began to make their name tags. Based on the discussion in the previous example, it might be clear as to what happened next. Making the name tags took several moments, while each person jockeyed for position around the small table. It took more time for people to write their names, and some students were even adding decorations to their name tags. While all this was occurring, the conversation level escalated as students chatted about what they had been doing over the past weekend. During this activity, students were *not* concentrating on remembering the directions, as simple as they may have been. So, when they had completed their name tags, they all turned and faced the teacher. She looked at them for a moment, and then repeated:

> "Please find yourself a partner!"

As soon as she said this, of course, they all remembered what they were supposed to be doing. They each quickly found themselves a partner, stood next to that person, and turned back expectantly toward the teacher. She looked at them with exasperation for a moment before saying:

> "Bring your partner over here and let's make a double line!"

Unnecessary frustration on the part of the teacher, and guilt and minor embarrassment on the part of the students, were the products of having provided too many directions at once. In this situation, there were, in fact, only three directions:

1. "Make yourself a name tag."
2. "Find a partner."
3. "Form a double line at the door."

However, because the first one took time to complete, the students forgot the two subsequent directions. And remember that these people were seniors! One would certainly hope that they could follow three simple instructions! Yet it is clear how quickly and easily students of *any* age can become distracted if the instructions are not presented in a clear, linear, one-at-a-time manner.

In this case, the teacher might have been better off giving the instructions in the following manner:

> "Please make yourself a name tag."

After everyone has made a name tag, she says:

> "Please find yourself a partner."

Finally, when each person has found a partner, she could complete the direction sequence by saying:

"Form a double line here at the door."

When they are presented in this way, the teacher has a better chance of having her directions successfully completed.

Despite the previous two examples, it is also useful to remember that not every situation calls for one direction to be given at a time. It is up to the individual teacher to determine how many directions students can handle in a particular situation. However, in general, directions relate to movement by the students. This movement can interfere with their ability to remember subsequent directions. To overcome this potential problem, when possible, *deliver one direction at a time*. Then patiently wait for the first direction to be accomplished before giving the next direction. Continue in this manner until the activity has been successfully accomplished.

While these examples demonstrate the logical and sequential nature of this concept, there is a hidden challenge in using this strategy. It lies in the ability of the teacher to successfully *pause* after a single direction has been given, and to wait in silence until it has been successfully completed. At first glance it may appear to be a simple thing to do, yet in practice it can prove to be a tremendous challenge, especially when you become fairly experienced in the classroom. It requires you to change the pace of your delivery when giving instructions, which has often become an unconscious pattern once we gain a foundation of experience. Breaking that pattern may take a considerable amount of conscious intention. However, believe it. The efficiency and positive effect it will ultimately create with a group of students will definitely be worth the effort to anyone who masters this skill.

Finally, a potentially useful way for teachers to consider whether or not they have provided clear directions is to view the results of their instructions through the lens of the following axiom:

The meaning of my communication is the response I get.

From this perspective, teachers can look at the result of their directions on their class, and, from the students' responses, decide how effectively the directions were communicated. If there is room for improvement, it is often learning to give directions one at a time, and allowing students to accomplish it before continuing to the next step.

SEE ME

Consider the following situation. Suppose a teacher, based on the previous section's discussion, is carefully sequencing the directions he needs to give to a class. The first thing he needs the students to do is to form themselves into groups, so he says:

"Please get into small groups, with approximately six to eight people in each one."

The teacher waits, and, when it appears that the groups have been properly organized, he gives the next direction:

"Please form your group into a circle."

Again, he is patient as the groups each form into a circle. When all groups are ready, he continues speaking. For his third instruction he begins explaining what they will be talking about in these groups. It takes him approximately thirty to forty seconds to describe their discussion topic. However, even before he can complete this brief instruction, he notices that he seems to be losing the attention of some members of his audience. Why might this be happening? Pause and consider the physical arrangement of the classroom before moving to the next paragraph. See if you can figure out the problem.

Did you see what was happening? While there might be many reasons why an audience fails to maintain their focus on the teacher, one cause stands out clearly in this particular example. It has to do with the physical arrangement of the students. The teacher has specifically asked them to move their chairs into a circle. This creates a unique problem. *No matter where he chooses to stand in the room, approximately half of the students will have their backs to him.* Why is this a problem? In general, being able to *see* the teacher strongly supports students' ability to understand and recall instructions and directions. It helps students maintain their focus and pay attention while the information is being presented.

If they find themselves unable to see the teacher, they may want to adjust their bodies so they can see better. However, this creates a unique problem. Examine what happens to one student in particular who is faced with this challenge:

Suppose a student happens to end up with his back to the teacher, just as the next set of instructions begins to be presented. He wants to see what is happening, but he can't move his chair. Why? Because he has just moved it into a circle, based on the previous instructions. Changing the shape of the circle would seemingly violate those instructions. He is stuck, uncertain what to do. Still, he wants to see, so he twists his body halfway around, until he can at least partially see the teacher.

But this is definitely an uncomfortable position to maintain for very long. Sooner rather than later he finds his body relaxing into a more comfortable position, which, of course, is facing *away* from the teacher. It is slightly more difficult to pay attention to the teacher now, because he is not facing in that direction. Also, he is now facing his peers, which makes it much easier to become distracted by engaging in a whispered conversation, or by exchanging a glance with another person sitting across the circle. These conflicts will further divert his attention from the instructions and increase the likelihood that he will be lost when it is time to begin the assignment. In addition, he has begun to distract those students who *can* see!

In the example at the start of this section, this may have been exactly what was taking place while the teacher was giving the third direction. However, keep in mind that that scenario is not happening to just one student; this phenomenon may be affecting as many as half of the people in the room—all those that ended up with their backs to the teacher. Once those students become disengaged, consider what effect it might have on the other students. It's easy to see how they would become distracted by the activities of the others; thus, even less of the entire group is attending to the information being presented. To a teacher this process of gradual loss of attention may or may not become apparent; at times it can happen gradually. Even a small loss of attention, however, may be enough to create sufficient distraction that it becomes necessary to repeat the instructions, and now we're back to having a frustrated teacher on our hands.

How can the teacher adjust to this potentially frustrating situation? Quite simply, by having the students turn and face him before continuing with the directions. For instance, in this example, once the students have arranged themselves into circles, his next direction could be:

"Please turn your body so you can *comfortably* see me."

With this statement, the teacher has given clear permission for the students to adjust their chairs so they can see him while he gives the next set of instructions. They will not feel as if they are failing to follow the previous direction asking them to form a circle. With the students facing him, there is less chance that they will become distracted by interactions with their peers. In this position they can focus their attention on the next set of directions.

While there are many phrases teachers could use to accomplish the objective of having their students face them, the one used above contains a key word: *comfortably*. It may be useful to include this word, or a similar one, in an instruction of this nature because it provides a clear visual image of what students are being asked to do. Examples of other phrases that might also be useful in this situation include:

- "Please adjust your body so you can see the board."
- "Move your chairs so you can face me."
- "Turn your body so you are relaxed while facing in this direction."
- "Please look up at me."
- "Make sure you can clearly see my eyes."

Any of these phrases, or others, would meet the needs of the teacher. The key is to make certain the students are given permission to face the teacher.

In the previous section, emphasis was placed on waiting until the first direction had been completed before providing a second direction. The same concept applies here. If teachers ask the students to turn and face them, they should make sure to *wait until everyone is facing in the desired direction before continuing* with the next instruction. If they begin talking too soon, they run the risk of having some students miss the first part of an instruction. For clarity, wait patiently until every student is ready before providing the next direction.

The opening example described a situation in which students had moved their chairs into circles. However, there are other times in a learning situation when the audience may not be facing the teacher. For example, students might be looking down at their notebooks or texts when the teacher is ready to give another direction. Or, they might be scattered around the room, working in small groups, talking in dyads, or perhaps working on a role-play scenario when the teacher needs to give them some additional information. In such cases as these, the teacher would be well advised to have them look up and wait until everyone's attention is focused before giving another direction. The teacher might say:

> "Please pause for a moment and look this way. [When they have paused . . .]
> Thank you. Let's take about one minute at this point and add some clarity to
> your discussions . . ."

There are certainly many similar situations during which students' attention will be focused on something other than the teacher. Whatever the physical situation, teachers might be well advised to first ask themselves if all students can see clearly and comfortably from the position they are in before continuing.

In summary, you can maximize the effect of your directions if you remember that the majority of students prefer to see you when you are giving directions. When students are in a position where they do not have a clear line of sight, go ahead and take the necessary time to have them adjust their bodies so that they can see, so they are in a comfortable position for maintaining their focus. When the students are arranged in this manner, they can better give you their full attention, at least at the start of the directions. Then it is up to you to keep it!

STEP CHECK

How long is it necessary to wait, after giving one instruction, before moving to the next one? How can a teacher verify that all students are keeping pace? The best way for teachers to be certain is to do a *Step Check*. A Step Check is a way to visually verify whether or not the students are keeping pace with the directions or the information being presented. Only once the teacher is certain that all students are at the same spot, does the class continue.

Example 1

I was in the back of the room, observing a teacher in a class that required the use of a workbook. There were approximately twenty-five students in attendance. The teacher wanted the students to consider a specific line from their workbooks. When she had opened her workbook to the appropriate place, she said to the group:

> "Please turn to page 12 and follow with me."

She then looked up from her workbook and glanced around the room. It was apparent, however, that her attention was on the workbook. From her quick look it appeared to her that everyone was following along. She continued, saying:

> "Now, look at the second paragraph. Do you see where . . .?"

However, as she began to discuss the designated line in the book, it was apparent that something wasn't right. As the teacher continued to explain her point concerning a quote on this particular page in the workbook, the class had fallen into three categories. One group of students had rapidly located the correct page and were following along. As you might imagine, there weren't many of these. A second group had found their workbooks, but had yet to locate the correct page or line. And the students in the final group *were still looking for their workbooks!* Yes, it's true. They were busily looking under their chairs, checking in their desks, or turning to see if they had left their workbook on a side table in the room. Can you guess how much learning was happening? You're right . . . not much.

Observing from the back of the room, I made a mental note to remember this for the future. It was obvious how much can be missed when teachers do not verify that all of the students are following along at the proper pace. As in the example above, for those who need an extra ten to thirty seconds to find their workbooks *and the proper page*, what will they have missed? Will they have failed to hear something important relating to an upcoming assignment? Will the information be critical to understanding material later in the class? For those without a book, when will they be able to take the time to locate their workbooks, catch up with the rest of the group, and pick up the information the teacher was explaining at that moment? If no time is provided, will they *ever* be able to catch up? What will it cost these students to have lost a link in the overall chain of understanding? Will the teacher be greeted at the break with a barrage of questions concerning the material that was just covered, and wonder why these people didn't hear what he or she remembers so clearly having covered?

A vital component in giving effective directions is verifying that each member of the audience is following along at the appropriate pace. Instead of continuing forward while leaving some members of the audience behind, this teacher could have done a *step check* by saying:

> "If you have found page 12, please hold your workbook up in the air."

Now she can carefully look over her class to determine which of the students, if any, require an extra moment to locate their workbooks. Taking the necessary thirty seconds at this point to make sure everyone is at the same place may save a much greater amount of time later in the day, when it suddenly becomes necessary to go back to concepts and ideas discussed earlier, reviewing each step for those people who may have missed some important elements during the day. This can be quite frustrating to teachers when they consider what else they could be doing with that time to further the learning in their classroom.

The idea of doing a *Step Check* is closely connected to a discussion later in this book on *Specify the Response*. If you have a moment you might jump forward to this section for the full discussion. If not, however, here's a brief explanation of the idea.

Each time the teacher does a Step Check, it is critical to specify the response. If the type of response is clearly indicated by the teacher, then the information on which students base their decision to move forward or to wait is real, not merely a "best guess." The worst case scenario would be if a teacher were to believe that he or she were doing a Step Check when saying:

"OK, did you all get that?"

This rhetorical question, while it may appear to be a valid Step Check, offers no clear way for students to respond. Teachers who find themselves asking such vague questions will frequently find the responses from their audiences equally vague. In the end, these interactions serve no purpose. Instead, when doing a Step Check, err on the side of being overly precise, such as:

"If you are 100 percent clear on what that term means, hold one hand high in the air."

This statement is both clearer than the previous one as to the question being asked as well as informing the students *exactly how they should respond.* The type of response the teacher expects has been specified. In the arena of effective directions, clarity should be one of the teacher's strongest focal points.

Example 2

The previous section focused on making certain that each member of the audience was able to see the teacher before giving a direction. In some cases it may be necessary to do a Step Check to verify that everyone can, indeed, see the teacher. This is especially true in larger group settings. For example, in a lecture class with fifty or sixty students in attendance, a teacher might want to say:

"If you can see me clearly, please raise your hand."

If every hand appears to be raised, then the teacher can continue with the next section of the class. If several students have not raised their hands, the teacher could ask them to move their chairs or desks so they can see more clearly. Once the students have done this, he might repeat the original Step Check in preparation for giving the next direction or showing an important visual.

Example 3

Suppose a teacher was about to lead a few stretches in the morning, just to wake everyone up, and the room was fairly full. The teacher might want to do a Step Check by saying:

"Please adjust your body so you can clearly see me. [When the students have relocated themselves . . .] Now, if you can see me, clap your hands twice."

If everyone claps twice, the teacher begins leading the stretches. If not, however, the appropriate changes need to be made. When everyone indicates they can see clearly, the stretching exercises begin.

Example 4

In a classroom setting, a teacher is about to administer a mathematics test. The students are only allowed to use a pencil to take this test. The teacher might want to verify that each student does have a pencil to use while taking the test. She says:

"Please hold up your pencil. Thank you, you may begin."

When their pencils are being held in the air, the teacher can be certain that all students have the necessary tools to begin taking the test. The teacher may have avoided having a student walk up after the test has begun, announcing that he or she doesn't have a pencil. Of course this won't help students who break the lead in their pencils during the test, but at least everyone will have gotten off to an organized start.

When first using Step Checks in the course of instruction, or when giving directions, teachers can expect to experience a curious staccato effect. Many teachers are quite used to hearing only their own voice in the room unless they are engaged in a question-and-answer session. When using the method discussed here, the experience is more of a brief period of instruction, or even a single direction, followed by a Step Check and then a return to the next direction. At first this may feel like an interruption in the teaching process. However, as both the teacher and the students become familiar with this style, the benefits this approach brings to long-term learning become readily apparent.

In summary, a Step Check is an invaluable tool for keeping all members of an audience moving forward at the same pace. It helps eliminate the occasional moments when a few students get left behind as a session is proceeding, because the teacher pauses to visually verify that all students have reached the same point in the instruction before proceeding with the next piece of information.

CLEAR AND CONCISE

In general, teachers tend to use far too many words when giving directions. As noted in the opening of this section, giving directions is much like speaking a different language. Contrasted to the mode of general instruction, or facilitating an interaction with students, the effective delivery of instructions necessitates choosing different words, different phrases, and sometimes even different sentence structures. Examine the following direction. Which words in this statement are not necessary?

"I want you to turn to page 42."

The first four words, "I want you to . . ." are not needed. This is one of the most frequently recurring unnecessary phrases in directions. What purpose do these words serve? In reality, they serve none at all. If one looks carefully at this phrase, these are redundant; of course, it is the teacher who wants them to turn to page 42! *He is the person speaking.* To say them becomes not only unnecessary, but eventually, over time, they can interfere with the intended communication because students tend to tune out repetitious phrases. Instead, stated in a clear and concise manner, the teacher giving this direction should simply say:

"Turn to page 42."

This is the essence of the communication. The goal is to be clear and concise, and only say what is essential. In this manner students can move immediately into doing what was asked of them.

Here is a list of words, phrases, or expressions that can get in the way of clear directions.

- "I want you to . . ."
- "I'm going to . . ."
- "What I'd like you to do is . . ."
- "What we're going to do is . . ."
- "What we have to do is . . ."
- "OK, now, we'll just need to . . ."
- "OK, everybody, here's what's coming next . . ."
- "In a few moments . . ."
- "Here's the plan . . ."
- "So, then, why don't we just . . ."
- "So . . ."

Teachers often develop an unconscious habit of using one or two "pet" phrases. These will begin to show up in the teacher's directions, as well as in other areas of their presentation. This can quickly become annoying to audience members, and dangerous to the long-term intentions of the teacher. If students hear a particular phrase too frequently, they may begin to stop hearing it at all. This is a dangerous trend. If they become accustomed to not listening at *certain points* during the teacher's presentation, then how long will it be before they stop listening during the spaces *between* those moments? Probably all too soon.

Being concise is also important as an approach to all instructions. How can the teacher say what needs to be said as briefly as possible? For example, notice all the "verbal garbage," the extra words, in this communication from a teacher:

"Well, then, it looks like it's time to move forward with what we're going to do next. I think you guys are really going to like this activity. So I guess what we'll have to do now is to just see if we can first of all get you to make sure that you have your textbook to look at, so you can all follow along with what is happening. Yes, that probably will be best. Why don't you just do that now? Go ahead and see if you can find your book."

I know what you're thinking. No one really talks like this! I can only say beware, because this is *not* an exaggeration. The above words were taken directly from a tape recording of a session led by an experienced classroom teacher who is quite skilled in almost every other area of instruction. The key is to choose words that will communicate the necessary information as briefly as possible. Instead, in this situation, the teacher might have simply said:

"Please make sure you have your textbook with you."

With these few words, the teacher has communicated basically the same information, but has left out anything that did not relate to the essential communication. Now the students do not have to sort through all the other words to figure out what they need to know. They can simply move into action.

In summary, avoid unnecessary words and phrases. Directions are more effective when they are presented in a clean and clear-cut manner. Say only what is necessary, and avoid getting caught in repeating words or phrases that fail to add anything to the communication.

CONGRUENCE

Great speakers throughout world history, such as John F. Kennedy, Martin Luther King, Jr., and Winston Churchill, all shared one critical characteristic: their ability to communicate a single message with power, conviction, and passion. This skill was not an accident. How did they make their audiences feel this way? How did they project their feelings to each and every listener, even when speaking before very large crowds? The key is that *every aspect of the delivery* was communicating the same message. Their choice of words, tone of voice, pacing, use of pauses, eye contact, and physical gestures were all focused on that one key idea. The term used to describe this effect is *congruence*.

This quality of being congruent is equally important in instructional settings. Teachers should strive to be as congruent as possible in their teaching. While it is certainly not necessary to teach on a daily basis at the same level that these speakers demonstrated, it is still a powerful tool that can be used to reinforce the retention of key points of information. High levels of congruence generate a strong impact on students. The stronger the impact, the more deeply they will encode the information, and the longer they will remember it.

In contrast, it is always humorous to see teachers begin leading a session by saying something such as

"I'm very pleased to be here."

when their tone of voice contains zero excitement, their facial expression is essentially blank, and their body language is indicating they've just gotten out of bed! Such a complete lack of congruence is always easy for an audience to spot, undermines the message in the words, and reduces credibility. Think of your own experiences. Ever had one of these teachers? (I'm betting you had *more* than one!) Then you know how critical this idea is for effective teaching. In addition, consider the effect of the following sentences, if they were delivered with very little emotion in the teacher's voice:

"History is such a dynamic subject."

or

"We're going to have so much fun today."

or

"You're really going to like this next activity."

Congruence is especially critical when giving instructions. Is the tone of voice supporting the primary message? Are the hand gestures adding to the students' comprehension? Is the teacher using his or her body language to further emphasize the idea? Each of these elements adds to the level of impact the teacher can create and should be utilized to the fullest possible extent.

Sometimes, keeping things simple is best. The following example shows how even in the smallest of moments, every detail is important.

The students are seated. The teacher wants them to stand in preparation for an upcoming activity. The teacher says:

"Stand up!"

Whether or not the students follow this instruction, and the manner in which they follow it, is entirely dependent on the degree to which all aspects of the teacher's communication are congruent with one another.

The first element to analyze is the tone of voice. This direction is not a casual request. It is an active command, and the tone of voice should be congruent with that message. Therefore, the voice should be powerful and commanding, a tone of voice usually referred to as *Command Mode*. Consider the range of tonality available to a teacher. The following diagram shows a continuum illustrating this concept:

Tonality Range

Soft & quiet - - - - - - - - - - - - - - (CM) - - - - - - -Loud & harsh

Command Mode (CM) is not quite loud and harsh, although it is located near that end of the continuum. It is clear and confident, while delivering an instruction that the teacher fully expects to be followed. It is emphasized here because most directions that ask audiences to shift into motion should be done in the command mode voice.

Command Mode is a certain tone of voice that is used only in specific circumstances. For example, it would certainly *not* be appropriate to use it when giving a lecture, facilitating a conversation, or sharing a metaphor with an audience. However, it may apply to a wider variety of situations than most teachers might imagine. For example, even asking the students to turn to a certain page in their text should be stated in Command Mode. This is, after all, a command that directs the audience to carry out a behavior requiring physical action.

It is frequently pointed out that the genetic differences between males and females plays a role in any discussion concerning the use of a strong voice. In some ways, this is true enough. It may appear that male teachers have a distinct advantage in projecting their instructions using Command Mode, because generally they have deeper voices. However, it has been my personal experience that gender is not the critical issue, nor even a very important one, in terms of delivering effective directions. In the end, the teacher's ability to be congruent using all aspects of delivery is the deciding factor. One female teacher specifically comes to mind. Although standing only 5'2" tall, she easily commands a room of 120 teenagers. Her strength lies in her ability to be absolutely 100 percent congruent when she gives them directions. She is never mean, never demanding. She's simply clear, precise, and speaks with a voice filled with conviction. She stands as a model from whom all of us can learn.

In this example, then, the teacher will want to say "Stand up" with a firm, commanding tone of voice. In addition, the voice can be used for including another auditory cue. Since the physical action is one of going from sitting to standing, it requires an *upward* motion. This message could also be conveyed by varying the pitch of the voice. The second word, *up*, is pitched slightly higher than the first word, *stand*. In print, that might look like:

"Stand . . . UP!"

At this point the teacher has provided at least three cues for the direction: the choice of words, the commanding tone, and a change in pitch. Consider three more cues that could be incorporated in this simple direction. First, there is the issue of proximity (see the earlier section on Bridges and Zones). Because this is an instruction, the teacher could move into the third zone (close to the audience) when speaking. This body language alerts students that the next words are an instruction.

Next, what about hand gestures? In what way could they be used to support the communication? Just as the pitch of the voice going up mirrors the required action, the hands could go from being at the teacher's side to being raised in front of them, approximately shoulder height, palms turned up. Now the teacher has added a powerful *visual* cue to the communication. For maximum effect, the hands would actually come up on the word *up* and finish firmly in that position.

The final issue is the teacher's stance. If he or she is slightly off balance, perhaps leaning to one side, or standing with one foot placed forward and one foot back, it can diminish the overall effect. Students need to know that the direction is complete when the teacher finishes saying the word *up*. To emphasize this point, he or she should be standing upright and evenly balanced on both feet.

At this point there are a total of *six* elements that are contributing to the impact and clarity of the direction. Imagine that the teacher puts them all together and delivers the direction. The words are spoken in command tone, the pitch of the voice goes up on the word *up*, and the teacher is standing clearly in the directional zone, balanced on both feet and with the arms extended, palms turned up. The powerful impact of the instruction should immediately spur the students into action!

The purpose of going into such minute detail in this example is to be extremely clear regarding the topic of congruence. However, it is understandable that the complexity involved in delivering a completely congruent direction appears overwhelming at first. Yet, the use of each of these elements offers another layer of impact to the directions a teacher provides, and, with practice, the style will soon become natural and easy. A conscious attempt to develop each of these elements will ultimately lead to greater levels of clarity and precision.

Additionally, it is important to point out that not every detail discussed here is needed for every direction given to an audience. For example, suppose a teacher says:

"Please turn to page 10 in your workbook."

Suppose that at the same time these words are spoken, the teacher uses one hand to mime the act of turning a page. With this single detail the clarity of the instruction is enhanced, and that may be enough for that particular moment. Or, perhaps the teacher might say to the class:

"Please move your chairs to the sides of the room."

The gesture accompanying these words might be a spreading of the arms. The fingers could be pointing to the walls of the classroom, indicating where the chairs are to be placed.

On a completely different note, if the class were moving from a more active situation into a quiet discussion session, the teacher might lower his or her voice and clasp his or her hands together in front and say:

"Please spend a moment thinking quietly to yourself about . . ."

Each situation is unique, and the teacher should become accustomed to considering which aspects would add the most effect to creating a congruent set of instructions. In summary, a teacher will deliver congruent directions if *all* elements of the instruction focus in a single direction, and function as a cohesive whole to create the maximum possible impact on the student.

DIRECTIONALIZE

In a learning environment, the teacher spends the majority of the time facing the students. For most aspects of instruction, this is a perfectly acceptable position; in fact, it is preferable. From this position students can access visual cues, such as nuances in the teacher's facial expressions. Conversely, the teacher can carefully monitor students' behavior. However, this mirror-image effect can also be an occasional source of confusion for students. For example, consider the following scenario, in which a teacher says to his students:

> "All the boys please form a group on the left side of the room, and all the girls please form a group on the right side of the room."

In this situation, what's the possible source of uncertainty? Given the fact that the teacher and students are facing each other, the problem is that it is in the students' hands to determine what is meant by left and right. Is the teacher referring to *his* point of view, or that of the students? These two perspectives are entirely opposite from each other; therefore, the distinction is an important one. If not clarified immediately, students will probably move tentatively toward one side of the room or another, watching out of the corner of their eye for the teacher's reaction to determine whether they have "guessed" correctly.

In choosing these words, the teacher has unintentionally introduced a factor that can undermine emotional safety in the learning situation. Forcing the students to guess at the true meaning of an instruction causes uncertainty and triggers a subtle game of right or wrong. Right or wrong situations are generally counterproductive unless they are introduced for a specific purpose, such as taking a test. Given that this is not a "test situation," it is much more useful to provide clarity in the original set of instructions. As has been mentioned several times in previous discussions, clarity allows students to feel comfortable with what is being asked of them, and when they feel comfortable they will tend to move more quickly to accomplish the task at hand.

In most learning situations, because the teacher is giving directions while facing the students, it may be useful to avoid potential confusion by eliminating the words *left* and *right* entirely. Instead, teachers might want to *directionalize* the instructions. This means that the teacher chooses some object that is readily visible to everyone, and incorporates it in the directions to ensure maximum clarity. For example, in this situation, suppose there is a clock on the wall to the teacher's left, and a large poster promoting health on the wall to the teacher's right. Given these large, visible items, the teacher could now directionalize the instructions by announcing:

> "All boys please form a group near the clock, and all girls please form a group near the health poster."

Now the instructions are much clearer to everyone, and students can quickly move to the appropriate side of the room.

Here's another example of a potentially confusing situation. Suppose a teacher raises a hand and says to a group of students:

> "Please raise this hand."

In this case, as he gives this instruction, the teacher raises his *right* hand. But the audience must once again quickly draw some conclusions for themselves. What does he mean by *this* hand? Is he referring to their right hands, because he is raising his right hand? Or, is he referring to the hand on that side of the body, mirroring where he is standing, which would mean their left hands? Once again it is up to the students to hazard a guess at the meaning of the instruction; thus, the directions are unclear. And, of course, at least one clown in the class will wonder aloud if the teacher meant *his* hand!

The teacher could avoid confusion by directionalizing the request. Suppose there is a large window on the right side of the room, from the teacher's perspective. If he originally meant for the students to raise their left arms—the one closest to the window—he could say:

"Please raise your hand which is closest to the window."

This directionalized instruction is much clearer and less confusing to students. Even though the teacher is raising his *right* hand, the inclusion of an object in the instruction provides the necessary clarity. Alternatively, suppose he actually does want to have them raise their right hands. In this case he could first *turn his body* so his back is to the audience. Now when he raises his right hand it will be much clearer what he is asking of them. He could actually now say what he said originally:

"Please raise this hand."

Because his back is to them and he is facing in the same direction they are, the instruction should be clear.

This idea of turning around so the teacher's back is toward the audience has additional applications for giving instructions. It can be useful whenever a physical motion is being demonstrated that the audience needs to copy. For example, it could be helpful when modeling a physical skill such as passing a football or hitting a baseball. Or it would even be useful if a teacher were leading a few morning stretches in class.

THE FOUR-PART SEQUENCE FOR MOBILIZING DIRECTIONS

When giving mobilizing directions, there is a particular sequence of phrases or sentences that can provide an effective organization of the information for the student, as well as help teachers structure their own thoughts.

First: Establish a time frame when the movement is going to occur.
Second: Imbed a trigger that will signal the start of the movement.
Third: Give the directions clearly and concisely.
Fourth: Pull the trigger.

To understand the use of this sequence in context, consider some of the possible problems in giving directions in the following situations.

Example 1

A teacher wishes to ask a group to move their chairs to the sides of the room in preparation for an upcoming activity. The teacher states:

"OK, we're going to move our chairs and . . ."

Imagine what happens in the room even before the teacher has a chance to complete that sentence. Suddenly, chaos reigns as students begin to pick up and move their chairs. Any other information the teacher has to deliver at this moment is lost as concentration shifts from listening to the teacher to the physical activity of moving the chairs. Why did this happen? Because in the original instruction *no time frame was given to indicate when the movement was to begin*. Therefore, most students will simply begin to take action. Now the teacher faces the challenge of regaining the students' attention in order to continue to the next section and to then provide the information she was originally going to cover before the students moved their chairs.

The importance of keeping students focused until they have clearly heard and understood the directions cannot be overstated. If students begin to move prematurely, thus missing even small pieces of information, a series of significant effects may occur. Most important is that the directions will almost certainly need to be repeated. As mentioned previously, repetition of instructions can be frustrating to both teachers and students. As frustration mounts, it can begin to interfere with hearing further instructions given to the class, in which case students understand even less, and a self-perpetuating cycle develops that is counterproductive to learning. Confusion from the students' point of view can be equally disorienting. As confusion grows, they may become less willing to involve themselves in the class. Giving clear directions allows students to feel confident knowing what is expected of them, and encourages them to involve themselves more freely in subsequent activities.

Example 2

A similar situation frequently occurs in a school setting when class is drawing to an end. What happens if, right before the bell rings, the teacher says:

"Well, we're almost done for today . . . "

As in the previous example, the time frame here is not clearly delineated. The word *almost* could refer to any amount of time. Given this ambiguity, students who are eager for the class to end will perceive this as the cue that the period has officially ended. They suddenly start to shift in their seats, rustle their papers, close their books, or organize their backpacks—whatever it takes to ready themselves for a quick departure from the classroom. As before, the key is to note what happens to their focus. It's certainly no longer on anything the teacher might have to say.

Example 3

In classrooms with older students, the situation may appear different to the untrained eye, although interrupted communication between the teacher and the student is still the result. Most teens have learned that the correct way to behave in school is to sit patiently until they are given the signal to move. However, their attention and concentration can be even quicker to wander than younger students. Here's one case in which this is likely to occur, similar to a situation described in the "One-at a Time" section but presented here to illustrate a different issue. The class is about to be divided into subgroups. The teacher states:

> "We'll be moving into groups shortly. The important thing is that . . ."

Because the formation of groups brings with it an array of complex social dynamics, such as choosing whom to include in their group, all the students hear is *moving into groups*. Lacking a clear time frame, they immediately begin to mentally form themselves into groups. Internally, they may be wondering:

> "Shortly? How long is that? Quick, there's not much time to think! Whom do I want in my group? More importantly, perhaps, whom *don't* I want in my group? And what are we going to have to do once we get into groups?"

While they are busy mentally organizing their groups, there is little focus on what else is being said. Any clarifying points the teacher may be providing before they move are lost in the maze of their mental consternation as they mentally formulate the possible composition of the group they are about to join. Much confusion can be avoided if the teacher uses a clear *time frame* when giving mobilizing directions. The primary point of confusion in most cases is that students lack a clear understanding of when the movement is going to occur. Teachers need to provide them with this information.

For example, in the situation where students were going to move their chairs to the sides of the room, the teacher might say:

> "*In ten seconds* we'll be moving the chairs to the sides of the room."

When the teacher uses those first three words, students now know approximately when the movement is going to commence. They know they have ten seconds to keep their attention on the teacher for further information. In the situation in which the students were to form groups, the teacher could add a time frame by saying:

> "In thirty seconds we will be reorganizing ourselves into groups of five or six. You will have as much time as you need at that point to decide which group you would like to join. For the moment, please listen to why we are going to approach this project as a group."

When students hear the announcement *in thirty seconds*, they know they will have the needed time for sorting out whom they would like to have in their group. This is further reinforced by the teacher's adding the next sentence, which lets the students know that the teacher understands this need on their part, and that sufficient time will be allotted for them to deal with it. Students are now free to concentrate on what the teacher has to say.

Adding a time frame to the beginning of a mobilizing direction is the first step of the four-part sequence. Subsequent steps follow along the same lines of thinking. When teachers clearly indicate when movement is going to occur, additional guidance will be provided if they offer a clear *signal*, which indicates when it is time for the movement to begin. This signal is referred to as the *trigger*. In the situation in which the chairs are to be moved, the *trigger* could be added both at the start of the instructions as well as at the end of the instructions when the trigger is metaphorically "pulled." Now the second and fourth parts of the sequence have been added. In this case, a teacher might say:

> "In ten seconds, when I say go . . ."

In this example, the word *go* has become the trigger. There are an infinite variety of possible triggers teachers can use. The word *go* is the most common encountered in this type of direction, but it can quickly become overused, thus losing some of its potency. Additional triggers may include the phrases "ready—set—go," or "on the count of three," or even a random word that the teacher identifies as the trigger. Some teachers will choose a word related to what is happening, such as "When I say *chair*, please move the chairs . . ." Variety in the choice of triggers helps maintain audience focus.

The third component of the sequence is to state the instruction clearly and concisely. This has been discussed in depth earlier, so we will now concentrate on how to use it in the four-part sequence. Putting all four parts together would result in the following direction:

> "In ten seconds, when I say go, please move the chairs to the sides of the room and stack them neatly. Go."

Now this teacher has incorporated all four parts in the direction. The same instruction, written another way, may more clearly illustrate each component of this directional sequence:

First:	"In ten seconds . . ."
Second:	"When I say go . . ."
Third:	"Move the chairs to the sides of the room and stack them neatly."
Fourth:	"Go."

A word of caution: Be sure to "pull" the trigger that was *originally embedded in the earlier part of the direction*! It is easy to imagine how confusing it can be to an audience if a teacher uses a sequence such as the following:

"In five seconds, when I say go, find a partner and stand with him or her—
ready, *move!*"

Because the word *go* was established as the original trigger, it is the word that the students are anticipating hearing. Vocal inflection on the word *move* makes it seem like this is the time to find a partner. But students may not be certain, because the embedded trigger has not been pulled. Pulling a different trigger may cause confusion, and in any case will certainly feel disconcerting to the audience. While at first glance pulling a different trigger may seem an unlikely occurrence, it is surprising how easy it is to forget the original trigger when teachers are first learning to incorporate this technique in an active learning situation.

Adding the trigger component to the example in this discussion where groups were to be formed means a teacher might say something like:

"In thirty seconds, when I say *reorganize*, we will be reorganizing ourselves into groups of five or six. You will have as much time as you need at that point to decide which group you would like to join. For the moment, please listen to why we are going to approach this project as a group."

Then, after the teacher has spent thirty seconds addressing why the class is approaching the project in this manner, she would say *reorganize*, and the class would begin to form themselves into groups. As with the previous example, it is rewritten here to highlight each component in the sequence:

First: "In thirty seconds . . ."
Second: "When I say reorganize . . ."
Third: "We will be reorganizing ourselves . . . (etc.)"
Fourth: "Reorganize."

A Final Example

Earlier in this discussion of effective directions, the example was mentioned of the potentially chaotic last few moments in a classroom, and the challenge of holding the audience's attention at this time. Naturally, this is one of the hardest times for students to concentrate, as they begin anticipating what they will be doing during the coming break. Anything that can be done to help students remain focused on the content during these times can be of immense benefit to both the teacher and the students. One option for using the four-part sequence in combination with an idea described in detail later in this book might be useful in such a situation. Given this tool, let's revisit that example. The teacher might say:

"There are two minutes remaining in this class. When the clock strikes 10:30 exactly we will be finished. However, during these last two minutes, there are three important things that you'll need to write down in your notebook."

By saying this, the teacher has clearly established a time frame. Students have also been made aware of the trigger signaling the end of the session. Although in many cases this is already known to the audience, it helps to reinforce the fact that the session is, in fact, not yet complete. And, the instructions for the remaining time period have been clearly stated—to write down the three important items. It's important that teachers communicate that they are aware of the needs of the audience and do their best to respond to those needs.

In summing up the Four-Part Sequence, it is apparent that each of the components plays an integral role in providing directions that are easily understood. Giving a time frame allows the students to fully understand when the movement is to occur, and the students can then focus more intently on the information the teacher is currently explaining. The inclusion of a trigger helps clarify when the movement is to occur. The instructions are then given clearly and concisely. Finally, the trigger is pulled, and the action begins.

While each component is a vital part of the overall success of the sequence, it should be noted that a teacher does not need to use *all* components of this sequence *every* time mobilizing directions are needed. It will be up to the individual teacher to judge when it is necessary to use all components, or whether the situation calls for a simpler instruction. For example, in a particular situation the teacher may simply need to say:

"Please move the chairs to the sides of the room."

These words may be sufficient to achieve the desired outcome. If so, they are all that the teacher needs to say.

To determine whether they are making accurate adjustments in the language of their directions, teachers should carefully take note of the success of their instructions. Do students stay focused after the time frame has been mentioned? Do students move immediately once the trigger has been pulled? Are teachers able to deliver their directions just once, and have them fully understood by all students? Feedback to self-monitoring questions such as these can help determine if adjustments need to be made. In this way, the clarity of the directions will be maximized as teachers learn to adapt to their own specific situations.

CHAPTER SIX

LANGUAGE ISSUES

Fourteen issues concerning effective language in the classroom are covered in this chapter. For clarity, each idea is explained through the use of specific words, phrases, or sentences. The ideas discussed here are arranged in alphabetical order.

ACKNOWLEDGMENT

In what ways are classroom students acknowledged during the course of a day? The teacher might write a nice comment on their papers, or perhaps a student answers a question and the teacher responds by saying "That's correct" or "Good." Maybe the teacher says "Thank you" when students return from a break on time. Or, in the case of younger students, they may even receive an occasional pat on the shoulder from the teacher. A consistent theme runs through all of these situations: In each of them, it is the teacher who provides the acknowledgment, and the student who receives the comment, reward, or verbal kudos. This is the norm in the majority of classrooms. When acknowledgment is to be given, the teacher does the giving, and the students do the receiving. Although the teacher-to-student flow of praise and reward is useful at times, teachers who remain stuck in this pattern will miss other opportunities for acknowledging students and creating a more dynamic learning environment.

Both the use and the effect of acknowledgment in learning settings, also referred to as *positive reinforcement*, is a widely debated topic and the subject of intensive academic research. The form that it should take, the frequency with which it is delivered, and the timing of the feedback are all specific areas of concern (Brophy 1979). Yet, it is not the intention of this section to cover the various concerns and beliefs about this complex topic. Rather, the intent is to broaden the range of options teachers have for providing acknowledgment in the classroom setting. There are other forms of acknowledgment that may be equally, or perhaps even more, effective than having the teacher be the only one to thank students when they have contributed in a positive manner to the class.

Reasons for Acknowledgment in Learning Settings

Why do people acknowledge each other? In a learning context, what triggers acknowledgment from the teacher? Does it only occur when students do something correct?

Will it only happen when they do something the teacher personally likes, appreciates, or values? While acknowledgment in these cases may be valid, if it stops there then a huge realm of additional possibilities is being overlooked.

What if acknowledgment was given for every small success, or even for honest endeavors that did not work out correctly? Is it possible that it could be effectively used even in these moments? Perhaps acknowledgment could be given regardless of results, based on effort expended. When people know their efforts are appreciated, it usually encourages them to try again, perhaps even harder the next time. Effective acknowledgment should span across situations and unite students in continuing to put their best effort into everything in which they are involved (Goleman 1995).

On the opening pages of this book, a sailing ship was mentioned. Return to that metaphor for a moment. If a ship is sailing forward and encounters heavy winds striking at it from all sides, its efforts to move forward will be severely hampered. In a classroom, the same idea applies. If students are acknowledged on an inconsistent basis, at other times ignored, and occasionally even reprimanded for what might be their best efforts, it is as if the ship of learning is being struck by winds from a variety of angles. Not all of them will propel the students in the desired direction. In fact, these ill winds probably end up canceling each other out; consequently, the learning stops dead in the water.

If, however, the ship encounters a single, steady wind that is blowing directly toward the identified goal, it can move in that direction with a minimum of effort from the captain. The goal of learning contexts is the mental, physical, and emotional involvement of the students so they can retain the information longer. If students receive a steady amount of encouragement and positive feedback for their efforts, the experience is akin to a steady breeze moving them rapidly toward the primary goals of the instruction.

If teachers utilize multiple forms of encouragement for students, and keep it coming steadily toward them, then the students are more likely to remain actively involved (Levenson, Ekman, & Friesen 1990). The encouragement must be genuine, focused on the efforts they are making, and provided frequently enough to keep the learning moving forward at the appropriate pace.

Examples

The traditional, primary form of acknowledgment in classrooms is from the teacher to the students. However, other forms of acknowledgment are possible, including self-acknowledgment and acknowledgment between students. Here are some examples of how these alternative forms of positive feedback and encouragement might work. You might consider which of the following could be useful in your situation.

- **Self-Acknowledgment**: Students can assess their learning by completing a form that asks them which aspects of the learning they fully understand at a given point. They can then grade their own paper and be given an opportunity to write three adjectives on the top of their paper that describe their success. With some groups it can be effective to have students reach over their shoulder and pat themselves on their own back, to thank themselves for successfully handling a particular challenge or task.

- **Peer Acknowledgment**: In most interactive learning environments, students will be working with each other in a variety of activities (Lazar 1995). They may be working in pairs, in small groups, or they may be simply chatting briefly with each other. After each interaction, it can be useful to have them thank those other people. The teacher might simply say, "Please say 'thank you' to the people you've been talking with . . ." or "Please thank your partners."

  The beginning and ending of each session, day, or program provides teachers with another opportunity for peer acknowledgment by having students greet and thank each other. At the start of a day, the teacher might say "Please shake hands with at least three people and say 'Glad you could make it today.'" Or at the end of a session the teacher could say "Please thank at least two people for being here today." After lunch, the words might be "Please tell two people you're glad they came back from lunch."

- **Physical Acknowledgment**: Physical forms of acknowledgment between students are another option. Athletes use a wide variety of actions to congratulate each other for their successes, some of which might work well in the classroom. The teacher might say "Pat at least two people on the back and say 'Well done!'" The practice of giving each other "high fives" (each person raises his or her right hand and these hands are slapped together) may also fit very well in some circumstances, especially if students have just been involved in a physical activity. Variations on this form of congratulations may also be effective, such as occasionally giving each other a "low five" or a "high ten" or even a "behind-the-back ten."

- **Compliments**: Compliments, even when done with humor, are another effective form of acknowledgment (Vergneer 1995). For example, one way teachers might distribute materials is by having several students hold the workbooks and stand throughout the room. To receive a workbook, the other students must approach one of these people and give a compliment, after which they are handed a workbook. One strategy is to take two minutes after they have received their workbooks to decorate and "personalize" them with magic markers. When this is complete, everyone stands up and holds their book in front of them. They then proceed to walk around the room showing their cover design to other students, while complimenting each other on their designs. This sequence takes less than three minutes, but helps create a playful, good-natured feeling in the classroom. This approach can set the stage for learning with a relaxed, comfortable tone that might continue for the duration of the class.

- **Feedback**: Students and teachers providing feedback for each other is a frequent component of many classes. One form this feedback can take is using the idea of "Gems and Opportunities." Gems are those things the person did that worked well. It is important to include the positive aspects in any feedback situation, because these are the things this individual is already doing well, and can build on in the future. Opportunities are those things he or she might want to consider changing for future efforts.

- **Young Student "Specials"**: Teachers of young students have a unique opportunity. These students rarely arrive with preconceived notions as to which forms of feedback are appropriate and which are inappropriate. In these circumstances there are a variety of options that they might find enjoyable, although they may only work occasionally with older students. For example, instead of applause, young students may be asked to snap their fingers, wiggle their fingers at the person, or give a "sitting ovation"—making a circle over their heads with their arms while saying, "Ooohh." They might want to give a quick three-clap acknowledgment after a person has spoken—where the group simultaneously claps three times quickly as a way of saying thanks. Or, in certain circumstances, if appropriate, they could even be invited to give each other a hug! In these cases, the *form* of the acknowledgment is less important than the fact that it is consistently given, and that they are a part of it.

The possibilities listed here are merely a sample of potential options for acknowledgment. Teachers are encouraged to continue seeking other ways of giving students feedback and appreciation for their contributions and their involvement in the classroom.

Some learning environments that last longer may use a particular form of acknowledgment that becomes standard for them. For example, students who will be together in the same classroom all year might begin providing acknowledgment for each other by simply saying "Thank you." when acknowledgment is needed. In these cases it is useful to occasionally switch from one form to another when needed to keep things fresh and alive in the classroom. Perhaps in the second month they might be asked to say "You're the best!" or "Thanks for your help" when acknowledgment is required. This will help students avoid falling into patterns where they are acknowledging each other simply because they are "supposed to," rather than meaning what they are saying. Variety is often the key to maintaining a genuine feeling in these interactions.

Acknowledgment in General

Several years ago I had an opportunity to attend a four-day personal development program in Southern California. One unique guideline for this program required all participants to put their hands together and bow before speaking with another person. This exchange was also mandatory after each interaction, whether within the context of the course, on breaks, or in the evenings after the sessions had concluded. The intention was to have us realize, at a deep level, how much value other people bring to our lives.

While this was a somewhat unusual situation, the tradition of acknowledging each other during those four days served its purpose by making all of us pause to consider how we have, or have not, been acknowledging people in our own lives. How often do we take people around us for granted? Simply because everyone is busy does not mean there is insufficient time to occasionally stop and thank others for who they are and what they bring to the world. The following story provides yet another viewpoint on this issue.

> Jeremy was in an advanced calculus class offered only to the most intelligent high school seniors. Near the end of the year, an important test was being given to all students in his class. After solving a series of challenging problems, he moved on to the final question, which simply asked:
>
> "What's the name of the custodian for this classroom?"
>
> Jeremy had absolutely no idea of the person's name. Because the question had nothing at all to do with math, he decided it must be a joke. He left the space for answering that question blank. As he was leaving the classroom, he asked the teacher if that final question would count toward his grade. The teacher replied:
>
> > Definitely. Success does not come just from *what* you know, it also depends on *who* you know. In your lifetime you will meet many people. Each of them is significant, and each deserves your attention and care, even if all you do is smile and say hello.

In Summary

Teachers might consider the issue of acknowledgment for themselves, on a personal as well as a professional level. Just as people appreciate being valued in their lives, they appreciate being valued in learning environments. Perhaps education can mirror how life *could be* in this regard. People could probably increase the quality of their lives simply by consciously acknowledging people five times each day. They could thank them for what they bring to their experience, for the way in which someone makes their day just a little bit better. A friendly smile, a casual wave, a firm handshake, or a word of thanks might go a long way toward improving everyone's attitude.

If people can come to value acknowledgment as a critical part of a positive learning environment, perhaps they will see its value in the larger world. If they find it enjoyable and useful in that context, they might begin to do it more frequently in their lives outside the classroom. What better lesson for them to experience in the classroom than meaningful, purposeful acknowledgment of other people?

APPROPRIATE ORIENTATION

Your brain is constantly being bombarded with input from your senses. If you tried to pay attention to all of it, all of the time, you'd go crazy. Instead, there's a portion of your brain that is dedicated to protecting your sanity by allowing you to pay conscious attention *only to what is important at that moment*. This wonderful mechanism is officially known as the Reticular Activating System, although everyone usually refers to it simply as the RAS. Earlier in this book, in the chapter on Principles of Effective

Instruction, the RAS was discussed in more detail. At this point, all you need to be reminded of is that the RAS is the focusing mechanism of the mind, sorting out incoming data and bringing to your conscious awareness only what it deems most important.

As a teacher, you can use this knowledge as a powerful tool in the classroom. The RAS can be used to deliberately shift students' conscious (and sometimes *unconscious*) energy and attention away from unwanted input and toward images that might be useful to them. As you increase your awareness of those thoughts, feelings, ideas, and reactions that help students stay focused on what they need to learn, you can turn their RAS in that direction. There are a wide variety of situations in which this skill may prove useful.

For instance, one of the more common places where this idea might be applied is in the dynamics of the teacher–student relationship. In the classroom, some students may occasionally have a negative reaction toward a teacher. Yes, honestly, this really does happen! Yet, there's frequently a very simple reason why this happens. One of the natural stages of development we all go through as teens is establishing our own identities. And one of the common ways to achieve this is to rebel against anyone in authority. In the classroom, that someone is you. As you might guess, that negative reaction can have a dramatic effect on a student's behavior. The key in these situations is to choose language that steers them away from these potentially disruptive thoughts. Suppose a teacher makes the following statement:

"I want you to go outside."

In what direction has the student's brain been oriented? The phrase "I want you to . . ." indicates that the teacher is the one in control, the person in charge. A teenager, or indeed any person who does not enjoy being ordered around, may have an instant negative reaction, *consciously or unconsciously*. Instead, the teacher might word the same request this way:

"Let's go outside."

Notice that, when using this language, the teacher is not specifically isolated in the statement as an authority figure to rebel against. Using *let's* also includes the teacher in the instruction, which may serve to soften the blow of the command. Some other phrases to be aware of, and to avoid when attempting to create a more appropriate orientation, are:

- "You should . . ."
- "I think you'd better . . ."
- "You need to . . ."

When possible, reword commands, by using one of the following two options:

1. leave off *I*, or any other related pronoun; or
2. use *let's*, *we*, or *our*"

When sentences are worded in this way, they are called "nondirective," or neutral statements. These kinds of statements contain less of a sense of inappropriate domination or control, to which some students may react negatively.

Appropriate orientation also includes another characteristic of language. Knowing that a teacher has the ability to direct a student's unconscious attention, the next question becomes one of knowing *where* to focus the student's attention. Consider orienting a listener's brain to one of the following:

1. something positive,
2. something humorous, or
3. something that provides a new way of looking at an issue.

Here are some examples that further illustrate this concept on a general level.

Example 1:   "All the short people over here."

Possible problem? Some students (and many adults!) have a belief that being described as "short" is derogatory. This would certainly be a counterproductive orientation. Instead, the wording could be:

"All the *less tall* people over here."

Delivered with an appropriate tone of humor in the voice, there's an excellent chance that good-natured laughter will follow, *while the directions are being carried out!*

Example 2:   "Would all of you who are bald please stand up?"

Possible problem? The use of the term *bald* might unintentionally come across as being negative or derogatory. Instead, the language used to communicate the same idea might be,

"Would all of you who have *chosen to have less hair* on your heads, please stand up."

Again, delivered with appropriate humor in the voice, there's an excellent chance that laughter will follow, while the directions are being carried out. (Of course, whenever I hear the word *bald* I am reminded of a teacher I worked with years ago who privately chose to refer to his hairless pate as his "solar sex dome." How's that for an entirely different orientation?)

For a teacher to constantly consider which orientation a student could hear might seem to be a demanding challenge at first. However, there are really only two keys to keep in mind when choosing which words to use: (1) be inclusive by using nondirective commands, such as *let's*, *we*, or *our* in the language; and (2) when possible, use humorous and creative rephrasing that allows people to feel good about themselves. These more appropriate orientations should direct students' thoughts away from potentially negative images and toward more useful ones.

Some Examples of Appropriate Orientation

Consider each example shown here. If stated as originally shown, the words might not create the intended results. What are some of the problems with each statement, and how could it be rephrased so that the actual message has a higher chance of registering appropriately in the mind of the student? As with the examples in the previous two sections on language, remember that there are an infinite variety of possible rephrasing options that might produce the desired result.

Example 1: "I want you to find your group and sit with them."

Possible problem? The use of the phrase "I want you to . . ." is potentially a negative orientation. Remove it, and the phrase reads:

> "Please find your group and sit with them," or simply "Find your group."

Example 2: "Raise your hand if you've only lived in this state for two years or less."

Possible problem? The word *only* may make it seem as if having lived in this state for less than two years is negative. One solution is to remove the word *only*. An even more elegant solution is to adjust the language so that being a resident of this state for less than two years appears to be a *positive* situation. Here are some words that could be used:

> "Raise your hand if you've arrived in our wonderful state within the last two years" or "Raise your hand if it's only been within the past two years that you came to this state and began sharing your talents."

Example 3: "You should leave the room now."

Possible problem? Use of "You should" can make this communication come across as more directive, authoritative, and possibly confrontational than the teacher may have intended. Rephrase the message:

> "Please leave the room now" or "Leave the room."

Example 4: "All the teenagers gather in one group, and all the adults gather in another. "

Possible problem? Suppose it is a situation in which teens and adults are in a room together, such as at an orientation meeting. Most teenagers would much rather be considered adults than teens. Interestingly, many adults would also gladly switch places with the teens! The trick is to be aware that they might interpret the use of either term in a negative way, and to address it in advance. In this case, the use of an age distinction may be helpful, such as saying:

> "All those slightly less than twenty gather in one group, and all those who are slightly over twenty gather in another group."

Most teenagers would be delighted to be considered *almost twenty*. And most adults would probably be pleased to be placed in a group that is *slightly over twenty*! This wording has elevated both sides and even brought humor into the instruction.

Example: 5:   "You have one more minute."

Possible problem? Use of the word *You* in this phrase makes a clear distinction between "them and us." It puts the teacher in the command role, and the student in the implied role of subordinate. This may be what the teacher wants to imply. However, if it is *not* part of the intended communication, simplify it by saying:

"Please take one more minute" or "One more minute."

Example 6:   "I'm going to give you a choice."

Possible problem? As in the previous example, the phrase "I'm going to give you . . ." establishes a clear dynamic in the relationship between teacher and student. The teacher is definitely in charge. This has been clearly demonstrated because the words identified the teacher as someone who has the "power to give." If the teacher wishes to avoid this more powerful/less powerful relationship dynamic, the language could be adjusted to:

"Which choice would you like to make" or "You have a choice to make."

Example 7:   "Who's experienced here and who's just a beginner?"

Possible problem? The use of the word *just* has put a negative emphasis on the category of beginner. From this statement, it appears that being experienced is good, and being a beginner is not so good. When a teacher needs to use statements like these that divide a class into subgroups, the key is to describe both sides so they have positive status in the minds of the students.

"Who's been fortunate enough to already have had the opportunity to look into this subject, and who's now bringing some new ideas to the table?" or "Who's experienced here, and who plans on becoming very experienced?"

In Summary

The use of an appropriate orientation removes a potential block in successful communication between the teacher and student, as well as during student-to-student interactions. The examples shown here are but a few of the many places this approach can be effectively employed. Teachers are encouraged to keep exploring other situations in which they can utilize this idea.

ENROLLING QUESTIONS

The teacher was welcoming a group of students to the beginning of a weekend workshop held in southern California. He started with a few brief opening remarks, then asked the following series of questions:

"I'm interested in knowing where some of you came from to be here today. Please raise your hand if you're from the San Diego area."

[Some students raised their hands.]

"Thank you. Raise your hand if you're from the San Francisco area."

[More students raised their hands.]

He continued asking these geographically oriented questions to the students, including one specifically for those who had traveled from out of the state. The sequence ended when he asked them:

"Finally, I'd like to see if anyone with us today is from this very city of Los Angeles. Please raise your hand if you're from here!"

[The remaining students raised their hands.]

"Thanks. It's nice to know that we have people here from so many different places. Let's give everyone a hand to thank them for making the effort to be present today from wherever they have traveled."

[At this point he proceeded to make some additional remarks.]

Was there a purpose in asking the audience these questions or, were they merely time fillers? Did the teacher really care where the people came from? The answer to these questions is apparent from the effect he has just created in the room. The students had relaxed and begun to warm up to each other. In fact, he had deliberately utilized a teaching technique known as asking "Enrolling Questions."

Defining the Term

Enrolling questions are a simple technique that can be applied in a variety of ways. These queries are designed to involve students at a minimal risk level during a presentation. The intention is to "enroll" them by bringing their backgrounds, skills, experiences, or knowledge forward and visible to the rest of the class. This information can then be used by the teacher as an integral part of the presentation.

Students usually come together in the classroom from a variety of backgrounds. In the early stages of developing a sense of class camaraderie, one means of building cohesiveness among them is to ensure that everyone belongs in some manner. In the above situation, when several people from the San Francisco area raised their hands, they became members of a distinct group. They could look around and see they had something in common with several of the other people present. Even if they are the only one from a particular area, at least they have been acknowledged and valued for what they bring to the larger group. The students have gained knowledge about some of the other people present, and the process of developing a sense of group camaraderie has begun, a critical ingredient in creating an effective learning environment (Corey & Corey 1997; Johnson & Johnson 1997).

While enrolling questions can be effectively used in the early stages of a group's development, it can also be used elsewhere throughout the course of instruction for a variety of purposes. At any point, when teachers want to involve the audience they can pose questions of this nature. The responses can be utilized to move the group forward, to include them in the overall discussion, or to check out whether they may have already been exposed to this information.

Examples

There are many times during the course of instruction that enrolling questions might be implemented. Below is a sampling of some categories that could be used in certain circumstances. Consider asking an enrolling question that asks whether:

- anyone has expertise in a certain skill area;
- they have had an experience, such as traveling internationally;
- they have ever been involved in a particular sport;
- they would like to finish a session early;
- they have seen a particular popular movie, from which the teacher is about to draw an important metaphor;
- they have ever experienced an interpersonal situation similar to the one being discussed in a communications class; or
- there are subgroupings represented that you would like to identify, such as asking members of a teenage audience if they are freshmen, sophomores, juniors, or seniors. In an audience of teens, each group would feel valued and acknowledged.

This is simply a small sampling of the numerous places where this idea could be used. Each teacher might want to examine his or her own content area to see if there are specific moments when this approach could be best utilized, given the subject matter and the student population.

The Issue of Divisiveness

The results of using enrolling questions are usually positive. Students enjoy being recognized and acknowledged for who they are and what they bring to the classroom. However, they can sometimes create a detrimental reaction in certain situations. Teachers should be cognizant of a potential roadblock and adapt their questions accordingly. The situations to be aware of are those in which, due to the question posed to the students, the class unintentionally becomes divided into "haves" and "have-nots." The hazard is that the group of "have-nots" may feel left out, and stop listening to any information related to that enrolling question.

For instance, suppose a teacher was about to tell a story. The location of the story is the islands of Hawaii. To maximize the impact of the story, the teacher wants to open this section with a question that makes students visualize the Hawaiian Islands. He asks:

"How many of you have been to Hawaii?"

At first glance, this may appear to be a simple enough inquiry. After all, it serves the purpose of acknowledging those who have been to the islands, and should get them thinking about that place. However, the problem with this question becomes clearer if, at this point, his next statement was along the lines of:

"That's good. I see some of you will know what I'm talking about."

He then launches into his story. However, he may have created a potentially negative emotional reaction for some of the students. Those who have not been to Hawaii may feel excluded. They may therefore conclude that this story must not apply to them. They may simply feel left out, or may go as far as feeling resentful that the teacher has just pointed out that they "haven't been fortunate enough to have traveled very often so far." By saying *good* in the second sentence, the teacher has also placed a value judgment on whether or not people have been to Hawaii. The enrolling question has been effective for a portion of the audience, but has actually created the opposite response from the other individuals. The group has been divided with potentially negative consequences.

In order to bring the group together again, the teacher needs to add an additional question, one that makes the rest of the group feel included. In this situation it might be something along the line of:

"And how many of you haven't been there yet, but would like to one day make it?"

No, saying this won't get them to Hawaii. However, he has now brought everyone *mentally* into the story. Most people would at least like to imagine that they will one day make it to Hawaii if they haven't been there yet.

Questions that divide the audience can be a tricky issue. The effect can happen so quickly that it may not even consciously register in the minds of the students. At the unconscious level, however, the result will be the same. If one part of the audience has been identified with something that can be perceived as more highly valued, then the remaining participants may feel excluded or diminished in some way. Basically, when asking questions that might be divisive to an audience, be certain to complete the sequence by asking a question that somehow values and includes the remaining students.

In Summary

The teacher in the original example used a particular phrase at the start of his questions. In each case he said the words "Raise your hand if. . . ." Another phrase that is commonly used to begin an enrolling question is "How many of you. . . ." Variations on this phrase might include "How many of you have ever . . ." or "How many of you would like to . . ." or even "How many of you are going to one day. . . ." Whatever the actual words, the intentions are still the same—to involve the students in the process of instruction and to value their ideas, experiences, and contributions.

Enrolling questions are a basic teaching technique that most teachers should be able to easily incorporate into their teaching style. However, a word of caution may be useful. Don't use them *too frequently*. Students will become tired of raising their hands, and may even stop participating. Teachers should gauge each individual class carefully with the intention of asking these questions only as often as needed to create the desired results.

GETTING RESPONSES

A teacher is giving a brief lecture. At the end of ten minutes, she turns to the audience and invites discussion by asking

"Any questions?"

Given that it is a classic *question*, often used in instructional situations, she probably gets the classic *response* to it, the blank, stunned stare from the students. If no one asks a question, she might wait through ten to fifteen seconds of silence, her impatience building, before saying something akin to:

"Come on, people! Weren't you listening? Don't you care? Listen, this is important material! It'll be on the test. You *must* pay attention!"

Finally, perhaps someone is brave enough to tentatively raise a hand and ask a question. The situation is strained, but at least the discussion has begun. Or, perhaps she simply gives up her quest for information and begins to lecture once again. Neither result is the reaction the teacher was hoping to generate from the students. How might this situation be handled differently? How might teachers open up a discussion with an audience and generate the maximum possible interaction?

Clarification

Why the blank stare, the "deer-in-the-headlights" look, from the students? There are many possible reasons, but, for the purposes of this example, let's assume that the teacher has indeed given a clear presentation on the topic, and that the students might have some questions to ask or thoughts to offer. What might keep them from responding in those first few seconds? To understand better, take a slow-motion look at what might be happening inside one student's head, when he is asked

"Any questions?"

Before responding, this student must make several mental adjustments. First, he must mentally switch gears. Keep in mind that, assuming he has been paying attention, he has been *listening* to the presentation, *processing* the information, and making his own mental connections to the material for the last ten minutes (Ruhl, Hughes, & Schloss 1987; Hughes, Henderickson, & Hudson 1986). Now, suddenly, he must bring that process to a quick halt. Next, he must sort through the material to see if he does have a question to pose or a comment to make. Suppose that something does occur to him. Now another step in the process must take place. He must find the words to express his idea. Finally, this student has to work up the courage to state his opinion in public.

Simply put, *this process takes time!* While the brain operates at a very rapid pace, it must still have a moment to prepare and organize itself (Calvin & Ojemann 1994). The blank stare from students is often simply the external expression of the fact that they are doing some internal processing. (Not always, of course. Sometimes that blank stare is a stunningly accurate reflection of what's going on inside that person's head—nothing! But we're talking about those other times . . .)

If a teacher does not offer students a way of dealing with this mental processing issue, another problem can quickly emerge. Teachers who typically use only that form of the question will find that only those students who are verbally quick will be involved in the discussions, and they will come to dominate all class discussions. A pattern will have been created that is hard to break once initiated, and students who are slower to respond the first few times will begin to believe that they shouldn't interact at all, and the verbally gifted students will continue to dominate most of the classroom interactions, further perpetuating and reinforcing this counterproductive cycle.

Suggestion

Because the hesitation to respond may be a by-product of both the mode students are in as well as the time needed to make the mental adjustment to conversation, it would be useful to give them a chance to *verbally prepare* their thoughts, in a safe way, before opening up the discussion to the large group. How might this be possible? Here's one method for achieving this outcome. When the ten-minute lecture has concluded, the teacher might say:

> "Thank you. Now, turn to one or two people near you and briefly discuss this issue."

Wait approximately twenty to thirty seconds, then ask:

> "What thoughts or questions do you have about this topic? What comments would you like to make? What areas, if any, might I clarify?"

In this situation, here's what tends to happen. Students begin by turning to someone near them. For the first few seconds they might be a bit hesitant as they organize their ideas and focus on the other person, but then the conversation begins to pick up pace. They are gradually switching into a verbal mode. When it appears they are sufficiently talkative, the teacher can now make the second statement, which helps bring the students' thoughts to a specific focal point. After giving them a brief amount of time to chat, the teacher would then say:

> "Please thank your partners. Face back toward me. Now, what questions or comments do you have?"

In an ideal world, most students have now made the mental adjustment from listening to talking, briefly organized their thoughts, and prepared a question or comment to offer to the discussion. Of course, it's not always an ideal world. However, by using this approach, students would at least have a *better* chance of being prepared to interact in the classroom by asking a question or making a comment.

How long might this process last? Interestingly, it should be fairly short. Perhaps no more than a total of sixty to ninety seconds are used for the entire sequence. Remember that the purpose of the interaction is *not to generate a lengthy discussion in the small groups.* The purpose is simply to give students an opportunity to make some mental adjustments and prepare themselves to be active in the discussion. This may feel unusual to some teachers, especially if, in the past, they have been used to having small groups discussions lasting five to ten minutes. The key is that the goal of the interaction between students has been changed, and all that is needed in this situation is usually a very brief period of time for them to prepare themselves.

Additional Thoughts

Now, ask yourself this question: Is it a waste of precious instructional time to give the students this sixty- to ninety-second period of time to converse among themselves? To answer this question it is necessary to consider the overall situation: What result does the teacher ultimately want from the learning situation? If the purpose in posing a question is to generate discussion, valuable time is often consumed anyway during the first few moments as students become mentally focused on interacting, move to a verbal place in their mind, and the conversation gains momentum. Using this approach makes the time spent well worth the final result.

However, it's interesting to note that some teachers tend to say "Any questions?" as an automatic reflex action, when in fact they really don't *want* any questions! It has simply become an ingrained part of their instructional delivery, their "patter." They say it without really thinking about it. Here's a simple key to success in the classroom. *If you don't really want audience interaction at a certain point, don't ask for it.* Then, when you actually do want interaction, and clearly ask for it, the chances of initiating a successful discussion will be significantly enhanced.

Note also that one of the potential side benefits of using this technique is that, in allowing all students the opportunity to talk, even briefly in the small group, gives each person the time to process the information in a manner different from simply listening. And when information is *actively* processed, even for such a short period of time, the chances that it will stay in memory are considerably increased (Ruhl, Hughes, & Schlass 1987; Hughes Henderickson, & Hudson 1986).

It's important to point out that using this technique is not necessary in every situation. For example, with a group of students who are quick to respond when given an opportunity to interact, or if a teacher should notice that students are already raising their hands to speak, obviously it would not be necessary to give the students time for mental preparation. They are already eager to begin, and the time would be better spent moving directly into the discussion.

In Summary

If, in your estimation, your audience may be reluctant to interact in a large group discussion, give them time to prepare first by having a brief preparatory discussion in a pair or trio with other students. This provides them with the opportunity to clarify for themselves what they are thinking. It also helps them organize their words so they feel more articulate and more confident when the discussion begins. Added confidence may also make it more likely that a reticent student will participate in the conversation. Even one minute of small group discussion may be sufficient to generate a higher level of interaction than might have been possible otherwise. Does it sound too simple? Sometimes it is the simplest of ideas that produces the greatest levels of desired change.

INVOLVE, DON'T TELL

An Example

Arizona's Junior Miss was touring her home state giving a series of brief presentations. The topic of this winsome young lady's speech was "Domestic Violence in the State of Arizona." At one point during the speech she informed the audience:

> "Did you know that of the number of women in Arizona who had to go to the emergency room in last year, 35 percent were there as a result of domestic violence?"

She then proceeded to continue with her talk. Her primary goal in the talk was to increase awareness of the severity of the issue of domestic violence in Arizona, and she had just made the single most important point of the presentation. Now, an important question could be asked: Had the effect of the impact of that information, the key statistic in her talk, been maximized?

The percentage she had stated was shockingly high, at least to me. It was also probably higher than most people in the room had expected. However, the statistic had been *told* to the audience, versus having them be *involved* in the discovery of it. Therefore, a considerable amount of impact had potentially been missed by simply telling the audience the key information. In a discussion later with her, the idea was brought up of involving the audience in the discovery of that same statistic to increase its impact. We generated a list of the options that might be used to meet this goal. Some that we came up with in that meeting included:

- polling the audience for what percentage they thought was accurate,
- asking a third of the audience to stand, pointing to them and saying "That's approximately 35 percent of the people in this room—the same percentage of all women who went to emergency rooms in Arizona who were there as a result of domestic violence"; or
- asking everyone to raise his or her hand, then having the presenter ask, "What percent of women . . ." and begin with 5 percent, then 10 percent, and continue

on in 5 percent increments, having the members of the audience drop their hands when the presenter had *passed* the percentage they thought was the correct answer.

In the end, the final option mentioned here was the one she ultimately chose to use and it achieved her intended outcome. It even led to a useful twist in her future presentations on this topic. She observed that, in the majority of her audiences, by the time she had reached 25 percent, no one's hand remained in the air. In these groups she was then able to say:

> "And that's a big part of the challenge; very few people are even aware of the seriousness of this critical problem here in Arizona."

Involving the audience creates a higher level of impact, which helps people easily and quickly recall the primary points of a talk (Cusco 1994). In transferring this idea to the classroom, the question to ask is:

> How can teachers isolate the key concepts within their presentation and focus the audience's attention on the importance of the point by engaging them in discovering, uncovering, or clarifying the information?

Theoretically Speaking

Memory researchers are convinced that students will remember only the "gist" of most things they hear and experience in a classroom (D'Arcangelo 1998; Jensen 1996). As silly as it may sound, *gist* is the actual scientific term they frequently use in articles and books on this topic. Essentially, *gist* means the basics, a general framework, or a vague impression. From this academically supported notion comes a clear issue for the classroom. Suppose teachers want to maximize the impact of their lessons on a class. If they isolate and highlight the key points of their presentation through involvement, students will have an easier time focusing on and encoding the main points. It will help them avoid walking away from the classroom with more than just a hazy sense of the lesson. Once the student is able to recall the key points, related issues will be easier to locate around it (Berstein 1994).

This idea directly supports one aspect of a popular theory of cognition (how we think) that predicts that memory is a function of "nodes" and "subnodes" and the connections between them, known as a "knowledge network" (Anderson 1990). But that's the kind of detailed information that only researchers get turned on by. As teachers, what we need to understand are the practical applications that come from this conceptual theory of learning.

In Summary

The bottom line for us as teachers is simple: We can assist students in encoding the primary pieces of information and building a knowledge network by having them involved with the information whenever possible. Teachers should carefully choose their most important points within a given speech or lecture, and devise a strategy to *involve* the audience in "discovering" the information, instead of simply telling them. This creates a more active mental process, one that is more likely to generate longer term memory.

LABELS

Imagine a classroom composed of high school seniors. The teacher begins the class by saying:

"OK, everybody, it's time to play a game!"

What happens when these individuals hear this announcement? As you might guess, high school students probably aren't exactly thinking positive thoughts at this moment. Perhaps they respond by groaning in dismay, or rolling their eyes. But the teacher plows ahead with the activity and the class grudgingly goes along. Does the teacher know that, even though the activity may have been successful, he made his job significantly more difficult by the words he chose to use? Probably not, but if you become aware of the issue here you might be able to save yourself a great deal of effort somewhere in the near future.

Simply put, this teacher had tripped over one of the common language challenges inherent to teaching. He used words that were inappropriate for this particular group of students. The words *play* and *game* may sound childish and silly to high school seniors. In their minds they may be "too old to play silly games." When they hear these words, they react negatively based on what they believe those words mean. Words that cause a reaction in us because we have had experience with them in the past are called "labels." By using labels that are inappropriate for this particular group of students, the teacher has made the job of engaging them more difficult than it might otherwise have been. Being aware of which labels work and which ones may produce a negative effect in your classroom is one of the keys to creating a dynamic learning environment.

Clarification

In the course of normal conversation, labels serve a useful purpose. They provide us with quick guidelines to understand the world based on our past experiences. For example, if you reach for a can labeled "Coke" you should reasonably expect to find inside the product known to you as Coca-Cola. You would have every right to be surprised if you discovered, instead, that the can contained only water, or worse, Drano! Examples abound in everyday life of how labels affect us, both for the better and for the worse, from ordering a type of wine with which we are familiar to deciding whether or not to see a movie based on its "type," such as action, romance, comedy, or mystery. In general, labels provide a service by preparing us for what is to come.

Can the definitions people associate with labels change? Consider the following three examples. In the 1950s a *gay* person usually referred to someone who was quite happy. Today that same word has a very different meaning. Or consider the label "Made in Japan." Forty years ago the first thought many North Americans would have had in connection with this label would have been *inexpensive* or *cheap*. Today, at least in the arena of electronics, the same three words frequently imply a high-quality product. The word *shout* in the United States means to yell loudly, whereas *shout* in New Zealand and Australia refers to buying someone something, such as a drink or dinner. Labels can change from group to group, from culture to culture, and over time. It is always wise to be acquainted with the associations and connections other people have with certain words before using them in your classroom.

Labels in teaching and learning can frequently be counterproductive, and it is wise to consider carefully the possible effects of a label before using it. When a label is spoken by a teacher, students immediately call to mind past experiences they may have had related to that label. For better or worse, they mentally prepare themselves for what they *believe* the label means. Without knowing the mental impression some labels may create with their students, teachers run the risk of calling forth an image that will inhibit the learning process, such as *play* and *game* used in the example that opens this section.

Examples

Labels are words that might bring to mind certain associations for students. In the case of potentially negative labels, teachers should either consider choosing a different word or avoid using any word at all if possible. The following is a list of words that, in *some contexts*, may trigger negative connotations for students. Each is followed by several alternative words or phrases. The teacher will need to decide which choice might best produce the desired results.

- Play   Action or involvement
- Sing   "A chance to share your musical abilities . . ."
- Game   Event, challenge, activity, or opportunity
- Fun   Enjoyment or pleasure
- Dance   Movement, action, or motion
- Homework   Studies, homeplay, or independent time activity
- Test   Assessment, analysis, or check-in time

These are just a few of the many words that have the potential to be counterproductive in certain learning contexts. At the same time, you may have noticed that, in the right situations, these same words may have *positive* effects. For example, the word *game* frequently creates positive associations with elementary school students, and so is a useful one to use. The key is to assess the effect of the words on *your group of students only* and use those that produce the result you want.

Here are some other places where word choice might be critical.

Example 1:   Suppose a teacher asks a group:

"Who here has ever heard of an 'Echo Clap'?"

Some students may have an inkling what this expression means, perhaps from some past experiences. However, because they are not entirely certain, they are likely to choose not to respond. Inside they may be asking themselves some questions, such as: Where has the teacher heard this term? Will it be the same place where I heard it? Because an 'Echo Clap' is not something people hear about every day, students may know it from an entirely different context, and, lacking confidence in their answer, they are less likely to respond to the question. Instead, the teacher might first demonstrate the action, in this case three quick claps to acknowledge a speaker. Only then might he say:

"That's what we at Camp Whittier like to call an 'Echo Clap'!"

When presented in this sequence, it becomes clear what action is being discussed, and students are not "put on the spot." Often it is better to assign a label only *after* students know what the word means.

Example 2:   Consider the potential risks in making the following announcement:

"This is an activity called Speed-Warp Time Juggling!"

While the teacher who uttered it may have been looking to generate excitement for the upcoming activity, many of the labels within the statement may give students a reason to hesitate. Pick any of the following words: *speed*, *time*, or *juggling*. Each of these could have negative contexts. "I hate to be rushed," "I'm not good at doing things fast," or "I can't juggle," are all possible internal reactions from students. The key here is that there are *many* possible negative labels. If they are nervous about even *one* of these words they may become resistant and end up not learning anything from the activity.

Example 3:   The teacher turned to her group of middle school students and asked the following question:

"Hey, you guys, what is a *wave*?"

She was quite startled when no one responded. The room continued to remain silent as she glanced around at the students. Finally she said:

"What? You've never heard of a wave? I'm amazed!"

To the teacher's way of thinking, she had asked a very basic question. In reality, however, the question was much more complex than it appeared at first glance.

The teacher hadn't taken into account how many *different definitions* there are for the simple word *wave*. For example, a wave might refer to the hand gesture people make when leaving, a wave in the ocean, a radio wave, a sound wave, or even a wave created by sports fans in a stadium, to name only a few of the many choices! To which one of these was she making reference? The audience didn't know, so they were confused. Therefore they simply chose not to respond at all. Labels with *multiple definitions* can also be challenging to use in a learning context.

Example 4: The scene was a ninety-minute class full of young people, eight to twelve years of age. They had been in the session for forty-five minutes, and it was time for a break. The teacher announced:

"OK, everybody, in just a minute we'll take a break."

However, to those young people the word *break* was a powerful label. In their minds they saw a chance to run around the room, play games, and have a great time. The instant they heard it they all raced for the door, not waiting for the teacher to say it was actually time to *go* on the break. The teacher had to tell them a few quick things first. But once she had spoken those words, it took over two minutes just to get them quiet enough so she could be heard. Had she never actually used the label *break*, they would have remained listening while she finished the directions, then been released. As it played out in this case, several important moments of the session were wasted. In certain situations, the accurate use of labels makes for improved time management.

In Summary

Words that can function as labels are commonplace in everyday life. In the course of instruction, however, they should be chosen with care. Without intending to, teachers may occasionally generate negative reactions from their students. Conversely, used with care they can become a powerful positive influence in the classroom. Labels are a language tool. Like most tools, they can be used for good or bad. In this case, teachers are smart to consciously consider the effect certain words might have on their students, and use them judiciously, as the specific moment dictates.

OPEN/CLOSED

A teacher wanted to engage her high school students in a discussion, so she opened the class with a question. To her surprise, no one responded to it. Examine what she asked them and see if you can spot the problem.

"What is the most important political issue facing the world today?"

Why might no one have responded to her query? Why was she faced with a room full of blank stares? To understand the difficulty she was having at this moment, let's look closely at the question she asked.

Two assumptions are implicit given the format of the question: (1) There exists only a single correct response to the question, and (2) the *teacher's* answer is the *correct* answer. These inherent assumptions may inhibit students from easily responding to the teacher, because they are now required to consider the following sequence of issues before responding:

- mentally generate several responses,
- evaluate which of these responses they believe best fits the question,

- decide whether their response may or may not match the response the teacher has chosen as the correct one, and finally
- risk participating in a game of right/wrong, when only the teacher knows the criteria for making the final decision.

These limitations to the responses students can offer, dictated by the form of the question, significantly increase the risk of participating. Indeed, based on the perceived risk, such questions may inhibit students from interacting altogether. To decrease the threat factor, thus increasing the likelihood of interaction, the same question might have been phrased:

> "What are *some* of the most important political issues *you* believe are facing the world today?"

The form of this question puts accountability in the students' hands, while making it clear that there is more than one possible correct response. Used together, these two changes in the form of the question should significantly reduce the amount of threat students perceive, and, thus, increase the likelihood that they'll participate in the discussion.

Definitions

A question posed in the Closed format indicates there is a single correct response, and may also imply that the teacher is the only one who knows it.

A question posed in the Open format (1) allows students to have accountability for the veracity of their response, and (2) indicates there are several correct responses.

Further Clarity

It is clear that there are times when a teacher should use the Closed form of a question. For example, consider the question "What's the speed of light?" There is probably only one correct response in this situation. (By the way, it's 186,000 miles per second.) However, in a surprisingly high number of learning circumstances, opportunities exist for thinking and reflecting on key ideas. This allows for deeper processing, which in the long term may result in higher levels of retention. Using a question stated in an Open format allows for a wider range of interaction with reduced risk on the part of the student.

Further Examples of Closed/Open Questions

Here are some examples of closed questions and how they might be rephrased so they are in an open format. Notice that there are probably many ways to adjust the words so the meaning stays the same while the format becomes more open. The ones included here are meant to show just some ways this *could* be done.

| Closed | "What's the best way to bake a cake?" |
| Open | "What steps would you use to bake a cake?" |

| Closed | "What's the best movie you've ever seen?" |
| Open | "What are *some of* the best movies you've ever seen?" |

| Closed | "Raise your hand if you're considering going to college." |
| Open | "Raise your hand if at least once in the past few years you've considered going to college." |

| Closed | "What are the rules to the game of Musical Chairs?" |
| Open | "Who's played musical chairs before? What rules did you use?" |

Notice how in the final example the original form of the question implies that there is a *single* set of rules, while in fact there may be a number of variations on the basic theme of the game. Think about it. In the whole world, isn't there a fairly good chance that there are *at least* two different ways of playing Musical Chairs?

Beyond Questions

The issue of an Open or Closed format extends beyond questions posed by the teacher. In the following examples, notice how the closed structure concept may apply to a wide variety of situations:

| Closed | "Turn to someone near you and compliment that person." |
| Open | "Turn to *at least* two people near you and compliment them." |

If there were an odd number of students in the room, the original statement would not work out; someone would not be participating.

| Closed | "In trios, discuss this question further." |
| Open | "In groups of three, four, or five, discuss this question further." |

Only if the number of students in the room was exactly divisible by three would the closed format actually be possible. Otherwise this might create an awkward moment while the groups get sorted out. One or two people might end up feeling "extra". It would also require more time for people to make sure *everyone* was in a trio.

| Closed | "Smile if you now know how to do the Twist." |
| Open | "Smile if at least once you've been able to do the Twist." |

The closed statement seems to imply that everyone can now do something called the Twist perfectly, while in fact some of the students may have been successful once or twice, but are not yet feeling that they have the movement down completely.

Closed   "What's the best place you've ever been to for a vacation?"

Open   "What's a vacation place you've really enjoyed?"

This closed format makes the student answering the question perform an evaluation process, knowing that when a final choice is made it must be better than *every* other vacation place he or she has ever been. The open format allows one of many enjoyable places to be picked.

Closed   "When should we use this communication skill?"

Open   "What are *some of* the circumstances in which you might use this communication skill to your advantage?"

The choice of the word *when* may imply to some listeners that there is a simple, specific circumstance when the skill under discussion should be used, and not at any other time. The use of the phrase *some of* relaxes this implied restriction, making a more open response possible.

Closed   "What is a Completion Circle?"

Open   "Has anyone heard of a Completion Circle? If so, what have you heard about it?"

The use of specialized terms in learning situations is frequently a dangerous choice. Students may have heard the expression in a different context from the one in which they currently find themselves. Not knowing precisely what the teacher is referring to may cause them to feel there is a risk of being incorrect. If so, it creates a game in which there are winners and losers. Students rarely enjoy interacting under these types of conditions, and it is doubtful they will respond.

In Summary

The issue of Open and Closed formats has wide-reaching implications. While clearly not a consideration for all circumstances in a classroom, teachers would be wise to be aware of the potential effect the format of their questions can have on their audience. Lacking this awareness, it is easy to see how they may sometimes become frustrated with their students for not fully participating, while, in fact, a simple adjustment in language and sentence structure may create a dramatic shift in the level of interaction.

POSITIVE MENTAL IMAGES

The human brain is constantly creating mental images. It is one of the primary ways we orient ourselves to the world. Mental structuring of images allows the brain to create relationships among the objects that our senses detect around us. Based on those images, we choose how to interact with the world. Another way of describing this process would be to say:

Images are a prime influence on behavior.

There are two main ways in which our mind receives data from the senses that it uses to create these images. One is from the sights we see, and the other is from the words we hear. The process of creating images from language is sometimes referred to as *verbal imaging*. Verbal imaging is the subject of this section. How can we consciously use our ability to turn words into pictures to communicate in the clearest manner possible?

First, here's some information about the process the brain uses to create images. While we will be focusing primarily on the *use* of images, understanding the process by which they are created can be important in understanding why individuals make certain choices when communicating with others. It is included here primarily as a means of providing background on the subject.

When students hear spoken words, a portion of the brain processes that "sensory data" as an image. In response to certain words, the image created in the brain can be contrary to the idea teachers are attempting to communicate. In fact, it's often the *exact opposite*! Therefore, in all areas of human communication it becomes important, if not critical, to consciously choose words to create the desired effect in a given situation (Bayor 1972).

A Demonstration

Here's a simple demonstration of this idea. One of the most curious words in the English language is *not*. This comes from the fact that, in terms of visual imaging, the brain *cannot process the word* not. It is as if, within the human mind, the word doesn't exist. When presented with *not*, the brain will immediately create the picture that the person speaking meant to avoid. For example, right now, try to follow these instructions:

"Do NOT imagine a huge pink gorilla!"

Most people have a very difficult time following these directions. When they read those words, the very first image that comes to mind is that of a pink gorilla. Once there, it's difficult to remove. Go ahead, try it right now. Can you erase the image of the pink gorilla? If you're having trouble with this, don't be surprised. It takes a while to clear the image from our mind. And, if you were successful in avoiding imagining the gorilla, you probably first had to see it, then replace it with another picture, and focus all your attention on it instead. The instant you stopped thinking about the other image, what happened? Usually, that gorilla big pink gorilla comes walking right back in!

No Use Crying over Spilled Milk

Here's another classic example of this situation. A mother has just handed her two-year-old daughter a glass of milk. She says to the child:

"Now honey, don't spill your milk!"

Based on the discussion so far, what image is instantly created in the child's mind? As you might have guessed, the child immediately sees . . . spilled milk! Now that the image is clearly embedded in the child's mind, what happens? Of course, she *tries* to keep the milk in the glass, but that picture keeps coming back to her of milk all over the table! Suddenly, apparently without warning, the little girl's arm flies out and knocks over the glass of milk. The mother, horrified, rushes over and says:

"I told you not to spill your milk! Weren't you listening to me?"

Actually, the fact that the child was listening quite closely to her mother's words helped create the final result, spilled milk. It was the mother's *choice of words* that led to the creation of an image in the child's mind, and that image ultimately influenced her actions. If the mother truly wants a different reaction, she needs to deliberately use language that will bring about the intended effect. For example, she might say:

"Honey, please be careful to keep the milk in the glass."

Now the picture is of the milk in the glass, and the odds that the mother will see the behavior she hopes for are greatly increased.

Watch These Words

Not isn't the only word that may create an effect opposite from what is originally intended by the speaker. Here are some commonly used negative words:

can't	won't	don't
shouldn't	couldn't	wouldn't
avoid	stop	never

It's helpful to become aware of when and how you use these words. The more aware teachers become of using these words in the classroom, the more their brains will begin to trigger more useful alternatives.

Accentuate the Positive

There is one additional component related to mental images that warrants discussion: the *type* of images conjured by a teacher's choice of words. The mental images teachers want to avoid are those that direct students' focus toward *negative* actions or consequences. Any time teachers can create images of *positive* actions or consequences in students' minds, they help stack the deck for success. Thus, a general term that describes the choice of words and phrases teachers should seek to use is:

Positive Mental Images

Positive Mental Images is one goal of all teachers who are consciously choosing their words to maximize the accuracy of the ideas they are communicating. Here's an example to illustrate this point; it includes two mental pictures that should be adjusted from negative to positive images. Suppose a teacher says:

> "Don't make a lot of mistakes, or you'll fail the test!"

What images are being created in the mind of the student? Obviously, mistakes and failure are being mentally highlighted, probably not the images the teacher was intending to create. Instead, the teacher might have said:

> "Be sure to get as many correct as possible, so you can receive an excellent score on this test."

With these words the teacher is focusing the students' minds in a more productive direction.

Some Examples of Positive Mental Images

Consider each example shown here. If spoken as originally shown, each statement may have some unintended, potentially negative results. How could each statement be rephrased so that the actual message has a better chance of registering in the mind of the listener? Remember, there are an infinite variety of possible solutions, and you should consider the ones given here merely as *options*.

Example 1:   "Don't look over there."

Possible problem? Where do a student's eyes immediately turn? Right to where the teacher does not what them to look. Reword this to:

> "Look here" or "Keep your attention focused in this direction."

Example 2:   "Try not to be late to class."

Possible problem? These words are creating a mental picture of being late, which may be exactly what happens. Reword this sentence to:

> "Be on time" or "Be prompt" or "Be early."

Example 3:   "Be careful during recess. We don't want sprained ankles or broken bones."

Possible problem? Students' attention is now firmly focused on spraining their ankles of breaking their bones! Their attention should be on safety. Reword this to:

> "Play safe" or "Be safe, healthy, and whole" or "Take care of yourself."

Example 4: "Please complete this assessment without looking at your notes, the board at the front of the room, or at anyone else's paper."

Possible problem? Now there are three things the students are thinking about, any of which may be strong enough to distract them. Suddenly they find their eyes wandering over to the paper nearest them, or discover that they are fixated on peeking at their notes. Keep their focus on what is most important. Three options include:

"Please complete this assessment with only the information in your head."

"Keep your attention on your paper as you complete this assessment."

"Keep your eyes on your own paper at all times."

Example 5: "Be aware of the danger of losing your patience."

Possible problem? This statement implies that most of us tend to lose our patience. To make matter worse, it focuses students' attention directly on the *danger* of losing their patience, a negative approach. Instead, say:

"Stay patient" or "Maintain your cool at all times."

Example 6: "At no time during an emergency should you allow panic and emotions to overwhelm you."

Isn't this is a wonderful statement! Look at all those negatives carefully compressed into a single sentence. Scary. Instead say:

"Stay calm at all times" or "In an emergency, remain calm and focused."

Example 7: "Avoid exiting this room by that door because you might set off the fire alarm."

Possible problem? Actually, there are two interconnected problems in this statement. The obvious one is that these words prompt an awareness of the fire alarm. However, the second issue is that, in some circumstances, a teacher must point out something that is potentially negative. If it is imperative to do so, the solution is to create a two-part communication in which the second portion is the positive image. The second image will be the one that stays with students the longest. In this case, the teacher might say:

"Everyone look toward this door. It is connected to the fire alarm, and should only be used in an emergency. Now, would everyone please point toward this other door. This is the door we will be using at all other times."

Using these words, students are now fully aware of the fire alarm connected to the first door. They have also been shown a clear image of the door to be used during normal operations. Because the more important image came second, it will tend to remain the longest in the students' minds.

These examples illustrate alternate wordings for communicating the ideas in a more positive format. Using this approach, students should now have an image in their minds that guides their behavior in the desired direction more effectively.

From the Opposite Direction

To complete this discussion, here's a unique example of how to incorporate this idea in the classroom. A science biology teacher once told me that he uses the same idea, but *in reverse*. Here's how he does it. On one of the days when students are going to be studying dissection, he sets the materials out in advance. For this lesson, they arrive at the classroom and find placed on their lab tables a real pig's heart. One of the first statements the teacher makes is:

> "It's very important that you *don't* squeeze the pig's heart."

Of course, as he expects, very soon one of the students (not surprisingly, it's usually a male) squeezes the pig's heart, and the blood squirts out all over everything. When this happens, the teacher is not upset. In fact, he calmly responds by saying:

> "What you've just done is shown the rest of us how a heart works. When it contracts it forces the blood out and into the circulatory system. Thank you for that very visual demonstration. Now let's all open one up and take a closer look at how it operates."

With that as an introduction, the lesson in dissecting a pig's heart has officially begun. The teacher's clever reverse use of the idea of mental images has served to begin the class with a bit of a surprise, and the students are now fully focused on the key points of the lesson.

QUESTION/CLARIFY/QUESTION

Suppose a teacher is giving a group of students a topic to discuss for a few minutes in a small group. In this situation, there is a questioning format the teacher can use to increase the level of involvement by students. Although it happens quite quickly, the sequence comprises three very distinct phases:

First:

Ask the general question.

↓

Second:

Provide details that clarify the question.

↓

Third:

Repeat the original question.

Each component plays an important part in achieving the desired result. In the first phase of the sequence, the question is stated clearly to allow students to see the overall picture. In the second phase, details are provided that will help students understand the type of responses that are expected. Finally, the original question is repeated, to serve as a springboard for the group to jump into the general discussion.

Clarification through Examples

Once you begin to use this idea on a consistent basis, it will quickly become apparent how the use of this structure can assist your students to both (1) rapidly engage in the conversation, and (2) be able to generate answers that respond to your intended line of instruction. Personally, I apply this sequence constantly in the in-service seminars I present for teachers. To illustrate the use of this concept in practice, here are three common situations from those programs in which this idea is utilized.

Example 1:   Effective Directions

One component of these seminars is a section focusing on giving effective directions, as discussed in Chapter 5. To introduce the topic, I first ask the teachers to engage in several brief activities that require me to give plenty of directions. At the end of this sequence they form small discussion groups, and are asked a question. Several years ago I phrased the question this way:

> "What do you notice about the way I give directions?"

Groups would spend a few minutes discussing the answers to this question. Then they were asked to share with the large group some of the answers they had generated. The purpose of the follow-up discussion was to focus on some specifics of giving effective directions such as word choice, vocal tonality, and the use of supporting body language. While many of the answers the students gave did match up with these specifics, others did not. Some of these responses that did not match expectations were:

- "They're pretty good, actually."
- "You do them very well!"
- "You are always nice."
- "I like them!"

These answers did nothing to move the conversation along the direction I had intended. In fact, they tended to distract from the key points, and time was wasted as these misguided comments were gently weeded out. Finally I narrowed their responses down to the useful ones and was able to proceed toward the desired outcomes. Over time, however, it became clear to me that it wasn't so much that their *responses* were incorrect. Rather, the issue was that the *question I had posed to the groups had not been specific enough to guide them in the intended direction.* At this point I made some changes in how I asked the question. Now teachers heard:

> "What do you notice about the way I give directions? For example you might consider my choice of words. Or is there something about my tone of voice that you've noticed that stands out? Or how have you seen me use my hands? OK, begin!"

This way of asking the question immediately produced significantly better results. Now the teachers tended to provide responses that were more specific and on target. At the same time I was getting better results; however, another issue emerged. In the above example, the original question is followed by three clarifying statements. It became apparent that some groups, while certainly having a much improved sense of what I was after, become stuck on the *last clarifying statement* that I had made. In this case, they became locked in a conversation about body language, and failed to consider equally other areas of the directions. In fact, it became apparent that the further away from the original question the word *begin* was placed, the longer it took the teachers to jump into the general discussion. The value of repeating the original question now became apparent. When I understood this, the instruction sequence had reached its final form. Currently, at this point in the seminar, I phrase the question the following way:

> "What do you notice about the way I give directions? For example, you might consider my choice of words. Or is there something about my tone of voice that you've noticed that stands out? Or how have you seen me use my hands? Discuss with your group what you've noticed so far in this program about the way I give directions. OK, begin!"

With the question repeated at the end, students jumped immediately into the discussion. Now all three phases of the instruction were being addressed. First, there was a statement of the overall question, next there were clarifying statements, and, finally, a paraphrased form of the original question was repeated.

Example 2:   Learning about State Changes

In Chapter 3 of this book there is a discussion on the instructional principle of the Crest of the Wave. This includes the topic of "State Changes." State changes are adjustments in modality from one section of instruction to another, such as changing from listening to a lecture to engaging in a small group discussion. When I cover this idea in in-service programs, it is clarified with a brief introduction to the concept, followed by a small group discussion. We are approximately an hour into our day, and I intend to ask the teachers a question something along this line:

> "What state changes have you noticed so far in the program today?"

But, the idea of state changes has only briefly been introduced to this audience. Therefore, it is understandable that their grasp of the concept is limited. To facilitate the conversation, I need to provide a few examples of some state changes that have been used in the opening hour of the program. And, I need to end with a paraphrased version of the initial question. Putting it all together, looks like this:

> "What state changes have you noticed so far in the program today? For example, when you stood up and introduced yourself to other people, that was a state change. When you took your books and moved to a new seat, that was another state change. The music provided a state change. And when I told the story about the old man and the gems, that was an example of a different type of state change, a more subtle one. Now, in your groups, see how many other state changes you can remember. Begin."

Again, notice that the first sentence is the overall question. It is followed by several clarifying examples, and concludes with a paraphrase of the original question. In practice, these examples provided sufficient clarity, allowing the groups to engage in a meaningful conversation regarding state changes. In cases where the students are encountering a concept for the first time, it is helpful to provide them with several very specific examples to further their understanding and promote a more useful discussion.

Example 3: How long can you pay attention?

This final example considers a related issue in this kind of situation. However, it uses the *Question/Clarify/Question* sequence to achieve a slightly different purpose. Another topic addressed in these seminars is how long students are able to pay attention to a teacher when they are listening to a lecture. Before explaining the results of several studies that relate to this issue, I find it useful to get the teachers to talk among themselves about how long they personally can pay attention in this kind of situation. The question I originally used in these circumstances was:

> "Discuss with someone near you how long you can pay attention when someone is lecturing at you."

While they were generally able to respond to this question quite well, a consistent theme often emerged in their responses.

> "It's always different—it depends on the situation!"

This, of course, is the truth. Our ability to pay attention certainly *does* depend on such factors as the teacher's presentational skills, the topic, and our internal motivation, to name just a few. However, while this was a topic that was going to be addressed later in the program, at this point the goal was simply to get a very general response. In order to achieve this, it was necessary to change the way the question was phrased. Eventually I changed it to:

> "Discuss with someone near you how long you can pay attention when someone is lecturing at you. While the truth is that many factors will play a

determining role in our ability to pay attention, for right now just consider this question on a broad basis. Later we'll look closer at some of these things, but for now, *in general*, how long can you pay attention?"

Acknowledging that complexity was an issue in advance allowed the teachers to avoid getting stuck on it, and they were able to stay focused on the question in general. As with this example, in some cases you may be able to anticipate that the audience could get stuck on a particular answer that will interfere with the upcoming conversation. Get ahead of the game by letting them know the issue will be addressed at a later point in the class so they can remain focused on the question that is posed to them at that time.

In Summary

The *Question/Clarify/Question* format is a useful sequence when giving groups directions for a discussion. It can also be changed slightly to be effective in other, related instructional moments. Remember that it usually works best when it is done in a concise manner. If the directions become too wordy, the original intention has been defeated. Use as few words as possible and move the group directly into the discussion.

SARCASM: DIVIDING RESPONSES

The situation: A teacher is leading a class in which a vocal minority tend to dominate by frequently making sarcastic, off-the-wall remarks. Every time the group is given an opportunity to share their thoughts these individuals make distracting, off-purpose comments. At first the teacher laughs along with the rest of the group, hoping it will cease as the class continues. When this proves not to be the case, the teacher tries to ignore this pattern of behavior, but to no avail. Finally, it detracts sufficiently from what is being taught, and the teacher realizes that something must be done about the situation.

Almost anyone who has stood in front of a classroom has encountered situations like this to some degree. There are some students who simply seem to find great joy in bringing attention to themselves by making fun of the topic, each other, or even the teacher. In the primary and secondary school years these individuals are known as the class clowns. As teachers, what can we do to limit the distraction caused by these individuals? There are many possible ways to curb this behavior, from addressing the situation in class to speaking to those students in private and asking for their help in making the class a success. However, I can't think of any strategy, including the one discussed here, that has been shown to be completely effective in every situation. The best idea is to have as many choices available as possible, and to keep trying them until something works.

There is one choice, however, that has not been mentioned in many of the source books on classroom management (that I am aware of). It is highlighted here because of its effectiveness as well as its applicability to groups of all ages. It is a suggestion that teachers might want to add to their tool kit in case they encounter a similar situation at some point in the future. However, as previously discussed, keep in mind that all of the suggestions in this book are to a large degree dependent on the teacher's skill in facilitating the particular situation.

The Suggestion

It's quite simple. Give those jokesters a forum in which to play. Focus their energy, while acknowledging the humor they bring to the situation. Here is a specific strategy that can do all of that. Suppose it is early in the class, and the teacher quickly realizes that there are some sarcastic members in the audience. At the next opportunity for group responses, the teacher might say something along these lines:

> "Why do you think we include a section on this particular topic in this course? Discuss this with your neighbor. See if you can generate at least three possibilities. However, at least one of these *must be a sarcastic response*!"

Then, when the time has come for the small groups to share their thoughts with the whole class, you begin by asking for sarcastic responses only. After these have been enjoyed by everyone, you state:

> "Those were great. Thanks. Now, let's move to the other point of view. In a more serious vein, why do you think we might include this topic in this course?"

Now the group can sense a clear shift in what is expected. Indirectly, although quite clearly, the teacher has identified the sarcastic responses as having had an appropriate time and place, while having set some parameters to limit their use. It has been clearly established that, if someone makes a sarcastic response at this point, it would be obvious to everyone that this is not the appropriate time. In a subtle manner, peer pressure has stepped in to assist the teacher in keeping the group focused in the appropriate direction.

Behind the Scenes

Offering students the opportunity to express their humorous, sarcastic, off-beat responses achieves several objectives simultaneously. First, it takes the energy away from the potentially disruptive nature of the remarks, given that they can no longer be disruptive if they are exactly what the teacher is seeking! Secondly, because humor now has the official "stamp of approval" at certain times, these dispensers of sarcasm often no longer find the same joy in it as they did before. It has been legitimized. Oddly enough, many will stop making those comments all together.

Some teachers may consider this idea a waste of precious classroom time. Yet, think about it more closely. If you were going to have to spend much of your energy all day trying to keep the class focused in a particular direction anyway, then this strategy may actually reduce the overall amount of time devoted to dealing with these distractions. Indeed, handled correctly it can provide light, relaxed moments that further enhance the learning environment due to their contrast with the more serious moments.

A Related Idea

A variation on this theme is the idea of *reversing* what students are normally expecting. In speech classes, for example, students are usually required to give the best speech possible. While this is perfectly acceptable most of the time, occasionally it can become much more stressful, because they are always being asked to do it the "right" way. For a change of pace, what if they were directed to give the most *awful* speech possible?

For those groups who have a natural inclination toward humor and sarcasm, give them the chance to role play in *reverse*. What would be the exact opposite of the "correct" speech? Students who are natural hams will instantly dive into such roles. And while everyone is laughing and enjoying themselves, they are actually reinforcing their learning, because they are becoming extremely aware of what strategies they are *not* supposed to use. When it is their turn, if they find themselves doing some of those incorrect behaviors, they will quickly realize it and be able to correct their actions.

In Summary

Humor is not necessarily a negative quality. Certainly most teachers could think of a worse situation to be involved in, such as working with a bored, indifferent, or even an outright hostile class. Individuals who bring humor to a group can be highly valued if their energy is focused in an appropriate direction. Remember that people who are "quick-witted" are often quite intelligent, and, if guided correctly, have the potential of becoming a powerful, positive part of any learning situation. Instead of attempting to shut them down, consider using this strategy, or others, to guide their humor so it can be acknowledged for the positive energy it brings. Doing this will also clearly delineate the times when humor is *not* the appropriate choice.

SPECIFICITY

When information is communicated, it is interesting to note how much of it is *assumed* to be understood by the student. Frequently, *mis*communication is merely the result of a teacher either using a "generality" or making the assumption that the student understands. For a moment, consider a situation at home. Suppose parents want their child to go bed. They could say:

"Go to bed soon."

Experienced parents probably caught the potential problem right away. Imagine the chaos that would ensue as the child create his or her own definition of what *soon* means. For improved clarity, the parent might say:

"You have five minutes left until 8:30, which is your bedtime. At that time you need to be in bed, under the sheets, with the lights turned off."

Anyone who has children knows the difference in the result of these two communications. The same approach is effective in the classroom. For example, a teacher might say:

> "Study hard tonight."

Students may indeed study hard, *if they already know what they are supposed to be studying*. However, if the teacher wants students to pay particular attention to certain aspects of the topic, she might more effectively say:

> "Study Chapter 5 tonight. Concentrate specifically on knowing the names of the people involved, and why they are important."

Now the students more clearly understand what is expected of them, and can focus their energy on the appropriate topic.

Goals

Goals are achieved more rapidly through the use of specific language. With a specific, clear image, the brain can begin to "bring that picture into reality." For example, if a teacher wanted to encourage a student to achieve a certain level of excellence, a more general statement might be:

> "Pay close attention so you can do well on the exam tomorrow."

As with the previous examples, this ends up being too general to produce effective results. What does the teacher mean by the words *do well*? A clearly identifiable goal enables the student to focus specifically on the outcomes and expectations of the teacher:

> "Excellence in this class is measured by getting 96 percent of the questions correct on the exam tomorrow. Every one of you can achieve this objective."

Compliments and Criticisms

When teachers give feedback to a student, there is a tendency to generalize the information. Specifics make feedback much more *useful* to the person receiving it. For example, a teacher acknowledging someone for giving an excellent presentation could simply say:

> "Very well done. I liked it!"

However, that kind of remark lacks specificity. How does someone respond to it? Instead, this communication could be phrased:

"Excellent presentation. I enjoyed your use of metaphor and the interaction you generated with the audience."

The same situation also applies to giving criticism to a person. For example, suppose the teacher observed a presentation that was not well done and was required to provide some feedback to the presenter. It would be ineffective to say:

"That wasn't the best you've ever done."

In fact, comments like this are possibly the most dangerous kind of feedback, because they leave the communication open to a great deal of misinterpretation. What wasn't good? Didn't the teacher like any of it? It's easy to see how people get defensive when put in this position. Feedback that is highly specific allows listeners to know exactly what wasn't done well, so they can avoid overgeneralizing. Here the teacher might have said:

"I felt that the visual aids were hard to see, and the presentation could have covered more details of the project."

Detail allows the listener to see areas for improvement, while not feeling that the entire presentation was a disaster.

Some Examples of Specificity

Consider each example shown below. If spoken as originally shown, the statement might not create the intended results. What are some of the potential problems with each statement, and how could it be rephrased so that the actual message has a better chance of being accurately interpreted by the listener? Remember that there are an infinite variety of possible solutions, and you should consider the ones given here as merely *options*.

Example 1: "See me after school."

Possible problem? Where? When? None of these important details are mentioned. Instead, be specific by saying:

"Meet me at 3:30 at my desk" or "Let's meet in the library at 4:30 p.m."

Example 2: "Stop fooling around."

Possible problem? There are two aspects of this communication that are unclear. What is meant by "fooling around," and what behavior is expected of the students? You could add specificity to both aspects of this statement by saying:

"Please stop talking and return to completing your worksheet" or "Please stop throwing your pens and return to working on the assignment."

Example 3: "You should try to be more positive."

Possible problem? What behavior would the teacher accept as being "more positive"? What behavior should be eliminated? A more precise communication might be:

> "Sit up and walk tall and you'll feel better" or "I would appreciate it if occasionally you'd thank me for what I've done.

Example 4: "My goal this year is to be more supportive of other students."

Possible problem? What does the word *supportive* mean to this student? What actions or behaviors would define the quality of being more supportive? A clearer definition of the word requires behavioral distinctions. Perhaps this person might say:

> "Three times a day I'm going to thank people for things they've done" or "I'm going to offer help to someone at least once a day."

Example 5: "I just want to say that you kids are so awesome."

Possible problem? What are these students doing that is so awesome? Specificity around the behaviors that generated this feeling adds value to the compliment. Use:

> "Thank you for coming here everyday this week to help us" or "I've really appreciated the way each person here has given so much of their time and energy to make this project successful."

Example 6: "Great job, everybody!"

Possible problem? What job did they do so well? What were the details that led to the overall success of the job? Add these details by saying:

> "As a team we've achieved more success because we've paid attention to the details, we've stuck with the deadliness, and we've been willing to communicate" or "This project only succeeded because everyone completed their individual part."

Example 7: "I don't think you handled that drama meeting very well."

Possible problem? What was it about the meeting that didn't go well? Given this broad statement, it would be easy to see how someone could get defensive. Clearly stating which elements of the meeting were not handled successfully would give the student receiving the feedback something specific on which to focus improvement, such as saying:

> "I felt there was too much talking and it might have been better for this topic if you had used handouts" or "People seemed to be repeating themselves, and as the student leader it might have been better if you had found a way to keep them on track."

In Summary

Conversations between teachers and students can easily go wrong. The best way to insure clear communication is to use very specific language that makes it easy for both people to understand the intent of the interaction. Specificity provides clarity.

SPECIFY THE RESPONSE

The teacher is about to ask a question of the class. However, he has noticed that when he has posed other questions to the group during the past hour, few students have been responsive. Why can he not get a greater level of response, even to some of his simpler questions?

Certainly, there may be many reasons for students failing to respond to questions. The earlier section on "Getting Responses" examined one option for handling this kind of situation. This section explores another, very specific reason why there may be hesitation in responses from students. If left unchecked, this particular issue can quickly build into an unnecessary, limiting factor in the classroom. If, however, these moments are facilitated appropriately by the teacher, they can actually become an essential building block in the success of the learning process.

Clarifying: The First Example

To understand some potential hazards in this situation, examine in detail a single student's response to a seemingly simple question. Suppose the class is asked:

"How many of you have been to Mexico?"

It appears to be a straightforward question, seeking a simple answer. However, is responding to this question really so simple? Consider the decision-making process the students must go through before making a response. First, they must decide if they have been to Mexico. Assuming they have been there, they are now faced with a critical decision. *In what manner are they supposed to respond?* Should they raise their hand? Should they nod their head? Should they speak out loud? Or should they do something entirely different, such as stand up? But the words the teacher used gave no clue as to the appropriate manner of response he expects, so it is left to each individual student to guess at what response the teacher is seeking.

Forcing students to play a guessing game in the classroom is a dangerous choice. As they consider their options, they know that one response may be right, while another may be wrong. When students sense they are running the risk of doing something incorrect, their willingness to engage is immediately reduced. The threat factor has been introduced into the situation; the fear of looking bad in front of others has reared its ugly head. It's important to note that most teachers never *intend* to bring these issues into the learning environment. They are simply a by-product of a particular form of question posed to the class.

As in the situation described above, when the type of response that is desired is unclear, what frequently happens is that the students who have been to Mexico will tentatively raise a hand, perhaps only halfway. They choose this option of how to respond because raising a hand in the classroom is the most common form of response. At the same time they are careful to avoid committing too strongly to a particular course of action, because it might be wrong. If the teacher were looking for people to answer out loud, then the one person who chose to raise a hand may look foolish. The uncertainty of how to respond results in a tentative response. In this particular case, the teacher might have avoided potential confusion and unnecessary complications by rephrasing the question:

"*Raise your hand* if you have been to Mexico."

With this slight change in the language of the question, the teacher has specified the desired response. The guessing game has been eliminated. Now everyone is clear what is being asked of them, and how they are expected to respond. Those who have been to Mexico can respond easily and with confidence. They might be even more inclined to respond if the teacher were also to raise a hand, because now students are seeing the desired behavior clearly modeled.

The Second Example

The class was using a sixty-page workbook. The teacher requested that the students turn to the top of page twenty-seven in their manuals. Then he said:

"Did you all find that? Great, let's continue."

What response was being sought by the teacher to verify that they had all found the proper page? Apparently, none. Unless someone were comfortable enough to quickly raise their hand, or to ask the teacher to pause for a moment, the class was going to continue forward regardless of whether everyone was ready or not. The danger here is that the teacher may proceed with the information, while several students are still finding the right place in their workbooks. While they are continuing to locate the appropriate page, they will not hear what the teacher is saying. They may have missed any important comments or instructions from the teacher, and a potentially vital link in the learning process may have been missed.

This situation highlights an important, although rarely mentioned, point about effective teaching. Far too frequently, teachers unconsciously operate in a vacuum as to how well their class is following along with the instructions. They *assume* that students are right there with them, because no one is protesting the pace of the instruction. However, on closer examination, those teachers weren't actually checking in with their students. In reality, they were asking a rhetorical question, never really expecting an answer.

Students are quick to pick up on whether the teacher actually does want an answer to a question. They will quickly adapt to the teacher's approach, for better or for worse. Specifying the response allows teachers to more closely monitor what is *actually* occurring in the classroom, and make the correct decisions based on their student's reactions. It also lets the students know that a response is genuinely wanted.

Given this discussion, several flaws should be apparent in the original form of the question used in the example. Instead, this teacher might have rephrased his question the following way:

"If you have found the second paragraph of page 27, please nod your head."

Presented this way, the teacher can watch the audience and wait until all students have nodded their heads. Now he is deciding when to proceed with the next instruction based on solid, visual feedback. When the situation has been handled in this manner, all students should be ready when the next instruction is introduced.

The Third Example

Even when simply asking students to raise their hands, by specifying the response teachers are asking students to be public. This can create a potentially negative situation. For example, what might the potential problem be with asking a group of students the following question:

"If you have not yet completed the assignment, please raise your hand."

Presented this way, those who are still working on the assignment must now raise their hands and, in a manner of speaking, "publicly confess" that they are slower than other students in the room! This puts them in a situation where they may feel embarrassed. Given this potential for public humiliation, some students who are still working may decide not to raise their hand. Now the teacher is making decisions based on incomplete information.

The key is to *focus on the positive*. For example, the statement used in this example could simply be rephrased as:

"If you have completed the assignment, please raise your hand."

Now the students responding will be those who are finished. From this statement, the teacher can still effectively extrapolate the necessary information of knowing how much more time to give the class, without running the risk of embarrassing those who are still hard at work.

Simply Stated

Specify the Response refers to situations in which the audience is being asked a question. In these circumstances, teachers should be certain to clearly specify how they are expecting the audience to respond. Knowing what they are expected to do will allow students to feel more comfortable with their interactions with the teacher. Repeated use of this technique will generate a heightened sense of security within the classroom, and may even lead to increased levels of participation by "less confident" members of the audience.

Further Examples

As stated previously, asking students to raise their hand is only one method of specifying the response. The following are some comparisons between statements that lack a specific response, and some options for how these statements might be rephrased. Note that there is no limit to the number of possible rephrasing options, and these examples should be considered as merely a starting point.

NO SPECIFIC RESPONSE	AN OPTION FOR REPHRASING
"Is everyone ready?"	"Smile if you're ready."
"Have you got the right page?"	"Nod if you're on page 16."
"Did you have a good lunch?"	"Hold your pen up and wiggle it if you had a great lunch!"
"Am I right?"	"If you agree with me on this, raise one pinky."
"Does this make sense?"	"If this concept makes sense to you, give me a thumbs up."
"Who's finished?"	"If you're finished, turn your paper over."
"Does everyone have the handout?"	"Hold up the handout if you have received one."
"Are there any questions?"	"Those of you who have a question, please come to the board and write it down."

Several of these options may seem silly to some more traditional teachers, and, given the environment in which they currently teach, they may be entirely correct. You are always responsible for creating options that fit your context, your audience, and your personality. However, while continuing to stay appropriate, keep in mind the value of finding unusual responses to ask for from your students. Creative choices can often keep the atmosphere of the room light and relaxed. This increase in the positive atmosphere in the learning environment has frequently proven to be useful to learning for students of all ages. Some choices can even function as state changes, such as asking students to close their eyes and relax when they have finished reading an article. Even in more serious, technical classes, specifying the response by asking students to look up if they have completed an assignment may be sufficient to achieve the desired outcome.

In Summary

At first glance, this idea may seem simple enough. But being simple to understand in a theoretical sense does not always equal being easy to master in a practical sense. For example, stopping smoking is very simple: Don't put the cigarette in your mouth! Simple, but by no means easy for serious smokers. Hopefully, this concept has been explained in a simple, clear-cut manner, though it may take time to fully master it in the classroom. Teachers who have considerable experience may find it especially challenging to create new speech patterns when posing questions to the audience. However, the benefit of consistently specifying the response should prove well worth the effort to those who spend the time consciously learning this skill.

Remember that a teacher does not *always* have to specify the response. The most obvious situation is one in which both the students and the teacher inherently understand what is expected, such as after several weeks have passed at the beginning of the school year. If the pattern has been set of raising a hand, students will already understand this, and it does not need to be repeated. Specifying the response may be most important early in the establishment of the dynamics of the relationship between teacher and students. The earlier this pattern of interaction is introduced and reinforced, the greater the potential for maximum results over the long run.

As with many of the concepts discussed in this chapter, there is often a great deal more involved than a single discussion can cover. With regard to the general issue of getting responses from the audience, some additional factors might include how often the teacher has asked the group questions, whether those responding might be expected to *do* something if they raise their hand, the level of trust the students have with the teacher, or even whether the audience knows the correct response to the question. This section is intended only to highlight some of the major issues related to the concept of Specify the Response, and to provide some options that might be helpful. As you begin to use it, continue to explore how to develop the idea within your own teaching style.

SUGGEST THE EXPERIENCE

The teacher walks to the front of the high school classroom. He is enthusiastic, energetic, and vibrant. He smiles at the students and says:

"You're going to have such fun today!"

While this statement may seem innocent enough on the surface, to the careful observer it is fraught with dangerous assumptions. For example, what does the word *fun* imply in this context? Do he and the students even share a common definition of that word? If not, is he referring to *his* definition of fun, or what *they* think might be fun? And how does he know this will be something they will *all* experience, each and every one of them? In making this statement, the teacher has actually shared with the students what *he believes* they will experience today. It's terrific that he feels this way, but the words he has chosen may end up working against what he hopes will happen.

The potential problem lies in the teacher placing his expectations on the students. They have been given something to push back against. Suppose a student finds that she is not enjoying the experience. She may think back to this statement. Obviously, he didn't know what he was talking about. If he doesn't know what he is talking about in this situation, what else is he just pretending to know? The teacher's credibility may begin to diminish in the eyes of this student.

Despite his obvious feelings regarding the day ahead of them, it might be more effective if he altered the wording of his statement slightly. Instead of *telling* the students what they will feel, he might instead *suggest the experience*. This allows them the freedom to create their own responses to the event. In this case, he might have said:

> "Today's class could turn out to be one the most enjoyable experiences you've had in a long time."

This statement is less overtly forceful than the original one. It may also serve a higher purpose in the long run by planting a suggestion as to how the students *might* view the impending experience. In many cases it's better to simply sow the seeds of what could happen, rather than exert pressure on the students to meet a stated expectation. Students are now invited to create their own reaction to the experience, possibly influenced in a positive direction by the teacher's words. From the lofty perch of possibility comes a much broader view of the world.

Clarification

Few people truly enjoy being told what to do, how they should feel, or what they will experience. When a solid wall is pushed toward us, the instinctive reaction is to push back against it. In learning situations there are many opportunities to present information in a format that *suggests* rather than *tells*. This approach allows students to have a personal investment in their reactions, thoughts, and feelings regarding the topic or experience. When students are given the chance to be mentally involved, chances for long-term retention of the information are significantly increased (Cove & Cove 1996; Cusco 1990; Jensen 1996).

Consider, for a moment, a farmer growing a crop of corn. The farmer cannot *force* the seeds to grow into mature plants. He cannot tell them how to develop, or how rapidly they can ripen. Instead, he carefully places them in the fertile soil. With sufficient nourishment and proper care, over time he will be rewarded with a bountiful harvest. When attempting to nurture concepts, feelings, and beliefs in students, the same process applies. Ideas can rarely be forced on them. Instead, they need to be "planted," offered as suggestions. Mental nourishment then comes in the form of examples, further clarification, and personal investigation on their own. This should ultimately lead to an understanding of how the ideas might work for the students. When they experience it on a personal basis, it will be a concept they can fully believe in and make a part of themselves. As teachers, this is our ultimate reward, the crop we seek to reap from the expenditure of our efforts in planting the seeds of information.

Teachers are frequently so certain of the validity of an idea, the applicability of a concept, or the value of an experience, that they push their views onto their students. Yet, if something is presented as an absolute truth, students might reject it entirely if they can come up just with one or two situations in which it doesn't apply. When presenting value judgments, it may be useful to remember they are simply our own thoughts and beliefs. If instead they are presented as *suggestions*, as opportunities to explore, or possibilities to investigate, the door to student ownership remains open. Teachers might be wise to present their entirely valid opinions in the form of recommendations for the purpose of communicating with greater influence and impact.

Consistent with this discussion is the idea that even this concept itself is meant to be taken as merely a suggestion for teachers to consider. In some situations they may believe it is better to tell students what they will experience, in the belief it will begin to guide them into a useful mind-set, a valuable framework for viewing the experience. In some cases, that can be an entirely correct choice. For example, suppose the students were developing their skills in the arena of computer software development. The teacher in this situation might say:

> "If you can successfully pass this course, your opportunities for finding a high-paying job will greatly increase."

The intention behind this statement is to provide students with an incentive to learn the material. In most cases, it should more than adequately serve that function.

However, even in this case there may be a hidden danger. What if a student does pass the course, but doesn't actually locate a high-paying position? Certainly the teacher was correct in *stating* that opportunities will have increased. Yet that person may perceive his or her lack of success in the job market as evidence that the assertion was false. When making any statements that are presented in the *tell* mode, teachers might be wise to be wary of the potential backlash.

Examples

Here are some pairs of sentences that illustrate how an idea stated in the *tell* format might be altered into the *suggest* format.

Tell   "You'll find this to be an incredibly useful tool."

Suggest   "You may find this to be a useful tool in certain situations."

Tell   "This activity will really wake you up."

Suggest   "This activity might allow your body to feel more energized."

Tell   "These ideas will be very valuable to you when you begin teaching."

Suggest "You may find these ideas valuable to you when you begin teaching."

Tell   "This is the most important idea in the entire course."

Suggest "You may find this to be one of the most important ideas in the entire course."

Tell   "This is the best way to approach serious communication problems."

Suggest "This may be one more useful ways of approaching some serious communication problems.

Tell   "This is the single most powerful model of effective instruction."

Suggest: "I've personally found this to be one of the most powerful models of effective instruction."

Tell   "Once you master this approach, you'll be able to quickly solve any problem that's in any way similar."

Suggest "Once you master this approach, you might have a better idea of how to approach similar problems."

The second line in each of these examples is only one of many ways in which the original statement could be changed to a suggestion.

Personal Word Choices

Readers may have noticed that words such as *may, might, could, perhaps,* and *consider* are woven throughout the text of this book (Poznar 1995). This is due to my personal alignment and agreement with the concept discussed in this section. Despite my strong feelings about the validity of the ideas presented here, my experiences with effective instruction and those of the readers will not always match perfectly. Therefore, it is useful to include these types of words, allowing each teacher to decide which aspects of the discussions might prove useful to them, given the unique parameters of their circumstances.

In Summary

Suggestions allow students to decide for themselves what they will take away from their experiences, while still helping create a perspective through which to view the event. Presenting ideas as possibilities acknowledges students as unique individuals, bringing with them their own valuable background, knowledge, and insights. The intention of *suggesting the experience* is to create an enhanced sense of personal involvement, leading to deeper levels of understanding and increased retention. Where possible, the suggestion is to . . . suggest!

VOCAL ITALICS

The student was in the final months of a high school honors class on economics. She had a unique opportunity to attend a lecture on international economics in the European Community presented by a prominent speaker from an Ivy League school. Given the nature of her current class and its relevance to the lecture topic, she was looking forward to the presentation with considerable interest. Of the eighty students present, most were quite interested in the subject, although none could have been called economic specialists. During the course of the presentation, the speaker naturally used a specialized nomenclature unique to that field of study.

Fortunately, due to her recent studies, the student was familiar with the majority of the terms the speaker used during his lecture. However, there were also a number of expressions and phrases that emerged during the course of the presentation that were entirely new to her. As she encountered each new word, she observed an interesting phenomenon. She seemed to experience a "mental pause" as she sorted through her knowledge to see if she had any understanding of the word. When her attention returned to the presentation, she found she had missed the next few words, or even entire sentences. These gaps in her understanding became disconcerting: They were like holes in a dam. The more holes, the more knowledge that leaked through, and at an ever-increasing pace.

The session lasted slightly over two hours. As she left the room, she mentally reviewed the lecture. While she certainly never expected to be able to recall *all* of the material presented, she was quite disappointed at how few important details she could bring to mind right them. If this was true even in the first few moments following the presentation, in spite of the careful notes she had written, what would her memory be like tomorrow? Or within a week?

The reason this had happened was clear. Those moments when she had encountered a new term—*but had not been given time to process it and make meaning for herself*—had significantly decreased her overall ability to recall the information. Even with her strong internal motivation to learn the content of the presentation, her learning had been significantly hindered by the gaps in her knowledge that were the result of her mental pauses. And if she, as an honors student, had experienced this phenomenon, what about other students who hadn't had the information from her class as background information to rely on? How much of the presentation would they be able to remember the next day? And if they couldn't remember any of the information, then why had they wasted their time?

Clarification

The goal of most teachers is quite simple. We want students to remember the material we've presented. Otherwise, why teach it? The question then becomes: How can teachers allow students to mentally process new terms and ideas at the moment they are introduced, and focus their attention on key concepts, so that at the conclusion of a given presentation the students have maximized their ability to recall the material?

In an educational setting, students will frequently encounter new terms, phrases, and ideas as they navigate the "uncharted waters" of the topic under discussion. When this occurs, they will need time to mentally define the terms for themselves and come to a full understanding of them before moving forward to related new thoughts and ideas. This is especially true given that many times a full understanding of the material is dependent on connections *between ideas* that are presented in a sequential manner.

Consider in slow motion the mental sequence of students encountering a new word. They might go through a variety of steps. Initially, of course, they must do a double-check and verify that they don't already know the term. When they realize it is new to them, they may move to comparisons between the sound of the word to other similar sounding words they do know (roots, suffixes, etc.) to see if it may have a related meaning. Failing this, most students will mentally do a quick check, to see if they can extrapolate the meaning of the word based on the *context* within which it was used. When, ultimately, no connections are made, most students will return their attention to the presentation and hope that the meaning becomes apparent later.

The fact is that *those steps take time*. And, during the time in which students are focusing their attention on making meaning out of this word, they are *not* focusing on what the teacher is saying, thus missing words, phrases, or even sentences in the presentation. All of this decreases what students are able to recall at the conclusion of a presentation.

Definition

When a teacher either (1) introduces a new word, or (2) needs to use a term that may be unfamiliar to a majority of the audience, it is helpful to make that word stand out in some way in the student's hearing. This process is referred to as applying "vocal italics" to the word, phrase, or expression.

From the Written Word to the Spoken Word

"Vocal italics" is drawn from a similar concept in relation to written words. Suppose an author wants a particular word or phrase to stand out to the reader's eye within a given sentence or paragraph. The author can choose from a variety of options as to how to highlight this expression. While perhaps the primary method in written work is the use of *italics* (as has been done throughout this book) there are many other options, including the use of underlining, bold print, quotation marks, or even a change in font type or size.

Similarly, in the verbal delivery of material, a teacher will want certain words to stand out to the student's ear. As with the example of the written material, there are also a variety of options that can be used to achieve this result.

Examples and Options

One simple way to verbally highlight a new term for students is the use of vocal inflection: changing the tone of the voice. This may be most effective if the definition of the word is explicitly stated, or readily apparent given the context in which it is used. For example:

> "Government hunters in Africa are said to be *culling* a herd of elephants when they kill certain ones to bring the size of the herd down to a number that can live on the available food and land."

Even here, it is advisable to place significant vocal emphasis on the word *culling*, allowing students to mentally focus on it, separate it from the other words, and encode it for later recall.

Another option is the use of pausing. When introducing a new word, consider pausing before saying the word, then again after the word. The initial pause informs listeners that the next word requires special attention. The second pause, following the word, allows students time to process it, time to remember both the word and it's definition.

> "When we consider the overall . . . *pedagogy* . . . of a particular teacher, it's necessary to include a discussion of classroom management techniques."

Note that pausing and vocal inflection could be combined together in this example by simply adding vocal emphasis on the word *pedagogy*.

A third option is the use of repetition and clarification

> "This is known as . . . *oxidation*. Oxidation is the process where by oxygen causes some metals to form rust."

Repetition of the key word allows it to become more familiar to the students, enabling them to practice recalling it. Further repetition of the word would be useful to allow them to verify its meaning for themselves.

Thus, the use of inflection, repetition and clarification, and pausing are but a few of the options for placing vocal italics on key expressions. The idea is simple: Place emphasis on the key word while allowing time for the students to process and encode the term and it's definition. Much as in writing, these options may be combined for increased effect. And, also as in writing, there are many ways that the end result can be achieved.

An Ancillary Concept

In a situation similar to those discussed above, even in the course of a brief lecture, a teacher can often isolate the single most important *fact* that students will need to recall at a later point in time. The same concept applies in this situation: The teacher must somehow highlight the key pieces of information so that the students can focus their attention on it, thereby heightening the opportunity for recall.

Further Thoughts regarding Vocal Italics

- It is perhaps critical to note the potential by-product of a student missing the definition of even a single word or phrase. Despite the best efforts of the teacher, students can often perceive a learning situation as a challenging, even threatening environment. Momentum can be created in either a positive or negative direction. Missing the understanding of one, then two, then possibly three key words could quickly initiate a negative mind-set in students concerning their ability to understand the material. An increased level of frustration could create an additional barrier to internal motivation toward learning. On the other hand, students who are clear regarding each key word used in a lecture may feel they are "really understanding this material," and increase their confidence and enthusiasm about participating and engaging in the learning process.
- There's a danger in learning to become aware of using vocal italics in presentations. Simply put, it's the fact that most teachers know their content very well. (Or at least they should!) Therefore, they will naturally be quite familiar with all the terms they intend to use. Which ones, then, will be unfamiliar to their *audiences?* Teachers must create a mental filter for themselves that allows them to analyze which terms, expressions, or ideas their audience might already be familiar with, and which ones will be new to them.
- Have you ever been reading along and suddenly realized that you have no idea what that last paragraph was about? Sometimes this is the result of our mind needing time to mentally process the material it has already absorbed. While the eyes continue to move forward, the mind is busy organizing the material, processing it, making meaning and connections between it and other related concepts you may have read. In a corollary to the concept being discussed here, it is often useful to *pause during reading*, allowing the mind to process the most recent material.

In Summary

The introduction of new terms can be disorienting to students. Teachers need to acknowledge that when words, phrases, or expressions are new to students, a few seconds are necessary for the students to process the information. A well-timed, brief pause may be critical to students' understanding of later information. If the speaker in the opening example of this section had merely paused before and after each new phrase, the honors student would have been able to significantly increase the amount of information she could remember. While it may have slowed down the pace of the presentation, the overall effect would have been to speed up her long-term learning process.

CHAPTER SEVEN

DESIGNING INTERACTIVE LESSONS

> This final chapter contains several strategies for putting together many of the various ideas explained to this point. The goal is to provide a variety of options for how to create an effective lesson plan.

THE FIVE-PART MODEL

There are many concepts and ideas contained in the preceding chapters of this book. Teachers will need to consider how best to weave them together for maximum impact, given the needs of the content and the learning context in which they are teaching. How can the general ideas of State Changes, Open Loops, and Frames, as well as many of the specific applications presented, be put into action in a learning environment? This chapter provides a format for developing a lesson plan that incorporates these essential elements for effective instruction. The following is a general sequence for designing a class.

The Five-Part Model: A Basic Lesson Plan

THE STEP	TIME	PURPOSE
1. Engager	1–5 minutes	Engage the student' attention.
2. Frame	Less than 1 minute	Create an appropriate perspective.
3. Activity	5–30 minutes	Introduce a grounded conceptual awareness
4. Debrief	5–15 minutes	Highlight and discuss major points.
5. Metaphor	2–5 minutes	Relate learning to a broader perspective.

It should be noted that this sequence is only a *model* of how the lesson plan could be designed in practice. The term *model* can be defined as "a preliminary construction that serves as a plan from which a final product is to be made." As such, this sequence for building a lesson plan is entirely open to adjustment given the specific needs of each situation. Times for each step may vary, the sequence itself may be adjusted or, occasionally, some steps may even be eliminated. Teachers should feel free to adapt the general format to meet their specific needs.

A Brief Overview of Each of the Five Steps

Step One: The Engager Stage. The idea of starting each learning session with some form of brief activity, essentially a state change, is based on the discussion from the "Crest of the Wave" principle in Chapter 3. This engager (or "energizer," as it is sometimes called) helps students mentally leave behind potential outside distractions, and bring their attention fully into the classroom. Clear directions, of course, will be essential for this interaction, as well as for the activity portion of the lesson.

Step Two: The Frame. As the session begins, provide students with an answer to the question, "Why?" Why are they going to spend time on this topic? How might it relate to material that has been learned previously or that may be covered later? If possible, how might the information be useful to them in their personal lives? What's in it for them to pay attention to this particular class session? The frame at this point can also function as an open loop for the activity that is to follow.

Step Three: The Activity. The experience used here introduces the basic ideas or concepts being taught. It should involve students in some capacity, whether physically, mentally, socially, or emotionally, making it also serve as a form of a state change as well. Students should feel or experience the importance of the concept by engaging in the experience (Gorman, Plucker, & Callahanj 1998; Stepien & Gallagher 1993). The activity serves as a demonstration of the "concept in action."

Step Four: The Debrief. This is the teaching component of the session in which the primary points of the lesson are highlighted and clarified. Based on the experience in which students have just participated, key points are illustrated and elaborated by the teacher. The idea of Involve, Don't Tell may be useful here. The teacher can ask questions that allow students to discover key aspects of the lesson for themselves. Specific practices such as Specify the Response and the idea of Getting Responses, as discussed in the previous chapter, would be included here.

Step Five: The Metaphor. In closing the lesson, broaden the scope of the students' understanding by using a metaphor or story. This allows the concept to be viewed from a wider perspective, perhaps as to how it applies to other areas of instruction, to the students' world at home, or to life in general. These connections can be made through the use of analogies, fables, fairy tales, or real-life experiences. Sometimes even jokes can serve this purpose, and end the session on a humorous note.

Examples

Four sample lesson plans will illustrate the Five-Part Model. They are outlined with the intention to provide a broad picture of how the learning session would be conducted using this sequence. If you were planning to teach the lesson directly from them you would naturally need quite a bit more information than is included in here. However, for the purpose of providing a general overview, only the essential aspects of each component are mentioned.

Example 1: A sixth-grade science class in Lake Tahoe looks at Watersheds

Overview: The primary intention is to have students understand what the term *watershed* means. They will also learn how they can help their community maintain a healthy watershed.

Engager Stage: Students are asked to hold out their hands, cupped together. The teacher approaches each student and uses a spray bottle to put some water on their finger tips, where it runs down onto the palms of their hands. The teacher then says, "When water runs over the ground from a high elevation to a lower one, the area over which the water runs is known as a *watershed*."

Frame: The teacher holds up two clear glasses of water. The water in one is clean while the water in the other one is a light brown and has particles floating in it. The teacher asks the students, "Which one would you rather drink? By understanding today's lesson, you are beginning to gain the power to decide which type of water you'll be drinking in the future."

Activity: In groups of four or five, students gather around trays containing a pile of flour. They then shape the flour into a topographic replica of the Lake Tahoe basin, consisting of a lake surrounded by a ring of mountains. Details are then added, including plastic trees, cars, homes, and some gauze pads representing meadows and wetlands. Finally, various shades of food coloring are added, representing pollutants in the environment such as fertilizer, pesticides, and car oil. When the students are satisfied with their model, they spray water all over it to simulate the effects of a rain storm.

Debrief: The teacher asks the groups to look closely at their model. The food colors have all collected in the lake area, creating a muddy brown puddle. The teacher points out that this is what happens to all pollutants when they are introduced into the environment; eventually they will wash down to the lake and become part of the drinking water supply. The teacher also notes how the gauze pads have absorbed some of the food coloring, demonstrating that meadows and wetlands can act as filters if they are left in their natural state. Finally, the students are given a list of ten things they can do to help protect the watershed in which they are living.

Metaphor: The teacher asks how many of the students have had an opportunity to eat fresh fish from the lake. Many of them raise their hands. They are asked if they would like to continue to be able to do this in the future. They all agree this would be great. However, the teacher says, Lake Tahoe is rapidly becoming polluted because of damage to the watershed. The only way for people to continue to eat noncontaminated, healthy fresh fish is if everyone becomes involved in cleaning up and maintaining a healthy watershed throughout the area.

Example 2:   A secondary health class on AIDS

Overview: The concepts to be taught concern the danger of contracting the HIV virus and AIDS, the rapidity with which it can spread, and the negative impact it can ultimately have on their lives.

Engager Stage: Students are asked to write down a list of things they want to accomplish at some point in their lives. They do this in silence for a few moments, then in small groups they share these lists with each other.

Frame: The teacher states that if they want to achieve some of these goals they should pay particular attention to the central theme of today's class. Their understanding of this issue may have a strong impact on whether or not they succeed.

Activity: Students are each given a file card. They each write their name in the center of the card. Everyone stands up and is asked to get at least two signatures from other students on their card. When this has been accomplished, everyone is seated.

Debrief: The teacher asks one person to stand up. This person then reads the two signatures he has gotten on his card. Those people stand up. They then read their signatures, and those people stand. This continues until, as usually occurs, everyone is standing. Then everyone takes a seat. The teacher points out that this is how sexually transmitted diseases spread. If only one person in the room had AIDS at the beginning, now everyone has been exposed to it and could, conceivably, be infected. The teacher points out that if a person has the HIV virus, their lifestyle might be dramatically altered, and some of those dreams may become impossible to achieve.

Metaphor: The teacher draws an iceberg on the board. She notes that, as most people know, only 10 percent of an iceberg is visible above the surface of the water. The same is true of the HIV virus. Only 10 percent of people who have it may show the external symptoms of AIDS. Therefore, everyone should be extra cautious when considering whether to have a sexual relationship.

Example 3:   The paradigm shift challenge

Overview: The concept to be taught is an awareness of how students may develop habits that unconsciously trap them into making ineffective learning choices. Challenging these patterns of behavior, or these paradigms, is important to success in school.

Engager Stage: Students stand in groups of four or five. Each group is given a hacky sack, and invited to play a game of "hand hacky," in which only hands are used to hit the sack back and forth. Music plays while they are engaged in the activity. They are subsequently invited to see the highest number of consecutive hits their team can reach before the hacky sack hits the floor.

Frame: The students are told that the best way to understand this concept is to involve themselves in the following activity. It is a puzzle, which they will solve as a group.

Activity: The group forms one circle. The group creates a pattern in which to throw the hacky sacks, and then reduces the length of time it takes to complete the pattern. Group times generally begin at one minute, and eventually take less than twenty seconds.

Debrief: The focus of the discussion after the experience is how the groups were able to reduce the time needed to complete the task. Eventually someone mentions that they had to "challenge the rules." More discussion follows concerning how the changes they ultimately made were never really against the rules at all; it simply felt that way because they had quickly acquired a "habit," a paradigm, as to the right way for the activity to be successfully accomplished.

Metaphors: What does this mean for learning? Small groups are formed to discuss "paradigms" related to school, such as the idea that studying is always best if it's done in silence. A list of these ideas is created on the white board. As the session closes, students are challenged to remain open to new ideas in learning.

Example 4:   The memory peg system

Overview: The concept to be taught is a "peg system." This is a study skill for memorizing lists of information.

Engager Stage: Two brief activities are used to engage the students' attention. First, they generate a list of twenty random items on the white board. It is mentioned that this list will be used shortly (an Open Loop). Second, in small groups, students discuss with each other what kinds of things they usually can remember easily, such as name, dates, or formulas, and what kinds of things are more challenging for them to recall.

Frame: The following observation is made:

"All learning is remembering.

If we can't remember it, then we never learned it!"

This approach to learning emphasizes how important it is for everyone to be able to easily and accurately memorize information.

Activity: The teacher demonstrates his ability to rapidly memorize the list of twenty that which was created earlier. He recalls the list in order, then at random. Students are invited to learn how to duplicate this feat. First they are taught the system, then practice using the system to memorize the same list of twenty items. The teaching process is highly interactive, both between the teacher and the students, as well as among the students themselves.

Debrief: When all students have demonstrated their ability to memorize information using this system, the teacher introduces the following idea:

"Memory can be easy."

The key is having a strategy. The method the students have just learned is one possible way of memorizing lists of information.

Metaphors: The teacher closes with a series of examples illustrating how to adapt this system for use in other situations. Brief examples are provided that demonstrate its applicability to studying for essay tests, making to-do lists, and learning a foreign language.

Adjusting the Model

The examples of the five-part model illustrated so far have each included activities that are meant to ground students in the central concept. It's critical to remember at this point that it's just a model, and *models are not the real thing!* Some lessons may not lend themselves to the use of an activity, and the teacher may need to simply present content. In these situations, the third and fourth steps mentioned previously can be replaced with an information component and a state change. The other three components can remain in their original locations because the overall purpose of each is still essential to the general learning process.

A Variation of the Basic Lesson Plan

THE STEP	TIME	PURPOSE
1. Engager	2–5 minutes	Engage the students' attention.
2. Frame	Less than 1 minute	Create an appropriate perspective.
3. Content	10–15 minutes	Introduce and explain the information.
4. State Change	1–3 minutes	Manage student's physical & mental state.
5. Metaphor	2–5 minutes	Relate learning to a broader perspective.

Because the presentation of material in a lecture format should be limited to a maximum of ten to fifteen minutes, longer sessions with more content may require that steps three and four be *repeated as often as necessary.* In this case the format might be:

An Extended Variation of the Basic Lesson Plan

THE STEP	TIME	PURPOSE
1. Engager	2–5 minutes	Engage the students' attention.
2. Frame	Less than 1 minute	Create an appropriate perspective.
3. Content	10–15 minutes	Introduce grounded conceptual awareness.
4. State Change	1–3 minutes	Manage students' physical and mental state.
5. Content	10–15 minutes	Expand on the information presented.
6. State Change	1–3 minutes	[Same as Step 4]
7. Content	10–15 minutes	Continue to expand on the information.
8. State Change	1–3 minutes	[Same as Step 4.]
9. Metaphor	2–5 minutes	Relate learning to a broader perspective.

Example 5:   Presenting content: A history lesson for secondary students

Overview: The concept to be taught concerns the history of the start of World War II.

Engager Stage: Students form small groups and discuss what they are looking forward to in the coming months. Have them form new groups to briefly share other future-oriented topics. Keep in mind that not all energizers need to be directly related to the content of the class. However, in this case it lays the groundwork for talking about how our hopes for the future are often dictated by the realities of the past.

Frame: The teacher asks if people think there might be a third world war coming soon. One way to predict such an event is through an understanding of the past. Our knowledge of the past can sometimes assist us in avoiding the mistakes of others.

Content: Lecture for ten to fifteen minutes on one important aspect of history that led to the start of World War II, such as Adolph Hitler's rise to power in Nazi Germany.

State Change: In small groups, students discuss what they have heard about Germany in World War II, and any effects it might have on their current opinions of that particular country.

Second Content Session: Lecture again for ten to fifteen minutes on another, related factor that eventually led to the declaration of war.

Second State Change: Distribute pictures from 1939 that depict locations in Germany, Poland, France, and England, showing some of the effects of the war. Students look through them and discuss them in small groups with each other.

Metaphor: The teacher tells the story of someone he personally knew who was a foot soldier in World War II and the horrific experiences this soldier endured. It is noted that only through an understanding of and a respect for the realities of war can people hope to avoid another one in the near future.

In Summary

The Five-Part Model discussed in this section is intended to provide guidelines or a basic template from which teachers can develop their own lesson plans. The examples provided are intended to show some specific ways the model could be adapted to meet the needs of different types of content areas. The model can be applied with equal success to such diverse academic subjects as math, science, physical education, and languages. Its usefulness is limited only by the range of each individual teacher's creativity, imagination, and willingness to explore new possibilities for instruction.

TEACHING DIRECTLY TO THE POINT

A little knowledge, as the saying goes, can be a dangerous thing. However, in some situations, a lot of knowledge can be an even *more* dangerous thing (Glaser 1984). How is this possible? Certainly as teachers we want to have a solid base of understanding of the material we are presenting. However, teachers frequently get so excited with their information that they forget one of the basics principles of effective instruction: Teach directly to the point! Beware of extraneous information that can cloud the students' understanding. The following example illustrates this important principle in detail.

The class was billed as an introduction on how to use the school's E-mail system. It was for beginners, with little or no experience using the Internet or even working on a computer for any purpose. It was scheduled to be a one-hour class, and was held in the Computer Hall, a large room dedicated solely to using computers and computer-based instruction.

The students for this introductory after-school session arrived and each person sat behind a computer. The teacher for the session was a young man who had been working with computers for a long time and was experienced with both computers and with the current E-mail system. He welcomed them to the course and began his presentation:

> "I'd like to start by saying that using this system is really easy. You'll get the hang of it in no time at all, and pretty soon you'll be able to move on to some of the more interesting applications, such as creating lists of people to send messages to, using an alias, or building databases. Why, you can even . . ."

At this point he listed a wide range of options the students might eventually come to use as they grew more familiar with the system. He spoke with enthusiasm and energy as he outlined the variety of ways these techniques would assist them in their education, from writing reports to getting advance copies of course materials. He spoke for the entire time allotted for the class, occasionally adding chalkboard diagrams to clarify his comments. At the end of the session he was smiling as he wished everyone well as they began to use the system. He invited them to return anytime if they had additional questions. The students then filed out of the room.

What's wrong with this situation? At the end of this class, how much had the students really learned? From their perspective, they walked away with very little usable information. Interestingly, from the teacher's point of view, he believed he had just done an excellent job in bringing a higher level of awareness about the potential of the system to the students. In fact, he was quite proud of the job he was doing, and pleased to be able to share his expertise of the subject matter. He enjoyed these classes immensely, and wanted to teach even more of them than he was currently doing.

To understand the magnitude of the problem in this scenario, the original purpose of the session should be considered. What did the students need to be able to do at the end of the class? Most of these computer neophytes had a clear agenda that had brought them into the room that day:

"I need to be able to send and receive messages using E-mail."

Could they accomplish that simple task based on the experience they had just had in this introductory course? Of course not! While they may have gained new ideas about what might be possible in the future use of E-mail and the Internet, what had been addressed regarding the single most important objective? Clearly, nothing. Students would therefore be unable to take even the first step toward using the system. This lack of understanding, at the most basic level, would limit their ability to consider any of the ideas the teacher had covered.

Several months later, an opportunity arose for me to redesign this one-hour introductory class. Based on comments received from students who had attended this particular session, I decided to try a unique approach. I put together an unusual sequence of instruction, based solely on the principle of teaching directly to the point, i.e., sending and receiving E-mail! I wanted students to be able to walk up to any computer at the school, turn it on, access their E-mail accounts, and read and send messages. To achieve this objective, I needed to approach it from a certain point of view. When the students had been seated, the first thing I said was:

"Welcome. Thank you for coming. Please turn the computer on that is sitting in front of you."

At this point I waited patiently while students searched for the appropriate button. This took some time. In the original class, *students never even turned on their computer*! Learning *how to do things,* such as using E-mail, is best accomplished if students can physically do it themselves. The first step in the process of learning to use E-mail is understanding how to turn the computer on. Yet, many of the students in this class were unfamiliar with the type of computer currently in use at the school, and they needed to know which button would activate their computer, so the whole process could begin. Finally, it was clear that everyone knew how to turn on their computer. At this point I asked them to turn it off again. Puzzled, the students complied. When all computers were off, I asked them to step into the hallway. This puzzled them even more, but eventually they were all standing outside the room. I joined them there, and said:

"Here are your instructions. When I open the door, please enter the room, go to *any* computer, and turn it on. Further instructions will be given once everyone has completed this task."

I then opened the door, allowing the students to enter. They each went to a computer and turned it on. When all computers were warmed up and ready, I congratulated the students on accomplishing the first step. Most of them felt a bit silly at being congratulated for doing such a simple task. However, they were assured there was a purpose behind each step, and the instruction proceeded.

Next, students were asked to open the general E-mail program. As before, confusion reigned until the E-mail icon was pointed out to them, and they were shown how to double click on it to open the program. I walked around the room until it was clear that all students had successfully opened the program. I then asked them to close the program, giving them the brief instruction that was needed to accomplish this step. All computers were turned off, and I asked them to once again step into the hallway. I joined them there and gave the next instruction:

> "This time, when I open the door, please proceed to a *different* computer than the one you were just using. Turn it on and open the E-mail program."

Why ask them to go to a different computer? I wanted them to understand that it did not matter which one they were using. All the computers were basically the same, and they could use any in the building to check their E-mail. Once they were at a computer, students turned the power on, then opened the E-mail program. When all students had successfully gotten this far, the next instruction was provided—how to open their personal account by entering their password and identification number. Several students required individual coaching at this point, but soon all had their own accounts open on the screen.

Once again, when everyone had completed this step, all computers were shut down, and the students gathered outside the room. At this point my directions were:

> "When I open the door, please proceed to different computer. Turn it on and open the E-mail program. Once you've done that, log on, using your password and identification number."

Again the door was opened. Students entered and completed the directions. The rest of the hour proceeded in a similar fashion. The completion of each step was followed by a trip to the hallway, then once again they entered the room and started from the beginning. At the conclusion of the session, students had demonstrated the ability to turn on the computer, open the E-mail program, open their account, send a message to one of the people in the room, read messages they had received, and delete messages. The basic objectives of the course had all been accomplished in the first class!

Why did students leave the classroom and go into the hallway each time a step had been explained? Was this a waste of precious time? In my eyes, starting new each time was exactly the point of the entire hour. I wanted students to be confident about how to approach any computer, how to turn it on, and how to open the necessary programs. If they had only done this once, at the beginning of the session, they may well have forgotten it by the time all other instructions had been completed. Firmly anchoring this sequence in their minds was one of the primary objectives of the entire exercise. If they had been unable to turn the computer on, they would have been returned to the starting point, with all other information lost along the way.

Another side benefit of this experimental format of instruction also became apparent over time. On an emotional level, one broad objective of the session was to have students become more comfortable entering the computer room and doing their work. Given the approach used in the initial example, it is quite likely they would have walked away feeling overwhelmed. This is exactly the opposite of what a teacher should want to achieve in this situation. Given this revised method of instruction, even the first-time students walked away with a feeling of accomplishment and a sense of certainty concerning at least one computer task. A positive association had been created for each of the students with the computer room by reinforcing the basic steps of the process.

It's important to note how long it took to achieve the stated objective. Originally, an entire hour had been spent with little or nothing accomplished. Now, in the same amount of time, all students were able to achieve the basic goal of the session. Primarily it was accomplished by (1) having them physically involved with the process, and (2) not adding any superfluous information to the instructions. While it is true that these students still had much more to learn about the potential of the E-mail program, at least a solid foundation had been built for subsequent learning.

Initially, this approach was greeted with skepticism by other computer teachers who felt I was taking the idea of physically involving the students too far. However, based on both the students' enjoyment of the course and the outcome it produced, they soon began using a similar method of instruction for their own classes. The expertise of the original teacher was wonderful, but unnecessary for achieving the outcome the students needed most at that stage in their development. Students would be better able to understand, appreciate, and utilize these more sophisticated functions if offered *after* a sufficient knowledge base had been developed.

What's the basic difference between the original approach and the new one described here? The key element is understanding the needs of the students, and gearing the instruction *directly toward meeting those needs.* This is the bottom line to this whole section: Regardless of the content, teach directly to the point. Avoid the temptation to add unnecessary information.

This is an especially challenging situation for teachers who enter the learning environment with a tremendous amount of knowledge about their subject matter. Contrary to popular belief, *knowing* the material does not equate with *teaching* the material. Expertise with the information is certainly a critical component in creating a successful learning experience. However, transmitting the information to someone else is an entirely different matter, and must be considered in a different light: What works for what the students need?

The situation described above is simply one example of directly meeting the needs of the students. For teachers of all subjects, the key is to remain focused on the behaviors, insights, and connections they expect as a result of their instruction. Consider how to approach these goals on a step-by-step basis, verifying along the way that *all* students are able to successfully accomplish each step before moving to the next one. The present example is included in this book because it demonstrates a creative way of meeting needs that may new to some readers. Meeting the objectives of a class may require innovation on the part of the teacher. However, experimenting with new strategies and approaches is one of the critical qualities of a successful teacher.

TEACHING BACKWARD

The following situation is probably familiar to most people. A student has a test coming up soon. He studies hard for it. He learns the material by heart. He takes the test.

He passes it, and does quite well. *He immediately forgets all the information!* Sound familiar? Why does this happen? What causes people to rapidly lose information they have worked so hard at remembering?

In retrospect, it may be easy to see a central factor that contributes to this phenomenon. The focal point of all the effort was the Test. The student was using a mindset of "pass the test," and all energy was expended toward that hurdle. The instruction was given in a *forward* manner, focused on the day of the Big Exam. When the Test was complete, and the grade had been posted, the goal had been met. Mentally, the exercise was over, so there was a subtle feeling that there was no need to continue remembering the information.

Teachers in these situations often base their long-term learning objectives on the depth of effort students expend in this memorization process. They believe that, by concentrating intensely on memorizing the material, students will encode the information deeply enough that they will be able to remember it when they need it. What actually happens may be something quite different. Students may have processed the information so that it is only accessible in a testing situation. This defeats the greater objective of having the information enhance the quality of the students' skills and abilities in real-life settings.

How can this trend be reversed? A starting point would be to keep in mind the higher objectives of each teaching situation. Where possible, teach to the *application* of the material. This is frequently called *teaching backward*. It means to start with the higher level objectives and end with the lower ones.

An Example of Teaching Backward

A teacher is teaching a course for teacher candidates. The material covered in the course will be part of a statewide certification test that all students must take at some point. She knows that students tend to forget the material immediately after the test. Yet, she also knows this material will be valuable to them at three distinct points in time namely, (1) for the test at the end of this course, (2) for the certification test, and, perhaps most importantly, (3) when they are teaching in a classroom full of students. She wants to avoid the "forget it right after the test" phenomenon. Knowing this, she chooses a different approach for the course.

At the start of the first class, she hands out the final exam. It even has the actual date written on it when the final will be given. She asks the students to look it over and decide which questions they don't know how to answer. The students are puzzled. Because they haven't even taken the course yet, how should they know the information? However, some of the terms are familiar to them, so a group discussion commences concerning some of the more easily answered questions. At the completion of the class, the teacher verifies that all students could correctly answer these questions. She notes that, as of today, this first day in the course, all of them could already pass 20 percent of the final exam. As the class ends, she gathers the final exams up, and gives the students some reading for the next class session.

The teacher's primary focus is on the students correctly answering the questions *as they are written for the test*. This is a critical distinction. As with all content, she could spend a great deal of time on elaboration, clarifying how it might be used in various situations, or how some of the finer points of the information might apply. She avoids this for the time being. Instead, she maintains a restricted focus on students learning how to answer the questions correctly as they are written, based on a very narrow definition of the information. The focus at this point is only on passing the test.

At the second class session, the teacher once again hands out the final exam. First everyone reviews the questions that had been discussed the last time. When all students agree that they could find the correct answers, she opens discussion on more questions from the final. These issues related to the reading they had been assigned. She clarifies as needed, again keeping their focus strictly limited to the test itself. At the end of this class session, more final exam questions are added to the list of ones that they could successfully answer. She notes that as of today, this second day in the course, all of them could already pass 40 percent of the final exam.

The next few class sessions continued in this manner. Soon, all students were confident they could score 100 percent on the final exam. At this point, only three weeks of a fifteen-week course had passed. The teacher then made the following statement:

> "How many of you now believe that you could get a perfect score on the final exam? [All students raised their hand.] Thank you. That's nice. Passing the test is useful for getting an excellent grade in this course, and for becoming certified to be a teacher. It also doesn't mean very much in the larger context of why we're learning this information. What we're really interested in here is how each of you can use this information in a classroom setting. How will it help you manage your students, or verify that what you want to teach is actually what you are teaching? Let's turn our attention toward making this information useful to you."

The rest of the semester was spent looking at how the information could be applied, how it could be of use to these teacher candidates. Demonstrations were conducted, field trips to local schools became frequent, and heated debates took place as students considered how the information might be useful to them. Occasionally, a class session would be spent in reviewing the final exam. Each time this was done, a broader understanding of the questions was apparent in the quality of the students' responses. However, most of the available class time was focused on making the material *meaningful* to the students.

Why did this teacher approach the class this way? Simply put, much of how the successful transfer of learning is evaluated through testing. But written, and even oral, tests are really only assessing a small part of what students know. Although they may be the best choice available in some situations, they are a very limited device for deciding how useful the material will be to some students. It also only looks at their understanding of the material in a testing environment. Having the test become the central focus of the course material detracts from the broader objectives of the learning process. Teaching backward allows the teacher to complete the aims of the course, and subsequently spend the remaining time on the greater issue of applicability.

Further Situations

Example 1:   Imagine that a teacher hands out the upcoming test. However, this time *the answers are included!* They are written out clearly, exactly as the teacher would like to see them worded. Now the role of the student for the test-taking portion of the class is even simpler than before—just memorize the information. Given this as a starting point, the teacher can begin with the very first class and spend the available time clarifying how the information is applied. Students are relieved of the stress of wondering what will be on the exam, and can concentrate on understanding the applications.

Example 2:   A high school math teacher in Texas uses a unique approach for teaching new concepts. Normally, problems are provided for the students and they must solve them to find the correct answers. However, this teacher occasionally hands the students a piece of paper that has three things on it for each question: (1) the problem itself, (2) two inches of white space, and (3) the answer to the problem. The students must then fill in the *steps* that were used to reach the answer that has been provided.

In certain areas of the content, he sees the primary need of the students as developing an understanding of the method used to solve the problem. If they are concentrating on solving the problem, as well as wondering if they have arrived at the correct answer, he believes they may become distracted. Instead, using this approach they are forced to focus on the issue that is of paramount importance to their comprehension of the material. Only when it is clear that they have learned this step will they proceed to the next level. At this point the more traditional approach is used, where students are only provided the original problems and must generate the answers entirely on their own.

Interestingly, one by-product of this form of teaching backward is that, when students see that the answer is already given to them, they have a sense of this material as being "easy." This outlook toward the content serves them well in terms of internal motivation. If they believe the material they are currently learning is simple, they become more willing to make an effort to learn how to be successful. Once students are secure in their understanding of the process necessary to solve the problem, the leap to arriving at their own answers seems to be a very small one. They are now able to answer all problems completely on their own.

In Summary

Not all material may be adaptable to this instructional approach. However, more than one might expect can be. Another high school math teacher even taught an entire year of algebra using this approach, and found it quite successful. Imagine giving the students a chapter exam on material they've never heard of! At the end, however, he found that they had been wrestling with how to solve these problems since the start of the chapter, two weeks before. This, in turn, gave them the entire time to develop mental frameworks for dealing with these questions.

MAKING IT MEMORABLE

The mathematics teacher was starting a new chapter. As the first class of this new session began, he welcomed the students by saying:

> "We're beginning a new section of the book today, and I have a story to tell you. You see, there was this really negative bee flying along. He flew up and down until suddenly he ran straight into a square root sticking up out of the ground. He looked inside and saw a really square bee. This square bee was dragging along behind him four AC batteries. He looked down and realized that he and the root were being balanced on a see-saw that had two apples holding it up at the middle."

As he told this story, students were staring at him, wondering what in the world he was talking about. However, he hadn't finished.

> "That was so fascinating, let me tell it to you again."

He repeated the same story a second time. When he had finished the story this time, he asked each student to find a partner and sit facing them.

> "Now, one person is going to tell the other person this same story, as exactly as you can. When they are done, the other person will tell that story back to them.

Although thoroughly puzzled, the students did as they were told. The entire process to this point took approximately five minutes. When each person had completed telling their partner this strange story, the teacher picked up a piece of chalk and turned to the blackboard.

> "Now, for the final time, let's look at that story. What was the first line in the story? There was a negative bee . . . [As he said this, on the board he wrote "-b"] who was flying along. He flew up and down [He wrote "+/-"], until suddenly he ran straight into a square root sticking up out of the ground [he drew the mathematical symbol for a square root]. He looked inside and saw a really square bee ["b squared"]. This square bee was dragging along behind him four AC batteries [which meant "-4ac"]. He looked down and realized that he and the root were being balanced on a see-saw that had two apples holding it up at the middle [all over "2a"].

On completing the story, he had written the following formula on the board:

$$X = \frac{-b \pm \sqrt{b^2 - 4ac}}{2a}$$

This is the quadratic formula, which was the basis for the chapter he was introducing on solving polynomials. For the next two weeks, each class session began with the students first telling that same story to someone near them, then writing the formula down on their paper. Knowing the formula rapidly became second nature to all students in the class.

In previous years, this teacher had noticed that even after two weeks of concentration on learning how to *use* the quadratic formula, students were still struggling to *remember* it accurately. Somehow, this initial step in the learning process had been passed over. The teacher realized that before students ever learned to apply the formula, they needed to be able to simply remember it and write it down. Now, by memorizing this story, students were quickly able to remember the basic formula. When these students had to solve any problem and needed to use the quadratic formula, the first thing they did was to write it down. From that point it became a simple matter of filling in the numbers for the variables and completing the mathematical calculations.

In this situation, knowing the quadratic formula was the key to solving the related problems. In many learning situations, there are several basic elements that students must know. These nuggets of information are the basis for all remembering, the building blocks on which all other information is built (Johnson-Laird 1988; Ormond 2000). Without this base being solid, any new information runs the risk of crumbling, falling through the gaps, and being forgotten.

Shared Responsibility for Memorization

Yes, students do have responsibility for remembering the information that is presented to them. Teachers, however, should remember that they play a key role in the ease with which this can be accomplished (Hansen 1998). A responsible teacher is accountable for the creative presentation of the material in a manner that directly assists students in encoding the material. To disregard this aspect of effective instruction is to avoid a major element in learning. The teacher's familiarity with the material makes them the perfect candidate to create the memory strategy best suited for the material. Leaving it up to the student may produce a wildly fluctuating range of results. How can a teacher make the information easily memorable for all students?

Telling a story, as shown in this example, is only one strategy for achieving this objective. Mnemonic devices abound that can be applied to a wide range of learning situations. The use of acronyms is one example. HOMES (something I still remember from my year as a fifth grader) was a common one used to help students learn the names of the five great lakes in the United States (Huron, Ontario, Michigan, Erie, and Superior). Also, applying the sound of a new word to a more familiar word assists the recall of definitions. Some students learn the names of the countries of a continent through the use of a song with an easy melody.

Interestingly, simple memory techniques such as those shown here may be familiar to the reader as strategies used only with young students. However, techniques such as these frequently work very well regardless of the age of the student. Most learning sessions, from academic classrooms to corporate seminars, have at least one key concept to which all other material is related. Easy access to this central piece of information opens the door to related images and ideas. Teaching students a simple method for recall of the material may make the remaining instruction a much simpler matter.

Involving the students in the presentation of the material is another approach that can be used with considerable success. An axiom from education states that *if you want to know something well, teach it to someone else.* Having students teach parts of the subject matter at hand involves them deeply in the material. They could teach the entire group, or to one other person. Engaging in the act of explanation will assist them in understanding it for themselves. Also, beginning a teaching section by allowing students to share what they already know about the subject may serve to engage them. Even simple group conversations about the material will involve the students and help them remember the material at a deeper level.

There are countless other methods of making information memorable. Here are two more examples. One is to facilitate recall by attaching emotions to the material. Emotional memory is a powerful device that can be called on to considerable advantage within certain contents. High levels of laughter, joy, or celebration can cause students to review those moments at a later point in time. While mentally reliving those pleasant experiences, students are also revisiting any key points demonstrated during the activities.

Another method is to limit all discussion of a topic until key ideas have been encoded by the students. In other words, suppose twenty new terms will be an integral part of a two-hour session. The teacher could spend the first portion of the session focusing specifically on the definitions of these words. During this time, *no other information is presented that might interfere with the process of memorization.* Only when they can demonstrate mastery of these key terms will further instruction be provided.

In Summary

Primary pieces of information should be easy for students to remember if they are presented in a memorable fashion. However, it is certainly not necessary to use memory strategies with all information that is being delivered. Such a presentation would be quite bizarre indeed. Instead, each teacher might isolate those elements central to the overall theme of the session, and highlight them in some manner for students. In general, the question, "*Is this material easily memorable to the students?*" should be at the forefront of all teachers' thoughts when preparing for their classes.

AN APPROACH TO CONSIDER

It might be useful at this point to consider how best to integrate the wealth of information this book contains into your personal teaching style. Perhaps the best way to explain this is through the use of a metaphor. Suppose you have a day free, and are going to spend it engaged in one of your favorite recreational activities, building a jigsaw puzzle. Recently you heard of a new approach to building puzzles. First, you dump all the pieces onto the table. Next, you pick up the two pieces closest to you and try to find a way for them to fit together. If they won't go together you drop one of them, pick up another one, and try to fit it together with the first piece. You continue in this manner until you finally discover two pieces that go together. But the odds of finding two pieces that actually do fit together are quite low, so the process is both time-consuming and frustrating. Not surprisingly, you soon find yourself losing interest in the project and become frustrated with the whole thing. You put it aside and move on to something else. Does this approach to building a jigsaw puzzle sound silly? It certainly should.

However, this is how some readers may be tempted to approach the material contained within this book. They may have already selected several ideas that they would like to try out in the classroom. They'll next begin to wonder how these various pieces of the teaching puzzle fit together. Yet while all of the pieces *are* important in the creation of the final product, understanding how and where they fit into the overall picture may require a different organizational strategy.

Here's how you would probably go about assembling a jigsaw puzzle in the usual, more rational manner. First you take the box and dump all the pieces onto the table in a heap. If you're like most people, you begin to sort for the edge pieces first, organizing them into a separate pile. Using the picture on the cover for a reference, you use these pieces to create the border. Then you might begin working on a particular portion of the puzzle that is distinctive in some way. When that part is finished, you move on to another section. You continue in this manner, gradually filling in the blank areas until the entire picture is complete.

A similar approach might be taken when considering how to look at the concepts and techniques you have been reading about. Some ideas contained here may provide a tip or idea that is useful in and of itself. You may find an immediate fit with what you are presently doing. At the same time, many of the ideas are interrelated. For example, giving effective directions in an active learning environment is a strategy that is closely connected with concepts presented in Question/Clarify/Question. While you are welcome to work at integrating the ideas in this book into your personal teaching style in whatever manner you feel most comfortable, it might be useful to approach it as if you are building a puzzle. Begin by "turning over" as many of the pieces as possible by simply reading about them. Patterns may eventually begin to emerge, and connections between ideas may become more evident the longer you consider the overall picture as well as the individual components.

One clear distinction, however, exists between building *someone else's* puzzle and the process of learning to use these ideas. The end result of building *someone else's* puzzle will be *someone else's* picture. The end product that emerges as a result of the process of training yourself in utilizing these ideas is a picture that is entirely your own. There is no single correct manner in which to use the ideas and skills contained here. How you choose to apply them will be a unique combination of your personality, your skill level, your learning context, your audience, and more! Keep creating and recreating until you reach the picture that works best for you!

THE MENU

What follows here is a "menu" of the ideas, principles, concepts, techniques, and strategies covered throughout this book. It includes a sentence or two describing what each one is, along with the page number where it is illustrated more fully. This menu is provided for two primary reasons. First, many of the terms used in the body of the text may have been unfamiliar to teachers before reading this book, and this section can provide a useful, quick review of the terms themselves and their definitions. Second, with this menu as a guide, readers can rapidly locate and review a section that may be of interest to them, or relevant to their current needs and interests. They can then turn directly to those pages and remind themselves of the specific points concerning that strategy.

CHAPTER TWO: INSTRUCTIONAL PRECEPTS

Teach People, Not Content (pp. 9–13)

While content is always important, it is never *more* important than people. Students are first and foremost individuals (a radical thought to some teachers), each one with a unique background and different life experiences. Teachers consistently produce a higher level of accomplishment when they mentally hold the students as the single most important element in the educational process, not the content they are teaching.

Awareness Leads to Choice (pp. 13–17)

The first step in making new choices is to become aware that they exist as options. The job of the teacher becomes easier when he or she understands that it is not always possible for us to *change* learners. Most often, the best option available is to simply expose them to alternatives and possibilities, so they can make the choice that is most useful to them.

Learning + Enjoyment = Retention   (pp. 17–20)

As human beings, we remember most clearly the things we experience on an emotional level. If enjoyment can be brought into the learning context, memory is naturally enhanced, without any increased effort on the part of the learner or the teacher. A sense of joy, laughter, and play encourages people to involve themselves, and they learn at a more rapid pace.

Application Is Everything   (pp. 20–23)

If students can *apply* the information that has been presented to them, it becomes useful and meaningful. Without the ability to apply the content, why have they bothered to learn it? Constantly bringing practical applications of the information to the attention of the students helps them see how it affects the world around them, and how they can use it to better their lives.

Stories Are Great   (pp. 23–26)

Stories and metaphors are everywhere in the world around us, from books to movies to our lunchtime conversations. They are the oldest known form of instruction, yet they are equally as useful in today's society as they were thousands of years ago. Weaving stories throughout a presentation provides a concrete foundation for understanding the information on a personal level.

CHAPTER THREE: PRINCIPLES OF EFFECTIVE INSTRUCTION

Crest of the Wave   (pp. 28–38)

Waves in the ocean build up, reach a crest, and then come tumbling down. Metaphorically, this is similar to what students and teachers experience in the classroom. Classes, lectures, and activities all have their own momentum, much like a wave of water. Does this seem familiar? We've certainly all experienced those classes that felt like a "tidal wave" of information! Teachers need to develop the ability to recognize the movement of the "waves" occurring in their room, the ebb and flow of students' interest and ability to pay attention to the information. They then need to respond when students' ability to focus reaches its crest. After all, we don't want them to *drown* in a sea of confusion and misunderstanding!

Open Loops

An "open loop" is any statement or action that indicates something that will be completed later. The human brain tends to seek completion, such as wanting to hear a favorite song all the way through to the end. Teachers can utilize this technique to keep learners focused in the classroom by using open loops on a frequent basis, indicating things that will be coming up at a future time in the class. This will help create an atmosphere of interest, enthusiasm, and excitement.

Frames Create Meaning

A "frame" is the perspective people take concerning experiences in their lives. Depending on the frame provided, the same learning activity can vary from being an excellent experience to one that is meaningless, or even negative. If a teacher does not provide a frame, the learners will make one up, *although it is rarely the same one the teacher would like them to create.* Becoming adept at framing learning experiences is perhaps the single most important skill teachers can develop in their tool kit.

CHAPTER FOUR: CLASSROOM STRATEGIES

Bridges and Zones

There are three distinct zones of teaching: (1) the instructional zone (closest to the chalkboard), (2) the facilitation zone (midway between the chalkboard and the audience), and (3) the direction zone (closest to the audience). Deliberate use of these zones builds bridges between the teacher's location in the room and the learners' emotional, physiological, and psychological states—and can lead to higher levels of learner participation and responsiveness.

Comfort Levels in Physical Situations

If learners are physically uncomfortable, they won't pay attention. They will be distracted by their discomfort. Some types of physical discomfort may be obvious to the teacher, while others may be less apparent. Teachers might want to be aware of and respond to subtle situations of potential physical discomfort, as they will interfere with the quality of the learning.

Completing Actions (pp. 65–67)

When learners are asked to do a particular action, it is necessary to *complete* that action. For example, if they are asked to raise their hands, it is important to tell them to put their hands down at some point! Failing to do this creates an awkward situation, and in the future learners may be reluctant to follow directions at all. Completing actions allows for a sense of comfort and ease on the part of students.

Contrast (pp. 68–72)

Blue writing stands out clearly against a yellow background. The contrast between the two colors is what creates the impact. To maximize the impact of key points in a learning context, teachers might consider what "background" and "foreground" have been created, and in what ways they could heighten the difference between the two so those important points will stand out as clearly as possible.

Distributing Resources (pp. 72–76)

Traditionally, resources are distributed to learners in one of several common ways. However, this is also a perfect opportunity for the teacher to add action and movement to the classroom. What innovative methods can the teacher use to accomplish the same goal, while allowing the natural energy of the students to be unleashed? This section contains a list of ideas for accomplishing this outcome, and gives examples of how to use them in a variety of settings.

Do It Standing (pp. 76–77)

Why do students spend so much time *in their seats?* Can learning actually occur while they are standing? If so, what are some typical situations during the course of instruction when it might be possible to include more movement, and, specifically, more opportunities for students to stand up?

Honoring Written Notes (pp. 77–79)

When students are taking written notes, much more is happening than most teachers realize. The process of taking in, analyzing, and recording new information is a challenging enterprise for most students. Those teachers who know how to successfully handle note-taking situations in the classroom can greatly contribute to the long-term learning of their students.

Layering (pp. 79–84)

"Layering" occurs when, within a single complex activity, there are a series of small steps designed to eventually come together to complete a complex action or product. It is an approach that helps learners to be successful in challenging situations. Layering is a flexible tool that can be used with an energizer, a lecture, or even a series of instructions.

Music (pp. 84–90)

The effective use of music in learning contexts has been a widely debated topic throughout the last two decades. Rather than consider the philosophical aspects of this issue, this section looks at four distinct places where music can have a positive impact on learning in any classroom, regardless of content. A brief discussion is also included considering which type of stereo is best for use in learning environments.

Ownership (pp. 90–95)

When learners feel that they are an important part of the process in which they are involved, interest and accountability go up and retention increases drastically.

Pause For Visuals (pp. 95–98)

If teachers simultaneously show a new overhead while continuing to speak, they are asking students to split their focus between their words and the new image being shown. This causes a reduction in the students' ability to focus in either direction, resulting in less retention of the information. There's a simple solution to this problem. Whenever an important new piece of information is visually presented, teachers could pause briefly until students have read it. If students have had time to construct a mental picture, they will then be able to concentrate more fully on the teacher's explanation.

Press and Release (pp. 98–100)

"Pressing" refers to the focused concentration necessary for learners to take in, process, and recall information. "Releasing" refers to the reaction that follows these moments. Both are necessary for learners to experience if they are to maintain a natural sense of balance and a healthy mental state that is conducive to learning. There are specific ways teachers can incorporate moments of release as a natural flow in the sequence of instruction.

Priming   (pp. 100–104)

Are students both mentally and physically ready to do what is asked of them? "Priming" is the concept of properly preparing learners so they can experience success. The better prepared they are, the less "threat" there will be in the situation. The more relaxed they are due to lack of threat, the more fully they can participate in the learning process. While the concept may seem simple at first glance, in practice it is a skill that needs to be clearly articulated and explained for new teachers to fully understand.

Step Down   (pp. 104–106)

Classroom management, as the novice teacher quickly learns, is frequently a challenge, regardless of the age of the learners. Step Down is a vocal control technique in which a single sentence is used to regain focus in the classroom, without the teacher needing to use common teacher phrases such as, "Please listen to me now," or "OK, everybody, let's move on," or "It's my turn now." Sound interesting? It's one of the most useful vocal tools new teachers can acquire.

Visual Field   (pp. 106–109)

The "visual field" refers to everything students normally see when they are in their seats. Visual fields can become boring to the eye if they remain constant for an extended period of time. There are a variety of ways teachers might consider changing the students' visual field throughout the course of a lesson. This change in scenery can help learners stay focused and attentive, thus increasing their retention of information.

Walk Away   (pp. 109–111)

When a student asks a question, it is a natural reaction for the teacher to walk *toward* the person speaking. However, moving this way may inhibit the rest of the class from participating in the exchange. There is, however, an alternative strategy walking in the opposite direction. There are multiple benefits of using this approach, and it can be done without disrupting the conversation.

CHAPTER FIVE: THE ART OF EFFECTIVE DIRECTIONS

(pp. 112–137)

Giving directions is one of the most critical issues in creating an effective learning environment. Despite the vital nature of this topic, it is rarely addressed in teacher education courses. A large part of communication in a learning setting involves the teacher providing the learners with directions concerning what they are to do. The effectiveness of these directions has a direct bearing on the experience of both the students and the teacher.

CHAPTER SIX: LANGUAGE ISSUES

Acknowledgment

(pp. 138–142)

The ways teachers should or should not acknowledge students, or provide "positive reinforcement," is a widely debated topic. Although both sides of the controversy are addressed, special attention is focused on those forms of acknowledgment that are generally viewed as effective, meaningful, and purposeful.

Appropriate Orientation

(pp. 142–146)

The use of phrases such as "I want you to . . ." or "I'm going to give you . . ." may unconsciously create a power struggle between the teacher and the student, interfering with the learning process. Teachers should know how to choose words that can help avoid this unnecessary complication in the classroom.

Enrolling Questions

(pp. 146–150)

There are many methods of involving students. This strategy is one of the easiest, and yet most effective approaches. Asking a designed sequence of questions of learners can help them personalize information and understand it at a useful level. Which form of questions to ask, how many to use, and what level of interaction are all important issues.

Getting Responses   (pp. 150–153)

As a teacher, have you ever experienced the "deer-in-the-headlights" stare from students when you've asked them if they have any questions? Why might this be happening? There are two possible reasons for this reaction, as well as ways to avoid falling into the common, although frequently unrecognized, teaching trap that often causes this reaction.

Involve, Don't Tell   (pp. 153–155)

The most common form of instruction is that of simply presenting material *to* learners. With key pieces of information, student recall will be heightened if they are somehow *involved* in the material. There are several methods for identifying the most important pieces of the presentation and involving learners in the discovery of that information. The result is higher levels of recall and retention.

Labels   (pp. 155–158)

A label tells people what to expect. In life, the use of labels is important, such as knowing the difference between "cola" and "root beer." In learning situations, however, labels can potentially inhibit a learner from fully participating. For example, some teens don't want to be told to "play a game," because this might imply that they are wasting their precious time with a childish activity. There are some potentially dangerous *labels* when used in the classroom and alternative words as well that can be used to ameliorate this effect.

Open/Closed   (pp. 158–161)

A question posed in a "closed" format indicates that there is only one possible correct answer, and the teacher is the one who knows it. Conversely, a question posed in an "open" format indicates there are multiple possible correct responses, with the learner being accountable for the "correctness" of his or her response. The difference between these two approaches in formatting questions is quite distinct, and the effect in the classroom can be profound. Where possible, open questions should be used to increase the likelihood that students will be fully involved in classroom discussions.

Positive Mental Images   (pp. 161–166)

The most effective words and phrases to use are those that help learners easily and quickly achieve the task at hand. In almost every learning situation, the teacher wants to look for words that create a positive, specific image in the mind of learners that will help guide their actions.

Question/Clarify/Question   (pp. 166–170)

This is a simple three-step sequence that can produce powerful results in a variety of circumstances. Each component plays an integral part in preparing learners to fully engage in an upcoming activity or discussion. Use of this format allows the teacher to clearly state the requirements and avoid unnecessary interruptions for clarification at a later point.

Sarcasm: Dividing Responses   (pp. 170–172)

Sarcasm, side comments, and off-the-wall remarks can be disruptive in a learning context if not properly handled. Interestingly, these are frequently the hallmark of high intelligence (although this is not always readily apparent, as I suspect many teachers will be willing to agree.) One solution is to allow responses from students to be subtly divided into "useful" and "less-than-useful" categories. The teacher can then focus on the appropriate comments without needing to visibly reprimand those more "creative" students.

Specificity   (pp. 172–176)

Conversations between teachers and students can easily go wrong. The best way to insure clear communication is to use very specific language that makes it easy for both people to understand the intent of the interaction. There are several common places where specificity on the part of the teacher can greatly increase the clarity of the communication.

Specify the Response   (pp. 176–180)

The teacher asks the group a question. Students either give a minimal response, or don't respond at all. Why? One reason might be that the teacher hasn't *specified what form of response* is required. Are they supposed to raise their hand, stand up, or speak out loud? If this is not clear, students are unconsciously being asked to guess which form of response is correct. This creates a threatening situation that learners tend to avoid by simply not responding at all. For higher levels of response, teachers might consider whether they are specifying the appropriate response.

Suggest the Experience   (pp. 180–183)

If learners are *told* what they are about to experience in a given situation, they may react negatively. This is analogous to having them put up a mental wall from which they can then push away. A more positive response is possible when the teacher simply *suggests* what might happen. Without the "wall" of being told what they will learn or experience, students are free to make their own choices, and are more likely to become involved in the discussion or activity.

Vocal Italics   (pp. 184–187)

When new or unusual words or phrases are introduced into a learning context, the student's mind requires a brief moment of processing time. They need a few microseconds to embed it in their memory if they are to recall it at a later point in time. Teachers can facilitate this aspect of learning by placing "vocal italics" around a significant word or phrase.

CHAPTER SEVEN: DESIGNING INTERACTIVE LESSONS

The Five-Part Model   (pp. 188–194)

The Five-Part Model is a basic model for designing instructional sessions. Its five components include (1) an energizer, (2) a frame, (3) an activity, (4) a debrief, and (5) a metaphor. Each component in the sequence plays an integral role in the success of the model. The model is highly flexible and can be adapted to fit a variety of classroom situations.

Teaching Directly to the Point   (pp. 195–198)

All too frequently, valuable time is wasted in instructional settings. When you were a student, odds are that you were a master at the lost art of wasting time. (What did *you* do to kill time in a boring classroom? Shoot rubber bands, doodle, write notes, or practice holding your breath?) However, as a teacher, time has become very important. We want to narrow our focus and teach precisely to the topic being addressed. Using creative ideas maximizes the time we have with our students, while keeping our more creative students from developing their own talents in the field of "time wasting."

Teaching Backward (pp. 198–201)

The traditional approach to instruction is to teach from the beginning to the end. Seems logical, doesn't it? While this approach is certainly useful in many circumstances, teaching from the *end* to the *beginning* is also an effective option in certain situations. Teachers can learn how to teach *backwards*, how to specifically design lesson plans to achieve this outcome, and the benefits and drawbacks of this innovative teaching strategy.

Making It Memorable (pp. 202–204)

Learning is directly related to remembering. If students can't remember it, then they never learned it! And memory Is Easy! Now, this may seem difficult to believe based on your school experiences of "remembering"; however, what if it were true? Contrary to the experiences of most new teachers who have just survived our current educational system, what if students could remember information quickly, easily, and naturally? Are there techniques teachers can use to make their classes naturally *memorable* to learners, and increase the efficiency of classroom time? How can teachers help learners gain long-term retention of the material? Several strategies for making things more memorable provide some introductory thoughts about the "lost art of memory."

A CHECKLIST

You may have noticed that there's a heap of information in this book. A simple way to insure that you are covering the majority of the key points when preparing a lesson is to generate and briefly review a checklist of some of the relevant concepts. Addressing each element in this checklist will assist you in creating the maximum possible impact for the lesson.

It is important to note, of course, that not all of the points listed here may be applicable for every lesson plan. This checklist is deliberately intended to be very broad in scope, providing a wide-ranging sequence of questions teachers can refer to if they want to be certain to cover most of the key concepts that have been presented. Given the unique nature of your own classroom, you might want to create a personalized list to refer to before each day of teaching, or prior to delivering a lesson for the first time. Consider asking yourself:

1. What engager will be used to start the class?
2. What frame will be used to create a useful orientation to the class?
3. How will the directions be given for each activity?
4. How will open loops be used, if at all?
5. Which state changes will be used during this class?
6. Where will these state changes be placed in the sequence of instruction?
7. What role will music play during this session?
8. In what ways will students receive acknowledgment during this class?
9. How will resources (if needed) be distributed?
10. What keys in language may be useful to consider?
11. Which labels should be used and which ones avoided in this session?
12. How will balance be maintained through press and release?
13. How will the debrief be handled after the activity, if one is used?
14. How will the key learning points be made memorable?
15. What metaphor, story, or verbal illustration will be used to end the session?

A quick review of these questions should help you avoid some pitfalls that might otherwise catch you by surprise. For example, if the directions are well prepared, the class should flow smoothly. If potentially hazardous labels have been considered in advance, the teacher can prepare other words to use in their places. If state changes have been selected and set for certain times during the lesson, there will be less likelihood of running out of ideas in front of the room. Taking time to check your own list prior to each class may become a useful, even essential component of your preparation.

CREATING A PRESENTATION

Teachers may occasionally be called on to give a presentation, perhaps to the student body at an assembly, perhaps to the faculty, or maybe even to the Parent Teacher Association. The ideas presented in this book can be applied to the creation and delivery of a speech, talk, or keynote address, as well as to classroom presentations. For example, the importance of adjusting for attention spans, the use of state changes, and the inclusion of stories and metaphors can be directly applied to the development of a powerful speech for a large audience. This section provides an outline for creating talks, presentations, and speeches based on the approach presented in this book.

THE BASIC SEQUENCE

Here's an overview of the basic approach to giving a high-impact speech.

1. an opening metaphor or example
2. a story used to introduce the main point
3. a state change, related to the main point
4. a story used to develop the main point (or secondary points)
5. a closing metaphor or example

Each of these elements plays an integral part in the overall structure of the speech. Longer speeches require the simple adjustment of adding more stories, metaphors, and state changes to the middle of this sequence.

As a general example, assume the speech to be designed is a keynote address twenty minutes in length. The opening metaphor should capture students' attention, allow the speaker to build rapport with the group, and announce the general theme of the talk (Evans 1988). Next, a story is used to explain the primary issue, the focal point of the speech. When this is complete, it is time for a state change, a brief activity or interaction that provides the audience an opportunity to process the ideas and "make meaning" for themselves. When the state change is complete, the main point is illustrated in further depth through the use of another story, or secondary points are made in the same manner. Finally, through a closing metaphor or example, the talk is brought to a conclusion. This last piece should leave a compelling image that will linger in the minds of the students long after the speech has ended.

The inclusion of stories, metaphors, and examples obviously plays a critical role in this approach to giving a talk. The value they bring to instruction will be discussed in more depth in the next section of this book. In the context of a speech, these qualities are even more important. Generally, speakers have a very limited amount of time in which to make an impact. Stories are easy for listeners to remember, and if they can be wrapped around the central point, the objective of long-term recall of the primary information is much easier to achieve. A very successful public speaker once made the following statement about giving speeches:

> "Giving a great speech is simple. All you have to do is open with a story, tell a few more stories, then close with a story!"

As a theoretical rule, this seemingly simplistic idea is actually quite close to the mark. In practice, however, the *sequence* of the stories, and the point each one makes, must be considered. Which story introduces the idea with maximum clarity? Which ones develop the more subtle points with the most clarity? Which images will work best for this particular audience? Answers to these questions should be considered in guiding teachers with the selection and sequencing of the stories they will use in their talk.

Two Examples

Understanding how to apply this concept to a specific set of circumstances may be easier if illustrations are included. The following examples are actual speeches I've delivered. The general approach to each component of the speech is described, although not every word is included here. The sequence that has been used to construct the speech, however, should clearly demonstrate how to put this approach into action.

Situation 1:   The setting was an annual conference for principles and district supervisors. Approximately 160 people were present. The scheduled length of the keynote address was forty-five minutes. The topic was "general motivation." The speech was to be held at 2:00 P.M., immediately after lunch, so it was apparent that some movement should be included to keep the audience awake.

1. Opening: General Welcome. Thirty seconds of comments concerning how this speech might be a bit different than the usual. Opening story: Meeting a particular person on an airplane. Key point: People are often not as motivated or excited about life as they think they are.   [5 minutes]

2. Opening examples and first major point: Are you living life to the fullest? Look around you. Are you seated in the same place you were this morning? Are you seated near the same people? Living life fully requires staying awake to opportunities to expand our horizons. Additional story: Taking the plunge and bungee-jumping in Australia. Still shaking about it, but it's a reminder to keep taking risks!   [5 minutes]

3. Brief state change: Take sixty seconds to stand up and meet at least five people that you don't know well in this room. After this is completed, challenge the audience to continue to expand their horizons throughout the conference.   [3 minutes]

4. Second major point: Everyone has a voice in his head. Is what it's saying a helpful thing or a hindering thing? Describe the example of standing in the middle of the road when a truck is coming at you—if your voice says move, that's good! But at other times it may tell you *not* to do something, when taking the risk to do something might be wise. Clarifying examples: Glass of water half full or empty, seeing is believing, and our beliefs as we grow up (Santa Claus and the Easter Bunny stories).   [8 minutes]

5. Additional example: Guiding a sailboat requires constant adjustment, and we are rarely actually on course. Instead, we need to keep adjusting for what is real, and that's OK! Quote: "You can be comfortable when you're dead. Life is for the living." Additional quote: "I'll sleep when I die."   [5 minutes]

6. State change: The pen twist. This is a simple challenge in which the students must rotate a pen from one position between their hands to another. After they have learned it, which takes several moments, the point is made about our feelings when we try something new—frustrating, challenging, and perhaps a little bit of fear. In motivating ourselves, recognize that this natural for all of us, and we must not be inhibited by it.   [5 minutes]

7. Third major point: Create an attitude that is useful to you. Stories from our youth of how we learned to *not* stay focused on the gifts of the present, such as always looking ahead to the next grade in school, or discounting a current partner for someone else who might seem better from a distance. How can we change this? Provide examples of looking for the positive in each moment, by telling the piano story—keeping the door of possibility open. Also do the myth of Sisyphus.   [9 minutes]

8. Summarize the three main points: 1) How much are each of us really living our life to the fullest? 2) Challenge the voice in our head! 3) Generate a useful attitude that guides you towards taking appropriate risks.   [1 minute]

9. Closing metaphor: Tell the Strawberry story. [Author's note: This metaphor is given in Appendix F.] The main point is that life is full of exciting moments, if we are only wise enough to reach out and take advantage of them when they come our way.   [4 minutes]

Situation 2:   The setting was the statewide annual conference of the California Association of Peer Programs (CAPP), held in Anaheim, California. Over 2,000 students were present. Approximately 90 percent of these were teenagers, the others were adult coordinators. Scheduled length of the keynote address was thirty-five minutes. The theme of the conference was "Making Connections." The organizers wanted an opening speech that would get the students thinking about how they could make connections with other students, programs, schools, and adult coordinators.

1. Opening: General welcome. Then a series of questions asking who was in the room, from freshman though seniors, and adults as well. Next tell the Strawberry story, making the connection that this conference could be a "strawberry" experience, a highlight in life, if they chose to make it that way for themselves, by creating significant connections with other people. [5 minutes]

2. The first example was a demonstration. Two teenagers were invited to come to the stage. They stood on chairs facing each other, approximately ten feet apart. Other teens were then invited onto the stage. These students stood in a ring around each of the two students on their chairs. The ring of students represented the boundaries of the two students' worlds. The students on the chairs were then challenged to make a "connection" with each other, without moving outside the boundary of their world. They accomplished this by having the ring of students pick up the chairs and physically move them closer, until they could reach out and shake hands. The key point: Connections only happen when we are willing to adjust the boundaries of our world.   [7 minutes]

3. State change: Students were invited to take thirty seconds and meet at least three people who were new to them, to practice "expanding their boundaries." When they had completed this, they were challenged: How far did you really go? Some people simply stood their ground and shook hands with a couple of people near them. Instead, try it again, and really extend yourself. At this point, the opportunity to meet people was repeated.   [3 minutes]

4. An additional state change: When they had returned to their chairs, they were asked whether they had returned to exactly the same chair. Most had, and the point was made that human beings get into habits that most of us must break in order to really reach out to others. They were challenged to practice opening themselves up right then and there by finding a new seat in the room.   [3 minutes]

5. Second major point: What stops us from connecting with others? Discussion about the voice in our heads and how we must challenge it. Relate stories and examples about the benefits of stretching boundaries, such as improved relationships with others.   [9 minutes]

6. State change demonstration: M&Ms. A three-pound bag of M&Ms is held up for everyone to see. The audience is asked if anyone wants it. Many people respond yes. The presenter keeps asking if anyone *really* wants it, until someone gets out of their seat, comes forward, and takes the bag of M&Ms. The point: It's not enough to simply say that you want something. If you really want it, you must be willing to take action.   [3 minutes]

7. Final metaphor: Tell the traveler story. [Author's note: This metaphor is given in Appendix F.] The point of the story in this context is that each person is a gem. The opportunity, in this situation, is to gather as many gems—as many friendships as possible—in the time available. Make as many connections as possible.   [5 minutes]

Both of these examples demonstrate one way in which I adapted the basic sequence to a particular situation. Given my knowledge of the content, my understanding of the audience with whom I was working, and my personality, I chose to develop and deliver these speeches as I've described here. When you are creating an effective presentation, you will naturally incorporate your own knowledge of content, and respond to the needs of your audience based on what you know about them and the circumstances.

MORE THOUGHTS ON DELIVERING
EFFECTIVE SPEECHES

Speeches given in the manner explained here may differ from those that you have encountered previously. Yet, perhaps that distinction is the key to understanding why this approach has been illustrated. In the more traditional mode of keynote address delivery, the speaker stands in the front of the room and talks from prepared notes behind a podium. While this may be effective in certain situations, for short periods of time, it can quickly become tedious for the listener. Be honest with yourself: How much do you enjoy this type of presentation? Because we know this is not an effective method of instruction in a classroom setting, how could it possibly be effective with a larger audience? Obviously, something different is called for in these circumstances. Consider this basic approach when planning a speech:

Speak *with* an audience, instead of speaking *to* the audience.

The more familiar form of presenting focuses on presenting *to* (or *at*) an audience, and information is being delivered from the mouth of the speaker to the ears of the listener. Contrast this with the idea of speaking *with* an audience. Within this framework, the speaker must decide what might work best for the listener. Stories and metaphors work well, state changes are useful, and allowing students time to process and digest the material allows them to transfer the key ideas into long-term memory. Speaking *with* an audience puts their needs and objectives at the forefront of all considerations.

Some presenters prefer the sense of safety and security that "notes" bring when they step to the front of the room. They clutch these papers or note cards firmly in their hands as they stand in the front, knowing that to lose them would bring about certain disaster. The use of note cards during a speech in front of a large crowd is not necessarily incorrect. However, reading from written notes can create an undesirable dynamic. It tends to separate the speaker from the audience and creates an invisible barrier between them.

If the presenter would like to take the risky, and highly rewarding, step of speaking without the aid of note cards, here's a suggestion . Consider developing a speech that includes brief state changes spread out every five to seven minutes. Have the speech written down on paper or note cards, set off to the side of the stage. When stepping to the front of the room, have memorized only what needs to happen up until the first state change. Then, during that state change, take advantage of the time by stepping to the side of the stage to review the notes for the next section, but only up until the next state change. Deliver that content, and at the next state change repeat the process.

Using this method has several advantages. Perhaps most important, it moves the speaker out from behind the podium. Now you are free to use large hand gestures, make greater use of the stage, physically contact the audience if necessary, and gauge audience reactions more carefully. With your hands free, you can involve your body more easily when you tell stories, and you only have to remember a brief segment of the content. Most presenters can quickly remember the next few minutes of their talk, so stress is significantly reduced. And, as always, the state changes serve the audience well.

I am frequently asked about the value of using graphics software for the delivery of speeches. There are people on both sides of this debate—those who are avid proponents of the use of this approach, as well as those who vehemently oppose it. In certain situations, graphics are undeniably a powerful tool for demonstrating statistics or providing stimulating visual images. The primary concern of those who oppose its use focuses on a speaker relying too heavily on the visual aspect of the presentation. It is not an exaggeration to say that some presenters will go through an entire hour speech with the room darkened, slowly reading every word from every slide as it appears on the screen. Despite its visual appeal, this is still an example of presenting *to* the audience, and, as such, its effect is quickly reduced.

The key is to remember the basic concepts of making an impactful presentation. The visual images generated by the computer can be quite stimulating to the mind, but should not be relied on as the sole means of instruction. For example, the presenter could show up to seven slides, turn the lights back on, and add a story for clarification or give the audience a state change. Later, when more slides are needed, the room could once again be darkened for a brief period of time while these images are presented, then turned on again for further explanation and clarification. This would make the very act of darkening and lightening the room a minor state change.

Here's another way in which one presenter overcame this challenge. He needed to rely heavily on the use of slides for his presentation. However, he was aware of the need for state changes. His method of addressing this issue was to, at random intervals, slip slides that were completely irrelevant to the topic into his presentation. These were such things as cartoons, shots of his family, or even occasional pictures of scantily clad men and women! Inevitably, as audiences figured out what he was doing, they found themselves focusing carefully on each new frame as it appeared, wondering what might be revealed next.

Even though graphics-dominated presentations do have a place in the world of speech-giving, they are still subject to the same principles as regular talks and speeches. The creation of a speech that uses computer software at any level should honor the parameters that guide all successful talks, including working *with* an audience, varying the presentation style to include state changes, and the use of metaphors and stories to help the audience recall the key points of the speech.

In general, giving talks, speeches, and keynote addresses can be an exciting and rewarding opportunity for teachers. A final reminder: The model introduced in this section is simply a general format. Individuals who find themselves faced with the task of giving a speech are invited to use it as a guideline for the development of their talk. Find stories and metaphors that address the theme of the talk. Consider what state changes might work best given the audience, the content, and the physical situation of the listeners. Then, simply organize those pieces into an appropriate sequence, and let the magic happen!

CREATING AN IN-SERVICE PROGRAM

The creation of an in-service program is another project teachers may be called on to do at some point in their careers. Whether one hour or a full day in length, these programs can also benefit from the concepts presented in this book. The principles of Open Loops, Framing, and Crest of the Wave can be employed in the design of the session, built on a solid foundation of the belief that awareness leads to choice, knowing how to use stories, humor, and action effectively, and a primary focus on the ability of the teachers to apply the information presented.

These guidelines are then brought to life through the use of many of the specific teaching practices already mentioned, such as getting responses, specifying the response, doing it standing, changing the visual field, and student ownership. Music and activities will naturally be incorporated throughout the entire workshop, consistent with the technique of involve, don't tell. With the important components clearly identified, it is now a matter of organizing them in an appropriate fashion to create the desired outcome of applicable information delivered in an enjoyable and memorable fashion.

As an example, consider the following hypothetical situation, in which a one-day in-service is created. The subject of the program is innovative teaching strategies for elementary school teachers. This imaginary seminar will be divided into four components of approximately equal length, two in the morning and two in the afternoon. Breaks will occur between each section. The focus of the in-service is how to creatively handle challenging situations in the classroom. Following is one way to use many of the ideas in this book to design the program.

AN IMAGINARY PROGRAM ON INNOVATION

MORNING SESSION 1:

Welcome and Greet: Create involvement and ownership through various activities in which teachers meet each other. Further ownership is developed as they ask the instructor questions about his or her background.

Content Introduction: The visual field is brought into focus as they are introduced to a variety of posters on the wall, all of which cover essential content of the program. A song is introduced that will be used to begin each session.

Opening Metaphor: "The Gem Story" is told (see Appendix F) indicating that the main focus is for them to gather ideas throughout the day.

Creative Distribution of Resources: Instructor has them "gather their first gem," which is the workbook they will be using, by finding them where they have been hidden throughout the room. This also functions as a state change.

Plant Open Loops: Mention that they might surprise themselves before the day is complete. Hint at what's coming up after lunch.

First Activity: The "Paradigm Shift" game. The challenge is to break through old habits and patterns and open up to innovative solutions. It's a fast, challenging activity that requires clear, precise directions. The sequence essentially follows the five-part model. The main point illustrates the challenge of most schools faced with a need for innovation, and sets the tone for the day. It also creates an Open Loop: How can teachers be more innovative in the classroom?

-Morning Break-

MORNING SESSION 2:

Engager: Teachers come back to a brief activity, the purpose being to get their focus back in the room. It lasts for two minutes.

Activity: This event is framed as a puzzle for the group to solve together. It clearly demonstrates the first main idea about innovation in today's classrooms. Clarity comes especially during the debriefing section of the activity.

Application: Teachers consider ways to apply this information to their present work environment through small group discussion. The technique of getting responses is then used to generate a large group interaction in which their ideas are gathered on a single flip chart and posted on an available portion of the wall.

Making It Memorable: Teachers are given the last five minutes of the morning to think quietly to themselves as to how the ideas presented up to this point might apply to both their professional and personal lives. They can use their own learning style and either jot these down or simply imagine them.

-Lunch Break-

AFTERNOON SESSION 1:

Opening Engager: It is soon after lunch, so they need to be physically engaged. A brief activity is introduced that achieves this objective. It takes approximately five minutes, is mildly active, and encourages social interaction among the teachers.

Open Loop Is Closed: Teachers are reminded of what was mentioned earlier concerning the after-lunch activity. Now is the time . . .

Activity: This event introduces and explains the second half of the innovation model. After the activity, further clarifying points are presented during the debriefing. The visual field is changed as this debriefing takes place facing the back of the room. On the wall behind the presenter are several posters and flip charts that are used to clarify the present concept. Small group discussions complete the learning as students examine ways to apply this aspect of the information.

-Afternoon Break-

AFTERNOON SESSION 2:

Final Energizer: A brief activity that reviews the principle model introduced during the day, the main content piece of the course. This take less than one minute.

Application: The various pieces of the model are pulled together for a final exploration of how to use them in practice. In small groups, teachers take a real issue from their school and apply the model to see what solutions might emerge. Answers from the group discussions are written on a flip chart and posted on the wall.

Review: Teachers do it standing by reviewing the posters on the wall and leafing through their book, looking for any questions they may have. These are then answered by the instructor. All open loops from the morning are closed.

Ownership: Open-ended evaluations are completed by everyone.

Closing Metaphor: "The Bicycle Story," which focuses on combining technology and effort to create the best outcome. The key in this context is that having the ideas is not enough in itself, and the technique that has been presented today can bring that idea into reality.

Final thoughts and thank yous

SUMMARIZING

This example is intended to demonstrate one way in which the material can be organized for a seminar. Certainly, there are thousands of ways to combine these ideas to develop a program that is effective, creative, and involving for the teachers who are attending, as well as enjoyable for the instructor to present. In-service leaders are invited to use this format as a starting point. Naturally, they will want to substitute their own energizers, activities, and metaphors.

STORIES

> This section contains ten stories that can be used in the classroom as analogies, metaphors, or examples. They come from a variety of sources, and all teachers should feel free to use them in their lesson plans as appropriate.

THE STRAWBERRY

There was a monk who lived in a small village in the jungle with a group of other monks. Each morning this monk would go out into the jungle and gather fruit for the other monks to eat for breakfast. One morning this monk went into the jungle and was beginning to gather fruit when he heard a sound behind him. He turned around, and saw a tiger. Not wanting to be breakfast for the tiger, the monk slowly began to creep away. But the tiger saw the movement, looked up, and began to walk toward the monk. The monk began to walk faster, and the tiger began to walk faster. The monk began to run as fast as he could, but the tiger began to run also, easily gaining on the monk. Suddenly the monk burst out of the jungle and found himself standing on the edge of . . . a cliff.

He turned around, and saw the tiger behind him, reaching through the bamboo with his claws. In this moment the monk decided it was time to take a risk. He saw a vine lying on the edge of the cliff, and he grabbed it tightly with both hands and jumped off the cliff. The vine held! And the monk began to climb down the cliff. He was halfway down the cliff when he heard a sound below. Looking down, he saw . . . a tiger at the bottom of the cliff! The monk said: "Wait a minute. Either that's the worlds fastest tiger, or . . ." and he looked up and saw that the tiger at the top of the cliff was still there! Now there was a tiger at both the top of the cliff and the bottom of the cliff! He clung to the vine, trying to decide what to do. As he was thinking, out of a small hole in the cliff right above where the monk was holding onto the vine, poked the nose of a very tiny mouse. It smelled the vine the monk was clinging to, leaned out, and began to nibble at the vine right above where the monk was holding onto it . . .

In this moment of crisis, the monk saw something. Growing out of a crevice in the cliff right near him was a strawberry plant, and inside of it was the biggest, most luscious strawberry he had ever seen! And this is what the monk did—he reached out, grabbed the strawberry, plucked it, ate it, and . . . here's the key . . . he enjoyed it!

Now it happened that, just as the mouse finished nibbling through the vine and it fell away, the monk found a tiny ledge to cling to. He held onto it for so long that the tiger at the bottom of the cliff got bored and went away, and the tiger at the top of the cliff got bored and went away. Very slowly the monk made his way back up the cliff, through the jungle, and back to his village in time for supper.

While they were eating, the monk told the other monks what had happened to him that day. They all smiled and said they were glad that he was safe. The monk thanked them, and then said: "Yes, I too am glad that I am safe. However, you know how we all try to learn something each day?" They all agreed with him.

"Well, I learned something today," said the monk.

"What did you learn?" they all asked.

"Life is precious, and time is short. Too often I spend my time worrying about everything that has happened to me in the past (the tiger at the top of the cliff). Too often I spend time unnecessarily worrying about what might happen to me in the future (the tiger at the bottom of the cliff). Or, perhaps worst of all, I spend too much time worrying about the nibbling, nagging worries of each and every day (the mouse). Then, when a true strawberry in my life comes along, sometimes I forget to pluck it, eat it, and most of all . . . enjoy it!"

"So not only should we wish for many strawberries in our lives, but also the wisdom to know they are there, to pluck them, taste them, and fully enjoy each and every precious moment."

THE TRAVELER

A traveler was on a long journey. Each morning he got up and traveled along his path. One morning he woke up and set out again on his journey. However, he soon noticed that on this particular morning the path appeared to be getting more and more narrow. He began to grow concerned that he had taken a wrong turn, and decided that he would ask the next person he saw that morning if he was indeed on the correct path. But no one else was on the path that morning. He walked and walked, and it wasn't until noon that he encountered the first person he had seen all day. It was almost noon when he entered a clearing, and there at the far side of the clearing sat a very old man. This old man had long, flowing white hair, and a white beard, and had his eyes closed.

The traveler was quite excited to see the old man. He hurried up to him and asked:

"Excuse me, but I was traveling along the path this morning, and it began to get very narrow, and I started to wonder if I was on the right path. Can you tell me? Am I going the right way?"

The old man just sat there in silence, his eyes still closed.

The traveler tried again, but could get no response. Finally, in frustration, he started to leave. He was at the far side of the clearing when he heard a sound, and he turned around. The old man had opened his eyes, and was staring straight out in front of him. And when he spoke, he said, very softly:

"You're on the right path. Keep going."

But the traveler was at the far side of the clearing, and wasn't sure if he had heard correctly, so he asked the old man to repeat himself. The old man did say something, but this time it was something quite different. This time he said:

"Gather what you find before you cross the river." And then he closed his eyes once again.

Now, the traveler had heard this last part quite clearly, but he was confused. What did it mean? But he could get nothing more from the old man, and finally the traveler did leave, continuing on the path as before.

It was hot on the path that day, and the traveler grew sweaty, tired, and thirsty. And the path, while growing ever more narrow, was still visible enough to follow. Finally, late in the afternoon, the traveler turned a corner and found himself in front of a river. He was so excited! He ran down to the river, drank some of the water, and used more water to wash himself. When he was fully refreshed he started to wade to the other side, but as he took his first step the words of the old man came back to him, and he paused.

"What did he say?" the traveler asked himself.

And then he remembered the words: "Gather what you find before you cross the river."

"Did he mean this river?" wondered the traveler. "Ah, he was crazy!" and he began to move again. But the words of the old man echoed so strongly in his mind that he found himself backing up to the bank of the river. He looked around.

"If I were going to gather something," he asked himself, "what would I take here?"

He looked around, and saw trees, shrubs, and pebbles by the river's edge, but nothing of any value. But the words of the old man were so strong in his mind that he said:

"This may be the strangest thing I have ever done, but . . ." and he bent down and picked up some of the pebbles and put them in his pocket. Then he waded across the river and continued traveling. However, at the far side of the river he soon lost his way and traveled aimlessly until he found another path to follow several hours later. He knew he could now never retrace his steps back the way he had come.

Late that night the traveler slept by the side of the road. He woke up in the middle of the night, but did not know what had awakened him. Then he realized that he had rolled over on the pebbles in his pocket, and he shook his head.

"That old man was crazy," he said aloud. "I don't know why I picked these up!"

He reached into his pocket and took out the pebbles. He was in the act of throwing them away when suddenly the moonlight shone down on what he held in his hand, and he paused.

"No," he said, "It can't be!"

Because what he was holding in his hand were no longer mere pebbles. Now they were diamonds, rubies, sapphires and emeralds, precious gems of all kinds. And he realized what had happened. They had been precious gems all along, but when he had first picked them up they had been covered in dirt, and in his pocket they had rubbed against each other so that the dirt had come off and he could see them for what they were.

And then the traveler said the most important thing of all. He said:
"Oh. Oh! I wish I had gathered more pebbles, before I crossed that river!"

THE ANIMAL SCHOOL

Once upon a time, the animals decided they must do something decisive to meet the increasing complexity of their society. They held a meeting and finally decided to organize a school. The curriculum consisted of running, climbing, swimming, and flying. Because these were the basic behaviors of most animals they decided that all the students should take all the subjects.

The duck proved to be excellent at swimming, better, in fact, than his teacher. He also did well in flying. But he proved to be very poor in running. Because he was poor in this subject he was made to stay after school to practice it, and even had to drop swimming to get more time to practice running. He was kept at his poorest subject until his webbed feet were so badly damaged he became only average at swimming. But, average was acceptable in the school and nobody worried about that . . . except the duck.

The rabbit started at the top of his class in running, but finally had a nervous breakdown because of so much makeup time in swimming . . . a subject he hated.

The squirrel was excellent in climbing until he developed psychological blocking in flying class, where the teacher insisted he start flying from the ground instead of the tops of trees. He was kept at attempting to fly until he became muscle-bound and received a "C" in climbing and a "D" in running.

The eagle was the school's worst discipline problem. In climbing class he beat all of the others to the top of the tree, but he insisted on using his own method of getting there. He received an "F."

The gophers stayed out of school and fought the tax levies for education because digging was not included in the curriculum. They apprenticed their children to the badger and later joined the groundhogs to start a private school offering alternative education.

So the animals held another meeting and criticized the failure of the educational system to produce successful members of society.

THE WHITE HORSE

In a small village there was a poor farmer who owned a beautiful white horse. One day a rich man from the city came through the village and saw the farmer's white horse. He was very impressed, and he went to the farmer to ask him if he could buy this lovely horse. The rich man said, "I will give you a huge pile of gold for your horse!" But the farmer loved the horse, and was not sure he should sell it.

"Well," he said, "this horse has been in our family since it was born. I'm not sure we could part with it, although it would certainly be nice have all that money. In my whole life I've never had much money. Still, we love this horse."

The rich man nodded his head and said that he understood the farmer's problem. "Tonight," he said, "I'm staying here in your village. I'll come back tomorrow and you can tell me what you've decided." So off he went into town.

Now, the farmer had a neighbor. He was a very nosy sort of person, always telling other people what to do and how to solve their problems. When he heard about the rich man's offer, he hurried over to the farmer's home.

"You must sell the horse!" he exclaimed. "When will you ever again have the chance to have so much money?"

"Yes, it is a lot of money," said the farmer, "but I'm not sure what to do. This horse is almost like a member of our family. We certainly need him when we plow the fields."

"Forget the fields!" said the neighbor. "With all that money you might never have to work again! You must sell the horse, or this will be very bad for you."

Then the farmer said something that he had believed in since he was very young. "Well, who can ever really tell what will be good or bad?" With that, he went back into his house.

The next day the rich man came to the farmer and asked him if he had made up his mind yet. The farmer said he was very sorry, but after thinking about it all night he had decided that he could not sell the horse. The rich man said that he was very sorry, but he understood, and off he went.

When the neighbor heard about this he was quite upset. He went directly to the farmer and said "Why didn't you sell the horse? That was crazy! You were very foolish! I have a bad feeling about this."

The farmer smiled and again said, "Who can tell what will be good or bad? All I know is that I've decided not to sell the horse." Having spoken these words, he went off to his fields and began working. But that very morning, as he and his son were plowing the fields, the white horse suddenly broke free of his harness and raced away into the woods!

When the neighbor heard this, he came over and said, "See! I tried to tell you! Now look what's happened. You don't have the white horse, and you don't have the gold. This is a disaster for you!"

But the farmer shook his head and simply said, "Who can tell what will be good or bad? All I know is that my horse has run away." And he went back to working in the fields with his son.

The next morning, as they were again out working in the fields, the ground began to shake, almost as if there were an earthquake! The farmer and his son looked up, and saw a sight that amazed them. Out of the woods came their white horse, being followed by one hundred wild horses! Being a smart man, the farmer hurried over to the corral and opened the gate. The white horse entered the corral, and the one hundred wild horses all followed it. When they were all inside, the farmer closed the gate.

The neighbor, of course, had heard all the noise, and saw what happened. Instantly he came over and said, "This was a great plan! Look, now you have your white horse back, plus all these other horses. Now you can sell them and become very wealthy! This is such a wonderful thing that has happened to you. You are so lucky."

But the farmer was not as excited. He simply looked at the horses in his corral and said, "We'll see. After all, who can tell what will be good or bad? All I know is that I now have one hundred wild horses in my corral." And with that he went back to work.

The next morning the farmer's son was out teaching the wild horses how to let a rider get on their backs. He was on one of the bigger horses when suddenly it bucked, throwing him high into the air. When he hit the ground, he broke both his legs!

When the neighbor heard what had happened he came over and shook his head sadly. "See," he said, "I knew you should have sold that horse in the first place. I just knew something like this was going to happen. I could just feel it! Now look, your son has broken both his legs! How will you work in the fields to bring in your crops this year? This is so terrible."

The farmer thought for a moment before speaking. Finally he said, "Yes, having my son break his legs is a terrible thing. But I won't worry about it too much. After all, who can tell what will be good or bad? All I know right now is that my son has broken his legs."

The neighbor threw up his hands in disgust and walked away, because he could not imagine how any good could come of having your son break his legs. But . . .

The very next day the army from the big city came sweeping through the villages in the countryside. They were taking all the young men and making them go off with them to fight in the wars in a faraway land. The families did not want their young men to go, because it was very dangerous, and there was a chance they could be hurt, or even killed.

When the army came to the house of the farmer, they saw that his son had two broken legs, and they said, "We can't take him! He's no use to us at all. In fact he'll just be a burden." They left the farmer's house in search of other men to take.

The neighbor heard about this and he laughed out loud. He told the farmer, "How clever. You must have planned this all along! What a great idea! Your son has two broken legs, and now he doesn't have to go off and fight in the war! How very fortunate for you."

As always, the farmer smiled and said, "One must never get too excited. After all, who can tell what will be good or bad? All I know is that my son doesn't have to go off and fight in the war."

The neighbor chuckled again, and walked away. But he shouldn't have laughed, for when he arrived back at his own home, he found the army waiting for him there. And because the army needed more men, they took the neighbor away with them, and he was never heard from again!

THE CASTLE WALL

The king had a beautiful daughter. It was time to find her a husband. But the king wanted to find someone who was very clever, someone with deep wisdom, because he knew that this man would one day become the king. How to find such a man? The king pondered at great length and finally came up with a plan. He would devise a test. Whoever could pass the test would marry his daughter.

The castle in which the king lived had huge walls surrounding it. One morning when he was out riding, he saw these walls and knew instantly what the test must be. That afternoon he made a proclamation throughout the land. Whoever could jump over the castle wall could ask for his daughter's hand in marriage.

When they heard about the test, many men came from all across the land to try and win the hand of the king's daughter by jumping over the castle wall. They all practiced very hard. They would build up their leg muscles as much as they could. They would take very long running starts. But despite everything they tried, a whole year went by and no one could jump over the castle wall. The king began to despair that anyone would be able to come forward and meet the challenge he had created.

One morning, however, a young man entered the castle. He was not as large as some of the other men who had come before, but he appeared very confident. He told the king he would like to marry his daughter. The king looked down at this young man and shook his head sadly.

"As you must have heard," he said, "I have issued a challenge to all the young men of my kingdom. Before you can marry my daughter, you must show your skill by jumping over the castle wall."

The young man looked at the walls of the castle for a long moment. Finally he said, "Very well, I shall jump over the wall."

Although the king very much liked this young man, he doubted he would be able to succeed. "You may certainly try," he said, "but I don't know how you could possibly do it when so many others have failed."

"We shall see," replied the young man, and with that he set off through the castle gathering as many wooden boxes as he could find. The king watched him and asked him what he was doing.

"Just watch," replied the young man. With that he stepped very far back from the castle wall and set down the first box. In front of it he placed a stack of two boxes. In front of that he placed a stack of three boxes, then four, then five, and so on until the final stack of boxes was so high that it came to just below the edge of the castle wall. On the other side of the wall he did the same thing. Then he turned and faced the king.

"You did say," he said, "that I must *jump* over the castle wall to marry your daughter. Isn't that right?'

Puzzled, the king nodded and said that was indeed the challenge.

"Very good, then." said the young man. "Here I go."

With that he went very far back to where the first box had been placed. He jumped up onto it. From that box he jumped up onto the stack of two boxes. He jumped from that stack to the one with three boxes on it. He continued jumping from one stack to the next tallest one until finally he arrived at the castle wall. With one last, small jump, he hopped over it, and began jumping down the boxes on the other side until he reached the ground. He ran back to the king.

"As you can see," he said, "I have jumped over the castle wall."

"Yes," said the smiling king. "You have indeed earned the right to marry my daughter. I believe that with the cleverness you have shown today you will not only make a good husband for my daughter, but you will also make a very wise king."

THE TWO SEEDS

It was springtime, and a lovely young woman planted her garden. Two seeds ended up lying in the ground next to each other. The first seed said to the second one: "Think of how much fun this will be! We will let our roots grow deep down into the soil, and when they are strong we will burst from the ground and become beautiful flowers for all the world to see and admire!"

The second seed heard this, but was worried. "That sounds nice," he said, "but isn't the ground too cold? I'm frightened to try to put my roots into it. And what if something goes wrong and I don't turn out very pretty? And what if the lovely lady doesn't like me? I'm scared of not succeeding!"

The first seed, however, was not about to be stopped. He pushed his roots down into the ground and immediately began to grow. When they were strong enough he burst from the ground and soon became a beautiful flower. The lovely young woman tended carefully to him and proudly showed him to all her friends. He was very happy. "Come on," he said to his friend every day, " it's wonderful and warm up here in the sunshine!"

The second seed was quite impressed with what the first seed had become. However, even though he could see what was possible, he was still very scared. He tentatively pushed one of his roots into the ground. "Ouch," he said. "This ground is still much too cold for me! I don't like it. I think I'll just stay inside my shell where I'm comfortable. Besides, I'm quite safe inside my own shell. I'll become a flower later. There's plenty of time." Nothing the first seed could say would change his mind.

One day, when the young woman was away, a very hungry bird flew in the garden. It scratched at the ground looking for seeds to eat. The second seed, still lying inside its shell, was terrified of what would happen if he was found. But this was his lucky day, and the bird did not find him. Finally it flew away.

When the bird was gone, the second seed breathed a sigh of relief. But he also had come to a decision. While hiding inside his shell he had realized that perhaps he had been wrong in thinking that there was always plenty of time to become a flower. Perhaps, he thought, no one should take for granted that there will be plenty of time to explore their hopes and dreams. Perhaps, sometimes, everyone needs to simply take a chance and reach for a goal. So that's exactly what he did. Without another word, he pushed his roots out into the ground and quickly grew into a beautiful flower.

THE 1958 WORLD SERIES

In the 1958 World Series, the New York Yankees and the Milwaukee Braves were tied three games each going into the seventh and deciding game. Warren Spahn, who was the 1957 Cy Young Award winner, was pitching for Milwaukee late in the deciding game. His team was up by one run when the Yankees star catcher, Elston Howard, came up to bat.

Milwaukee manager Fred Haney came to the pitching mound and told Warren Spahn, "If you throw it high and outside he'll hit it out of the park." That statement did it! Spahns mind was programmed and the next pitch was high and outside and Elston Howard blasted it for a home run. The Yankees went on to win that game, and the World Series four games to three.

As Elston Howard triumphantly rounded the bases after his home run, Warren Spahn threw his mitt down in disgust and shouted something. Reporters later asked what he had said. He replied "Who would ever tell somebody what to do by telling them what *not* to do?"

THE EIGHT COW WOMAN

Serrita lived on a quiet island in the South Pacific many years ago. In her village there was a unique custom when women reached the age they could be married. If a young man was interested in a young woman, he would go talk to the father of the girl. He would then offer some cows to the father of the family in exchange for the young woman's hand in marriage. The more beautiful the girl, of course, the more cows that were offered. If his offer was accepted, the marriage was arranged.

Serrita saw many of her friends become married. Sometimes the young men offered three cows, sometimes four, and once a young man even gave six cows for a young woman! But no one came forward to make an offer for Serrita. She was too wild, they all thought. She would never be a good wife. Besides, some of the meaner ones said, she wasn't even very pretty. Her father became very concerned. "Will no one offer me at least *one* cow for my little Serrita?" he thought worriedly. "I must find her a husband!"

So Serrita's father let all the other villages know that she had reached the age where she could be married. But still not a single young man came forward with an offer. Then one day, just when he was certain she would never be married, a miracle happened. A young man from the other side of the island came to the village and asked to speak to the father. The two men sat and talked for a while before the young man asked to be introduced to Serrita.

She came into the room very slowly, keeping her head bowed low. She knew that she must not be very beautiful, because no one had come to ask for her hand in marriage. She stood there in silence for several minutes while the young man looked at her. Finally he spoke to Serrita's father.

"Yes, yes, I think we will do quite well for each other," he said. Serrita's father was surprised but very relieved. He decided to see how much he could get in exchange for her. He knew he would probably get only one cow, but had to try for more to help out his family.

"Two cows," he said boldly, while secretly crossing his fingers and hoping for the best. "I couldn't possibly see her married for less than two cows. She's is a very special young lady."

The young man looked at her for a long moment before turning back to him. Finally he said "No, no, I don't think that will do at all."

Serrita's father groaned on the inside. Oh, well, he thought, I had to try. At least my little Serrita will have a husband. To the young man he said, "Very well, one cow it is then." But then the young man surprised him completely.

"No," he repeated, "I agree with you that she is a very special young lady. I couldn't possibly take her for less than eight cows." Both Serrita and her father gasped. Eight cows! But this was impossible. No one had ever given eight cows to a family for a young woman! But before the young man could change his mind Serrita's father quickly agreed and the deal was done.

When the young men of Serrita's village heard how many cows the young man had given for her, they laughed at him. "She's not an eight-cow woman," they shouted. "We wouldn't even offer one cow for her! You paid far too much."

"We shall see," said the young man.

So Serrita and the young man went to his village and were married. Everyday he told her how lucky he was to have found her, and what a great deal he had made in only giving eight cows for her. As for Serrita, she could not believe it. Was she really worth eight cows? For many weeks she did not accept it, but her husband kept telling her how very valuable she was, repeating what he had said before.

One day Serrita was by herself and began to think. Am I really worth eight cows, she thought? After all, she thought, if my husband was willing to exchange eight cows for my hand in marriage, perhaps I really am worth that much! If so, how should an eight-cow woman behave? How would she help her husband? What could she do to make herself so valuable? And after that day, Serrita began to act as if she were really worth eight cows. She did all the things she felt an eight-cow woman would do to help her husband.

One year later, Serrita and her husband went back to her village to visit her family. Her father could not believe what he saw. His little Serrita had become an elegant young woman. All the young men in the village were equally impressed, and each wished that he could have taken her as his wife. But it was Serrita herself who was most pleased. Her husband's belief in her had been the beginning point from which she had stepped forward to truly become an eight-cow woman. She had come to understand a very important lesson in life: Sometimes all we need is for someone to believe in us.

THE CATERPILLARS

Processionary caterpillars feed on pine needles. They move through the trees in a long procession, one leading and the others following, each with its eyes half-closed and its head snugly fitted against the rear extremity of his predecessor.

Jean-Henri Fabri, the great French naturalist, after patiently experimenting with a group of these caterpillars, finally enticed them to the rim of a large flower pot, where he succeeded in getting the first one connected up with the last one, thus forming a complete circle that started moving around in a procession with neither beginning nor end.

The naturalist expected that after while they would catch onto the joke, get tired of their useless march, and start off in some new direction. But not so . . . through sheer force of habit, the living, creeping circle kept moving around the rim of the pot. Around and around it went, keeping the same relentless pace for seven days and seven nights, and would doubtless have continued longer had it not been for sheer exhaustion and ultimate starvation. An ample supply of food was close at hand, and plainly visible, but it was outside the range of the circle so they continued along the beaten path. When Jean-Henri realized that if they were left alone they would follow this circle until they perished, he gently broke the chain and led the entire procession to the food and water

The problem is that they were stuck firmly in a habit (instinct, custom, tradition, precedent, paradigm, past experience, standard practice—whatever you may choose to call it) but they were following it blindly. They kept expending their energy in a quest that was ultimately taking them nowhere. They failed to see the larger picture. In the end, they simply mistook *activity for accomplishment.*

THE BICYCLE

Imagine that you were digging through your garage one day, and came across an old bicycle. Perhaps it looks to be as much as twenty-five years old. But you're pleased with your discovery, so you move aside everything else and pull out this classic contraption. It's so old that it only has three speeds! And there are even some worn playing cards still stuck to the spokes so that they make noise when you pedal! You apply some much needed grease to the chain, and off you go. It works! While you're pedaling around you notice that there's a race being held shortly down at the local school. Eager for some exercise, you head there and enroll in the race. When the race begins, you give it all you've got, pedaling as hard as you can. Will you win this race, even giving it 100 percent of your effort and energy? Well, probably not, given that the *technology* you are using is lagging significantly behind the other competitors. Your bike is just too old . . .

Now imagine another scene. One day you go to the sports equipment store and buy the latest bicycle available, one with all the bells, whistles, and gadgets. It has thirty gears, an aerodynamic shape, and weighs so little that you can lift it with just your pinkie finger! You happen to notice a sign indicating that there's that same race at the local school, so you head there at once. You are confident, given that you have the latest technological wonder to serve you. The race begins, and you are so confident you will win that you don't even make much effort, relying on the technology to take you across the finish line first. Will you win this race? Again, probably not, because technology in and of itself is simply not enough. It takes the effective *application* of the technology to make the real difference.

To be a contender in the race described here would take, at the least, a combination of technology and effort. Just putting in a tremendous amount of energy would not be enough, nor is it sufficient to simply possess the appropriate technology. It is the combination of both, applied in the correct manner, that helps one maximize the effort for the best result.

To succeed in life requires that we have two things, and that we use them together. The first is the drive, the willingness, the energy, and the enthusiasm for the task. The second is the technology. One must have the proper tools for success. These tools, can take many forms. They could be physical tools such as a technologically advanced bike, or they might be interpersonal skills, such as knowing how to communicate effectively with another person. Putting these two things together makes for people who are the most successful in many aspects of life.

REFERENCES

Anderson, J. R. (1990). *Cognitive psychology and its implications.* 3rd ed. New York: W. H. Freeman and Company.

Bayor, G. W. (1972). A treatise on the mind's eye: An empirical investigation of visual mental imagery (Doctoral Dissertation, Carnegie-Mellon University). Ann Arbor, MI: University Microfilms, 1972. No. 72–12, 699.

Berliner, D., & Biddle, B. (1995). *The manufactured crisis.* Reading, MA: Addison-Wesley.

Berlyne, D. E. (1965). Curiosity and Education. In J. D. Krumboltz (Ed.), *Learning and Educational Process* (pp. 67–89) Chicago: Rand McNally.

Berstein, D. (1994). Tell and show: The merits of classroom demonstrations. *American Psychology Society Observer, 24,* 25–37.

Brigham, F. S., Scruggs, T. E., & Mastropieri, M. A. (1992). Teacher Enthusiasm in Learning Disabilities Classrooms: Effects on Learning and Behavior. *Learning Disability Research and Practice, 7,* 68–73, In W. Gage & D. Berliner (Ed.), *Educational Psychology.* Boston, MA: Houghton Mifflin.

Brophy, J. E. (1979). Teacher Praise: A functional analysis. *Review of Educational Research, 51,* 5–32.

Bucko, H., & Elliot, R. (1997). Hands-On Pedagogy vs. Hands-Off Accountability. *Phi Delta Kappa, 80*(5), 394–400.

Bucko, R. (1997). Brain Basics: Cognitive psychology and its implications for education, *ERS Spectrum.* Summer, 20–25.

Calvin, W., & Ojemann, G. (1994). *Conversations with Neil's Brain.* Reading, MA: Addison-Wesley.

Campbell, J. (1983). *Man and time.* Boston, MA: Princeton.

Canfield, J., & Hanser, M. V. (1993). *Chicken soup for the soul.* Deerfield Beach, FL: Health Communications.

Cialdini, R. (1984). *Influence: The new psychology of modern persuasion.* New York: Quill.

Corey, M. S., & Corey, G. (1997). *Group process and practice.* (5th ed.). Pacific Grove, CA: Brooks/Cole.

Cove, P. G., Cove, A. G., & Goodsell, A. (1996). *Enhancing student learning: Intellectual, social, and emotional integration.* ERIC Digest (ED400741).

Covington, M. V. (1992). *Making the grade: A self-worth perspective on motivation and school reform.* New York: Holt, Rinehart & Winston.

Covington, M. V., & Omelich, C. (1987). I knew it cold before the exam: A test of anxiety–blockage hypothesis. *Journal of Educational Psychology, 79,* 393–400.

Cusco, J. B. (1990). Cooperative learning: Why does it work? *Cooperative Learning and College Teaching, 1*(1), 3–8.

———. (1994). Critical thinking and cooperative learning: A natural marriage. *Cooperative Learning and College Teaching, 4*(2), 2–5.

D'Arcangelo, M. (1998). The brains behind the brains. *Educational Leadership, 56*(3), 20–25.

Dastoor, B., & Reed, J. (1993). Training 101: The psychology of learning. *Training and Development, 47*(60), 17–22.

Deporter, B., Reardon, M., & Singer-Noire, S. (1999). *Quantum teaching: Orchestrating student success.* Boston, MA: Allyn & Bacon.

Diamond, M. (1988). *Enriching heredity: The impact of the environment on the brain.* New York: The Free Press.

Driscoll, M. P. (1994). *Psychology of learning for instruction.* Boston, MA: Allyn & Bacon.

Evans, G. E. (1988). Metaphors as Learning Aids in University Lectures. *The Journal of Experimental Education, 56,* 91–99.

Fisher, K. W., & Rose, S. P., (1998). Growth cycles of the brain and hand. *Educational Leadership.* November, *56*(3), 56–60.

Fisher, R. P., & Geiselman, R. (1987). *Enhancing eyewitness memory with the cognitive interview.* Proceedings of the Second International Conference on Practical Aspects of Memory. England.

Gage, N. L., & Berliner, D. (1998). *Educational psychology.* Boston, MA: Houghton Mifflin.

Gagne, R. M., & Glaser, R. (1987). Foundations in learning research. In R. M. Gagne (Ed.), *Instructional technology: Foundations.* Hillsdale, NJ: Erlbaum.

Glaser, R. (1984). Education and thinking: The role of knowledge. *American Psychologist, 39,* 93–104.

Goleman, D. (1995). *Emotional intelligence.* New York: Bantam.

Gorman, M. E., Plucker, J. A., & Callahanj, C. M. (1998). Turning students into inventors: Active learning modules for secondary students. *Phi Delta Kappan, 79*(7), 530–535.

Greeno, J. G., Collins, A. M., & Resnick, L. B. (1996). Cognition and Learning. In D. Berliner & R. Calfee (Eds.), *Handbook of educational psychology* (pp. 15–46). New York: Macmillan.

Grinder, M. (1988). *Righting the educational conveyerbelt.* Portland, OR: Metamorphous Press.

239

Hansen, E. J. (1998). Creating teachable moments . . . and making them last. *Innovative Higher Education, 23*(1), 7–26.

Hart, L. (1975). *How the brain works: A new understanding of human learning.* New York: Basic Books.

———. (1983). *Human brain and human learning.* White Plains, NY: Longman.

Hughes, C. A., Hendrickson, J. M., & Hudson, P. J. (1986). The pause procedure: Improving factual recall from lectures by low and high achieving middle school students. *International Journal of Instructional Media, 13*(3), 217–226.

Jensen, E. (1988). *SuperTeaching.* Dubuque, IA: Kendall-Hunt.

———. (1996). *Brain-based learning.* Del Mar, CA: Turning Point for Teachers.

———. (2000). *Music with the brain in mind.* San Diego, CA: The Brain Store, Inc.

Johnson, D. W., & Johnson, F. P. (1997). *Joining together group theory and group skills.* (6th ed.). Boston, MA: Allyn & Bacon.

Johnson-Laird, P. N. (1988). How is meaning mentally represented? In U. Eco, M. Santambrogio, & P. Violi (Eds.), *Meaning and mental representations* (pp. 318–324). Bloomington: Indiana University Press.

Keller, J. M. (1987). Motivational design of instruction. In C. M. Reigeluth (Ed.), *Instructional design theories and models: an overview of their current status* (pp. 384–434). Hillsdale, NJ: Erlbaum.

Kincheloe, J., Slattery, P., and Steinberg, S. (2000). *Contextualizing teaching.* New York: Addison-Wesley Longman.

LaBerge, D. L. (1990). Attention. *Psychological Science, 1*(3), 156–162.

Larkins, A. G., McKinney, C. W., & Oldham-Buss, S. (1985). Teacher enthusiasm: A critical review. In W. Gage & D. Berliner (Ed.), *Educational Psychology* (pp. 240–247). Boston, MA: Houghton Mifflin, 1998.

Lazar, A. M. (1995). Who is studying in groups and why? Peer collaboration outside the classroom. *College Teaching, 43*(2), 61–65.

Levenson, R. W., Ekman, P., & Friesen, W. V. (1990). Voluntary facial action generates emotion specific autonomous nervous system activity. *Psychophysiology, 27*, 213–215.

Litecky, L. P. (1992). Great teaching, great learning: Classroom climate, innovative methods, and critical thinking. *New Directions for Community Colleges, 77*, 83–90.

Loftus, E. (1992). When a lie becomes memory's truth: Memory distortion after exposure to misinformation. *Psychological Science, 1*, 345–349.

———. (1993). The reality of repressed memories. *American Psychologist, 48*(5), 518–537.

Lozanov, G. (1979). *Suggestology and outlines of suggestopedia.* New York: Gordon and Breach.

Maslow, A. H. (1968). *Toward a psychology of being.* (2nd ed.). New York: Van Nostrand.

———. (1970). *Motivation and personality.* (2nd ed.). New York: Harper and Row.

McConnell, J. (1978). Confessions of a textbook writer. *American Psychologist, 33*(2), 159–169.

Ormond, J. E. (2000). *Educational Psychology: Developing Learners.* (3rd ed.). Upper Saddle River, NJ: Prentice-Hall.

Plyshyn, Z. W. (1973). What the mind's eye tells the mind's brain: A critique of mental imagery. *Psychological Bulletin, 80*(1), 1–24.

Poznar, (1995). Goals for higher education from technique to purpose. *Current,* (October), 3–7.

Ready, M. (1978). The conduit metaphor: A case of frame conflict in our language about language. In A. Ortony (Ed.), *Metaphor and thought* (2nd ed.), (pp. 164–201). Cambridge, UK: Cambridge University Press.

Ruhl, K., Hughes, C., & Schloss, P. (1987). Using the pause procedure to enhance lecture recall. *Teacher Education and Special Education, 10*(1), 14–18.

Sapolsky, R. M. (1999). *Why zebras don't get ulcers.* (4th ed.). New York: W. H. Freeman.

Schmier, L. (1995). *Random thoughts: The humanity of teaching.* Madison, WI: Magna Publications.

Sfard, A. (1998). On two metaphors for learning and the dangers of choosing just one. *Educational Researcher, 27*(2), 4–13.

Shatz, C. T. (1990). Impulse activity and the patterning of connections during CNS development. *Neuron, 5*(6), 745–756.

Smarginsky, P. (1998). The social construction of data: Methodological problems of investigating learning in the zone of proximal development. *Review of Educational Research, 65*(3), 191–212.

Squire, L. R. (1987). *Memory and brain.* New York: Oxford University Press.

Stepien, W., & Gallagher, S. (1993). Problem-based learning: As authentic as it gets. *Educational Leadership, 50*(7), 25–28.

Sviniki, M. D. (1990). *The changing face of college teaching: New directions for teaching and learning.* San Francisco, CA: Jossey-Bass.

Tomlinson, C. A., & Kalbgleisch, M. L. (1998). Teach me, teach my brain: A call for differentiated classrooms. *Educational Leadership, 56*(3), 52–55.

Vergneer, G. W. (1995). Therapeutic applications of humor. *Directions in Mental Health Counseling, 5*(3), 1–11.

Vygotsky, L. S. (1987). *The collected work of L. S. Vygotsky,* Vol. 3. R. W. Rieser & A. S. Carlton (Eds.). New York: Plenum Press.

Weinberger, N. M. (1998). The music in our minds. *Educational Leadership, 56*(3), 36–40.

Wolfe, P., (1998). Revisiting effective teaching. *Educational Leadership.* November *56*(3) 61–64.

Woolfolk, A. (1998). *Educational psychology.* 7th Ed. Boston, MA: Allyn & Bacon.

Yerks, R. M., & Dodson, J. D. (1908). The relation of strength stimulus to rapidity of habit formation. *Journal of Comparative Neurology, 18,* 459–482. Also in A. Wolfolk (Ed.), 1998. *Educational Psychology,* 7th Ed. (pp. 218–220). Boston, MA: Allyn & Bacon.

INDEX